Day Trips® From Phoenix, Tucson, and Flagstaff

"The introduction is practically worth the price of the book with its vital information on when to travel where in Arizona. Thirty-five day trips follow and special directories of 'festivals and celebrations' and the 'great outdoors' complete the picture."

—Family Travel Times

"A calendar of seasonal festivals and celebrations is appended along with lists of national parks, Indian reservations, and tour associations. A valuable adjunct to more general books on the Southwest."

—ALA Booklist

"The trips are planned within a convenient drive from the cities, though there are 'worth more time' sections for not-to-be-missed attractions."

—The (Chicago) Star

"Presents a diversity of explorations including Indian ruins, ghost towns, lost mines and artist colonies."

—The Los Angeles Times

"A must for those planning a trip to Arizona."

—Bridgeport (CT) Post-Telegram

D0092545

Shifra Stein's Day Trips® Series

GETAWAYS LESS THAN TWO HOURS AWAY

Shifra Stein's

Day Trips®

from **Phoenix, Tucson, & Flagstaff**

Fifth Edition

by

Pam Hait

The Globe Pequot Press

OLD SAYBROOK, CONNECTICUT

Section on Flash Floods, Desert Survival, The Climate of Arizona, and Heat Wave Safety Rule is reprinted with permission from the 1984 *KOY Almanac,* by Pam Hait for KOY radio.

Cover photograph copyright © 1996 (IMA) Kaoru Mikami/Photonica

Cover design by Freeborn Design

Library of Congress Cataloging-in-Publication Data is available.
ISBN 0-7627-0111-0

Manufactured in the United States of America
Fifth Edition/Second Printing

Contents

Preface

Arizona. The name sings with romance. This is the landscape celebrated in western films where rugged cowboys still ride a vast, rolling range. This is a countryside blessed with sunsets that burst upon the horizon spilling apricot and purple hues as far as you can see. This is a land of immense physical size and unparalleled variety. Mountains and desert, cities and wilderness— Arizona has all of them.

While directions are as clear and exact as possible, you should refer to an Arizona road map as you travel. Write to the Arizona Office of Tourism, 2702 North 3rd Street, Suite 4015, Phoenix, AZ 85007, or call (602) 230-7733 to request a map. You may also write or call the communities or regional tourism information offices of the specific areas you plan to visit and ask for city maps. Read these and refer to them as you travel. Always note the scale of the map. If you are accustomed to eastern maps, you're in for a shock. With 113,909 square miles of land, Arizona is one of the largest states in the nation. Once inch on the state road map equals approximately 16 miles!

In addition to its sheer physical size, Arizona is dazzling in its infinite sights, sounds, and moods. In a short two-hour trip from the urban centers of Phoenix, Tucson, or Flagstaff, you can drive from the floor of the desert to a rocky red precipice and travel in time from pre-historical to frontier days.

There's variety in the climate, too. Wide travelers will consider both the season and their destinations when they plan day trips in and around the three metropolitan areas. Plan summer trips in the Phoenix area with special caution. Because of its low elevation and irrigated Sonoran desert location, the capital city can sizzle under extremely hot daytime temperatures from late May through mid-September. Getting in and out of a hot car saps the enthusiasm of even the most dedicated tourist. In contrast, the fall, winter, and early months of spring offer warm days and cool evenings that guarantee almost ideal conditions for driving and sightseeing.

Although Tucson and Phoenix have similar desert climates. because Tucson is about 1,200 feet higher than Phoenix, Tucson's summer temperatures generally are about ten degrees cooler than those in Phoenix. Tucson is less humid as well, making summer sightseeing more comfortable there than in Phoenix. Winter temperatures in both cities, however, are comparable.

On the other hand, the Flagstaff area offers travelers a radically different experience. Perched at an elevation of over a mile high, Flagstaff's climate is similar to that of Michigan or Wisconsin. The cold winters can come complete with deep snows, making winter day trips around Flagstaff risky. However, a delightful climate with warm, sunny days and cool evenings makes northern Arizona a perfect vacationland during spring, summer, and fall.

Be prepared for some local idiosyncrasies. For instance, if you ask a direction, you'll generally hear, "It's just twenty minutes down the orad," or "That's only a couple hours away." Arizonans measure distance in time more frequently than in miles. And they think nothing of driving two hours to a destination—that's hardly even a jaunt—which is why many of the day trips included in this boo stretch the two-hour getaway time to three hours and sometimes more.

Once you venture even a few miles outside of the three major cities, you'll often encounter open, empty country. This is a treat for people who love the wild, untamed outdoors, but it can pose challenges for those who prefer urban conveniences. One delightful way to handle the great distances when planning day trips is to carry a picnic lunch. Frequently you will find good restaurants few and far between, so you can eat at any of the scenic roadside rest shops. You bring the food: the state provides the ambience with shaded ramadas and sweeping vistas.

Heed the road signs at *all* times of the year. If you see a warning: "Not recommended for sedan travel," believe it! Arizona roads can be rugged and extremely rough on automobiles. When driving through country marked "open range," be alert. Although a rare occurrence, you could encounter loose cows, sheep, or other livestock wandering across the road. Obey both flash flood warnings and dust storm warnings. That dry wash may appear harmless, but a wash can quickly turn into a deadly torrent to cross flooded areas. Specific directions for dealing with flash floods are included in the back of this book.

Safe driving in the desert demands that travelers take certain precautions. Arid lands can be unforgiving, especially during the hot summer months. Always carry water in your car for emergencies. You may need it for drinking during the early morning hours or after the sun sets. Always tell someone where you are going and when you expect to return. If you are overdue, somebody will know when to start worrying and can alert the authorities. If you have car problems, stay with your vehicles. Don't wander off for help; let help find you. Refer to the back of the book for desert survival tips.

Finally, don't hike into the wilderness alone. Even experienced hikers get lost.

You can take every day trip and hike described in this book without running into any of the emergency situations mentioned above. Arizona is not hazardous to your health. If you treat this unique and often untamed landscape with the respect it deserves, however, you can have safe and exhilarating experiences. What's more, you will be free to appreciate its magnificence and learn to love it as I do.

Pam Hait

Using This Book

Restaurant prices are designated as $$$ (Expensive, $15 and over); $$ (Moderate, $5 to $15); $ (Inexpensive, $5 and under).

Lodging rates are designated as $$$ (Expensive, $100 and over, per night); $$ (Moderate, $50 to $100, per night); $ (Inexpensive, $50 and under, per night). Rates often change seasonally, so be sure to call first fort prices.

The symbol (CC) denotes that at least one credit card is accepted.

Highway designations: Federal highways are designated U.S. State routes use A. County roads are identified as such.

Hours: In most cases hours are omitted in the listings because they are subject to frequent changes. instead, phone numbers are provided for up-to-date information.

Help Us Keep This Guide Up to Date

Every effort has been made by the author and editors to make this guide as accurate and useful as possible. However, many things can change after a guide is published—establishments close, phone numbers change, hiking trails are rerouted, facilities come under new management, etc.

We would love to hear from you concerning your experiences with this guide and how you feel it could be made better and be kept up to date. While me may not be able to respond to all comments and suggestions, we'll take them to heart, and we'll also make certain to share them with the author. Please send your comments and suggestions to the following address:

The Globe Pequot Press
Reader Response/Editorial Department
P.O. Box 833
Old Saybrook, CT 06475

Or you may e-mail us at:

editorial@globe-pequot.com

Thanks for your input, and happy travels!

Phoenix

Welcome to Phoenix, capital city of the state of Arizona and hub of "The Valley of the Sun." The valley is surrounded by mountain ranges, clear cool lakes, and more five-star resorts than any metropolitan area in the country—a veritable paradise for tourists. Because visitors have such a choice of accommodations, it is suggested that you write to the Arizona Hotel & Motel Association, 2201 East Camelback, Suite 125B, Phoenix, AZ 85016, and request a brochure describing the hotels, motels, dude ranches, and cabins in the state. Or you may call (602) 553–8802 for information.

Because of the way this book is organized, some of the best Phoenix attractions are listed in the section, Day Trip 1 Northwest From Tucson. You'll want to check out this Day Trip if you are planning on staying in Phoenix!!

With Phoenix as your starting point, you'll be amazed to discover how much variety awaits you even in a two-hour drive. Some easy day trips can take you to urban areas, such as Scottsdale, Mesa, Tempe, or even Tucson. On other trips, you can climb quickly from the desert floor to mountainous pine forests, or you can enter a time warp that takes you back to pioneer and ancient Indian eras.

Ideally, visitors to Arizona should plan to spend some vacation time in Phoenix, Tucson, and Flagstaff, taking day trips from each. In this way, you'll get a true flavor of the state. A second plan could include Phoenix as your hub, because it is centrally located and is the largest metropolitan area in the state. As you journey around the Phoenix environs, you'll soon discover that many of the Phoenix-based trips easily fall within the two-hour limitation. In some cases, you'll need to drive longer than two hours; however, each trip is worth it.

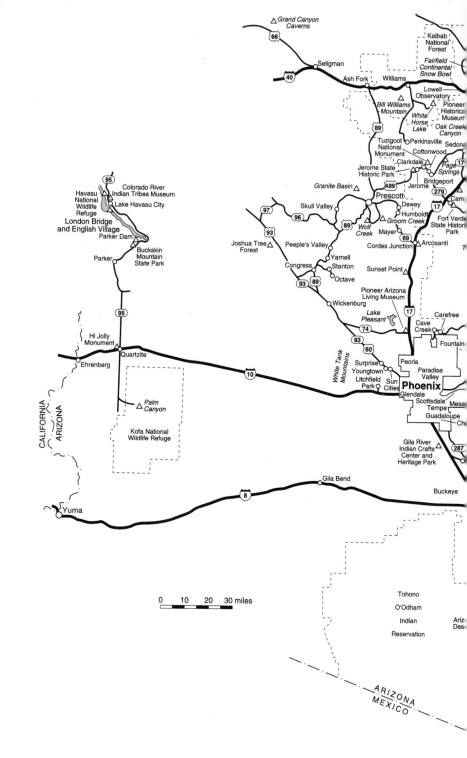

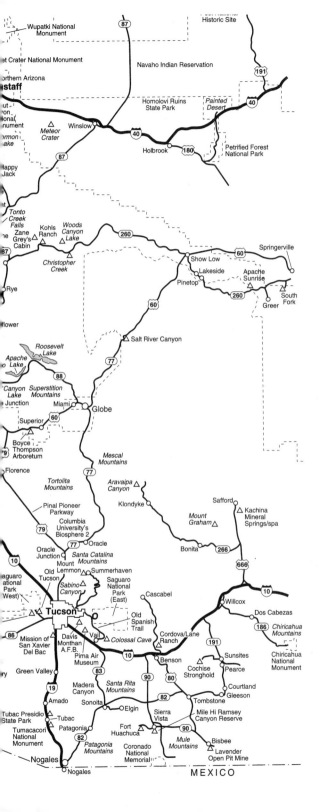

If you use Flagstaff as your starting point for several of the Phoenix-based day trips, you can cut your travel time by an hour or even more. The vast majority of tourists, however, start their day trips from the Phoenix metropolitan area, rather than from the smaller northern Arizona community of Flagstaff.

As you read along, you'll note that many of the itineraries described can be done as an overnight instead of a single day's journey. If you have the time, it's always nice to stay over in a destination town. That way you can spend more hours seeing the sights and exploring the area, and proportionately less time on the road.

One last piece of advice: As you peruse the Phoenix section of this book, you'll read about sights to see, canyons to explore, side roads to wander along, shops not to miss, and special trips to take. In your enthusiasm to do it all, don't overload yourself. This is especially true when traveling during the summer, because the high desert temperatures can be extremely tiring. If you decide to visit a museum or Indian ruin, allow enough time to study the exhibits or soak up the atmosphere of a few selected attractions rather than rushing from point to point. The essential Arizona experience is a casual, laid-back lifestyle. Whether sitting at a sidewalk cafe in Scottsdale or standing silently before Montezuma Castle, don't push yourself to cover too much too fast.

For brochures, maps, and specific information on the fascinating Phoenix metropolitan area, contact the Phoenix & Valley of the Sun Convention & Visitors Bureau, 1 Arizona Center, 400 East Van Buren Street, Suite 600, Phoenix, AZ 85004, or call (602) 254-6500, or for general tourism information: (800) 842-8257.

PRESCOTT

This trip covers some of the same territory found in Day Trip 2, North from Phoenix. However, in this itinerary, Prescott is the primary destination. A pine-studded jewel of a town two hours north of Phoenix, and once the capital of the Territory of Arizona, it is the seat of Yavapai County. It's famous for its Victorian-style homes, Fourth of July celebrations, and temperate climate. Since there are so many scenic drives in the Prescott area, you may want to spend the entire day there.

The town of Prescott was founded not too long after gold was discovered in nearby hills in 1863 — the same year that Abraham Lincoln signed an act to create the Arizona Territory. Prescott has approximately 525 buildings on the National Register of Historic Places and is a favorite destination for Phoenix residents who enjoy the cool summer days when Prescott's high temperatures average in the 80s. Visitors will especially enjoy the Fourth of July weekend which is Prescott's Rodeo. This is billed as the World's Oldest Rodeo parade and festivities.

Prescott offers cool summer days and moderate winter days, so it's always safe to take a sweater or lightweight jacket with you. If possible, visit during any of the festivals and celebrations that occur during every month of the year. Obtain details from the Prescott Chamber of Commerce at 117 West Goodwin Street, 86301, or call (520) 445-2000.

To reach Prescott, follow I-17 north to Cordes Junction. Take A-69 northwest and meander past the small towns of Mayer, Hum-

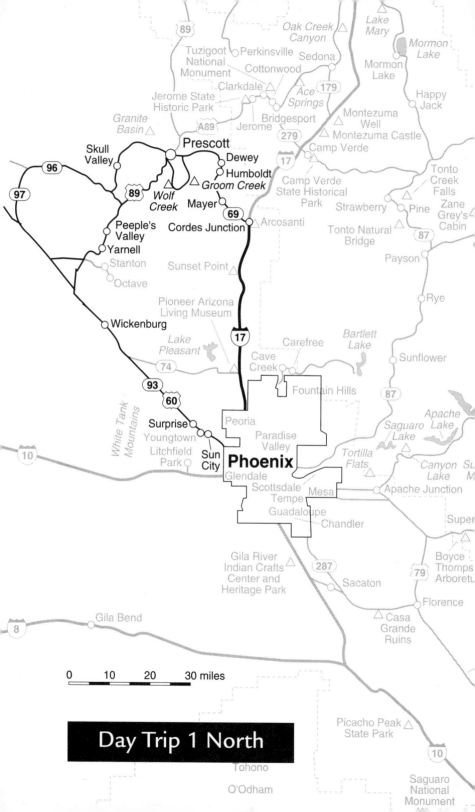

Day Trip 1 North

boldt, Dewey, and Prescott Valley. The largest of these communities is Mayer, which is located in the foothills of the Bradshaw Mountains. Founded in 1881 by Joseph Mayer, it began as a store, saloon, and Wells Fargo Stage station. Mayer was a stop along the stage line between Phoenix and Prescott. Today, it continues the tradition as a stop along A–69 for motorists.

Enter Prescott on A–69 west until it meets Gurley Street. Travel left on Gurley past Marina Street and you're in the heart of town. Park anywhere between Cortez and Montezuma streets for your tour of this historic area.

As you gaze at the gingerbread homes and tall brick buildings, you may think that Prescott is an unlikely Arizona town. Remember that the desert, with its low-slung adobe structures, is only one Arizona image. In the more northern parts of the state, two-story brick and wood buildings are just as appropriately an "Arizona" style.

Here territorial Arizona springs to life. Prescott flourished when the area was a wild and untamed place. As military personnel and miners moved in, no doubt they were anxious to make it seem like home, so they built what they knew: "back-East" buildings, proper brick and two-story structures reminiscent of Ohio or Pennsylvania.

The first capital of the Arizona Territory, Prescott ultimately lost its bid to become the permanent state capital. The honor went to Phoenix instead. Still, much Arizona history was made here and fortunately, for visitors, remains well preserved.

WHERE TO GO

Courthouse Plaza. This is the area bounded by Cortez and Montezuma, Gurley and Goodwin streets. It's a real town square that functions much as it did during territorial times. During festivals, the grassy square is lined with booths, and people sprawl on the lawns. In more quiet times, you can soak up the serenity that the solid courthouse building exudes. After you've enjoyed the courthouse, wander through the streets to explore the galleries and stores. Although Prescott is a tourist mecca, it has resisted ticky-tacky tourist shops. You'll find a real community here, not cardboard storefront images.

Sharlot Hall Museum. 415 West Gurley Street, Prescott 86301. This museum is actually a number of separate buildings grouped together to give visitors a living panorama of Southwestern history.

Spanning the years from the founding of Prescott in 1864 to the present, the buildings appear to be in architectural sequence. You can tour the Governor's Mansion, which was built on this site in 1864 from local ponderosa pine. Several territorial officials, including Governor John Goodwin, lived in this mansion.

The John C. Fremont House. Built in 1875, it is constructed of wood and reflects the rapid growth Prescott experienced during its first ten years. Fremont, known as "the Pathfinder," served as the fifth territorial governor of Arizona from 1878 to 1881.

Arizona became a state on February 14, 1912. The William C. Bashford House represents the type of architecture common to the area during the two decades before statehood. Complete with a solarium, this house was built in another location and moved to the museum grounds in 1974.

The **Sharlot Hall** building, completed in 1934, is the primary exhibit hall and includes the Museum Shop and display rooms for pre-Columbian artifacts, historic southwestern items, and old photographs. These pictures capture the essence of what it was like for white and red men to live in this territory over 100 years ago. This exhibit is all the more remarkable when you realize that Indians feared—and some still do fear—the camera, believing that it takes away a man's soul.

Who was Sharlot Hall that an entire enclave of a museum is devoted to her? She was an outstanding woman—a writer, poet, collector of Arizona artifacts, and territorial historian—who moved to Arizona from Kansas in 1882. She remained fascinated with Arizona until her death in 1943.

As you stroll along the sidewalks, which circle and connect the museum's major buildings, you can visit other memorials and exhibits, including the Blacksmith Shop; one of the town's first boardinghouses, which the frontiersmen called "Fort Misery"; a replica of Prescott's first public school; and the Pioneer Herb and Memorial Rose garden. The Museum is closed Mondays, but the grounds are open. Donation requested. (520) 445-3122.

Bead Museum. 140 South Montezuma. The museum is in a double store front right on Whiskey Row and is combined with a bead shop. On display are beads from all over the world, proof of the ingenuity and imagination that have gone into human adornment throughout history. Special exhibitions are mounted and there is even a reference library. Free. (520) 445-2431.

Smoki Museum. 147 North Arizona Street. Designed to resemble an Indian pueblo, this museum opened to the public in 1935. Thousands of pine logs were used for the columns, *vigas* and *latillas* of the ceiling, and for the *slav* doors and window enclosures. A Hopi-style kiva is in the center of the building, and a Zuni-style fireplace extends along the north wall. The museum houses collections of pre-Columbian and contemporary pottery, pre-Columbian jewelry of shell, stone and turquoise, and an outstanding collection of basketry, kachinas, stone artifacts and textiles all from the southwest. A collection of war bonnets, costumes and beadwork are from the Plains Indians. Open daily in the summer and weekends during the winter, visitors can also arrange tours by appointment. Donations accepted. (520) 445-1230.

Phippen Museum of Western Art. 4710 A-89 North. George Phippen was one of the founders of Cowboy Artists of America. Western art buffs will enjoy the collection of works by Phippen and other Cowboy Artists including Joe Beeler and Frank Polk. Bronzes, paintings, and Indian art and crafts are on display, and special exhibitions are mounted. A major art show and sale on Courthouse Plaza is held every Memorial Day. Call ahead for hours. Fee. (520) 778-1385.

Whiskey Row. Montezuma Street between Goodwin and Aubrey streets. This is Prescott's famous "wicked" street. The name says it all. Everyone needs to walk up Whiskey Row, even if he or she isn't thirsty. Today, it is more sedate, except during festivals and celebrations. Then the Old West springs to life again as cowboys belly up to the crowded bars.

Prescott Historical Tours. Prescott and the Bradshaw Mountains. Several years ago Melissa Ruffner, dressed in authentic period costumes, began giving tours of Prescott's Victorian homes. Since then she and her husband have offered walking tours of the four-block historical district.

Call ahead to find out more about this trip. You'll need good walking shoes, a sack lunch, and, if you care about your manicure, gloves. Ms. Ruffner also puts together specialty tours of Prescott, which can cover anything from how the frontier settlers used solar energy to the area's early religious or ethnic populations. Fee. Contact Melissa Ruffner, (520) 445-4567.

WHERE TO STAY

Forest Villas. 3645 Lee Circle. Take I-17 North, and exit at Cortez Junction (A-69) going toward Prescott. After you pass the town of Prescott Valley, you will see the mauve-colored Forest Villas on your right. Prescott's newest hotel brings European ambience to this small western town. Guests can enjoy rooms with great views, fireplaces and whirlpools. The hotel offers a mountainside heated pool and spa, and complimentary continental breakfast. (800) 223-3449 Ext. AZR.

Hassayampa Inn. 122 East Gurley Street, Prescott 86301. Established in 1927 and recently renovated, this is Prescott's historic Grand Hotel. It is centrally located in the heart of town and offers a step back in time to the West of 1927. Rooms are spacious and accented with lace curtains, comforters, and period furniture. Charming and comfortable, the Inn provides complimentary breakfast in the graceful Peacock dining room. $$-$$$; (CC). (520) 778-9434; or in Arizona, (800) 322-1927.

The Prescott Resort. 1500 A-69, Prescott 86301. As you head into town, look up at the intersection of Highways 89 and 69 and you'll see this resort nestled high on a hill. The Sheraton Prescott offers rooms with views of Prescott, large suites, a full health club, dining room, and two lounges. $$$; (CC). (520) 776-1666.

WHERE TO SHOP

Downtown Prescott. Prescott is a great place to hunt for antiques. The town is filled with converted homes that offer "treasures." In addition to antiques, Prescott has two stores you shouldn't miss and a mini-mall that is fun to browse through.

The Llama House. 108 South Montezuma. This is a fun shop filled with beautiful women's clothes and accessories at very reasonable prices. Proprietor Marsha Rishar has assembled a varied collection. The earrings and jewelry are great. (520) 445-9689.

SCENIC DRIVES

Granite Dells. Drive east on Gurley Street, and north on US–89 for about 4 miles. Just north of Prescott, nature has carved a sculpture garden of ancient rock formations. As you approach, you'll notice that the rocks appear to have human or animal forms. That's Mother Nature, the artist, at work. Centuries of wind, rain, snow, and sun worked on these granite cliffs to form eerie figures. Formerly known as the "Point of Rocks," the Granite Dells is set off by Watson Lake, a clear blue pool that contrasts vividly with the subtle colors of the smooth, round boulders.

Granite Mountain and Granite Basin. This trip will take about twenty minutes each way. Drive west on Gurley Street to Grove Avenue. Turn right on Grove and continue out Miller Valley Road. Bear left at the junction of Iron Springs and Willow Creek roads onto Iron Springs and continue to the Prescott National Forest sign on the right side of the road. Turn right and continue to Granite Basin Recreation site, a unique geological and historical wilderness area. Long before Congress declared the Granite Mountain Trail a national recreation area in 1979, hikers and rock climbers were well acquainted with its spectacular scenery. If you are in good shape and dressed for outdoor action, you can hike to the overlook. Otherwise, walk along the trails and marvel at the sheer, smooth cliffs.

Lynx Lake. Fifty-five acres of lake just fifteen minutes away! Follow A–69 east for 4 miles to Walker Road. Turn right for approximately 3 miles. Lynx Lake, which is fed by nearby Lynx Creek, has a rich history. Gold was discovered at the creek during territorial days, giving frontiersmen and women even more reason to make the trip to Prescott. Fishing is good year-round, and during the summer, you can rent a boat from the lakefront concession. Take your sweetheart on a moonlight cruise across the smooth, clear waters.

Senator Highway Drive. This is an hour's round-trip but well worth it, especially if you like to relive history. Drive east on Gurley Street to South Mt. Vernon/Senator Highway. Along the way, you'll pass by Groom Creek, which was a Mormon settlement. Turn right on South Mt. Vernon/Senator Highway and head south to Wolf Creek picnic grounds. If you are so inclined, head for either Wolf Creek or Lower Wolf Creek campgrounds where you can hike, picnic, or do some four-wheeling on all-terrain vehicles (ATVs) if you trailer them in with you. Continue following this road to the right as it goes down the pine-studded mountain to the Indian Creek picnic grounds. Join US–89 6 miles from Prescott. Turn right and continue back to town. This used to be an old stage route connecting Prescott with Crown Point. As you make this drive, you can imagine how the pioneers felt as they bounced along on rutted roads shaded by these tall ponderosas.

Skyline Drive (also called Thumb Butte Loop). Plan on forty-five minutes to cover this truly spectacular drive. Head south on Montezuma Street (US–89) to Copper Basin Road. Turn right on Copper Basin Road, make a circle, and return to Thumb Butte Road. Along the way, you will see the Sierra Prieta Mountain range, which overlooks Skull Valley. As you approach Thumb Butte, you'll have a panoramic view of the San Francisco Peaks. These mountains are sacred to the Hopis, who believe that these peaks are home to their Kachina gods. During this drive, you'll ascend some 1,500 to 1,700 vertical feet. If you think this is a steep drive, imagine what it's like to *run* up this road. The Whiskey Row Marathon Society uses it as its course.

Along the way, you'll see a number of places to pull off to drink in the views. Be sure to do so when you see a viewpoint for Skull Valley. The name, Skull Valley, came from a group of cavalrymen who discovered mounds of sun-bleached skulls there in 1884. Later it was decided that these were the skulls of Apache and Maricopa Indians who clashed over stolen horses.

If you're dressed properly and not bothered by the altitude, take advantage of the hiking trails. These are well marked. A 2.3-mile trail leads to Thumb Butte. It begins easily. For almost a mile you can stroll along shaded ponderosa pines and three kinds of oak trees. Gradually, the vegetation changes . . . the pines recede and junipers, prickly pears, pinyons, and other scrub vegetation gain on you as the trail approaches the exposed ridge. You'll come to a junction at 1.1 miles. To the left, the trail rises to the base of the butte. This climb involves 200 feet of steep cliff and is not recommended for non-climbers. Instead, hikers should follow the right fork and continue about 150 yards to a vista point. When you reach it you'll understand why you've made this trip.

Short trails also lead to Mount St. Francis and West Spruce Mountain. When you're tired and hiked out, head back to your car and continue into Prescott on West Gurley Street.

The city of Prescott is virtually surrounded by the Prescott National Forest. Just a few minutes outside of town are campgrounds, picnic sites, lakes, and areas for nearly every kind of outdoor activity including exploring, prospecting, rockhounding, backpacking, horseback riding, and fishing. If you do any of these drives, wear comfortable shoes so you can get out of the car and walk around. The views are breathtaking.

WHERE TO EAT

Murphy's. 201 North Cortez Street. In this general store setting, you can munch on mesquite-broiled seafood or chow down on a variety of entrees, including excellent prime rib. $$–$$$; (CC). (520) 445–4044.

The Porter House Prescott Mining Company. 155 Plaza Drive. Great for fresh fish, prime rib, and steaks. The outdoor patio is a standout. Eat amidst a sylvan setting of flowers and trees (and ignore the new condos in the distance). $$; (CC). (520) 445–1991.

Note: both the Hassayampa Inn and The Prescott Resort have beautiful dining rooms. See "Where to Stay."

YARNELL-PEEPLES VALLEY

To return most directly to Phoenix, head south on US-89 through Yarnell and Peeples Valley. The road bisects the densely wooded Prescott National Forest and is exceptionally scenic. You'll be looking at the Sierra Prieta Mountains or the Black Mountains named by the Spaniards who explored this part of the state. The Black Mountains owe their dark color to their volcanic origin.

Peeples Valley is named for Abraham Peeples, who supposedly gathered between $4,000 and $7,000 worth of gold nuggets before breakfast one morning when he was walking on Weaver Mountain. Not surprisingly, the area commemorating Peeples's find is called "Rich Hill."

For more scenic beauty, follow A-96 (a back road) west from Prescott as it meanders past Iron Springs and into Skull Valley. The views are as great as the names. Where A-96 intersects with A-97, follow A-97 toward Phoenix for 16 miles to where it joins US 93-89. Follow US 93-89 to Wickenburg, Surprise, and Sun City; about 60 miles northwest of Phoenix the route becomes US-60.

PIONEER ARIZONA LIVING MUSEUM

Prepare to move through time from a prehistoric era to the future. The drive begins in rolling desert but climbs into steep mountain terrain in Jerome. You'll begin with endless vistas, and, as the mountains close in around you, saguaros give way to scrub and ultimately to sycamores. This landscape is filled with silent memories of the Sinaguas, an ancient Indian tribe who lived here hundreds of years ago. During the late 1800s, this countryside was alive with the ring of picks and shovels and the shouts of prospectors who worked in Rawhide Jimmy Douglas's silver mines.

Although the driving time from Phoenix to Jerome is three hours, this is considered a full-day trip in this land of wide open spaces. Should you choose to hike and sightsee, you'll arrive home in the evening tired but happy.

Start off early and take I-17 north toward Camp Verde to the Pioneer Arizona Living Museum. Plan to arrive around 9:00 A.M. to do this trip easily in a day.

WHERE TO GO

Pioneer Arizona Living Museum. 3901 Pioneer Road, Black Canyon Freeway and Pioneer Road. On I-17, 12 miles north of Bell Road, take exit 225 and follow signs to the museum. You'll spend a good hour touring the many authentic and replicated buildings on the grounds of this privately supported museum. Although a restau-

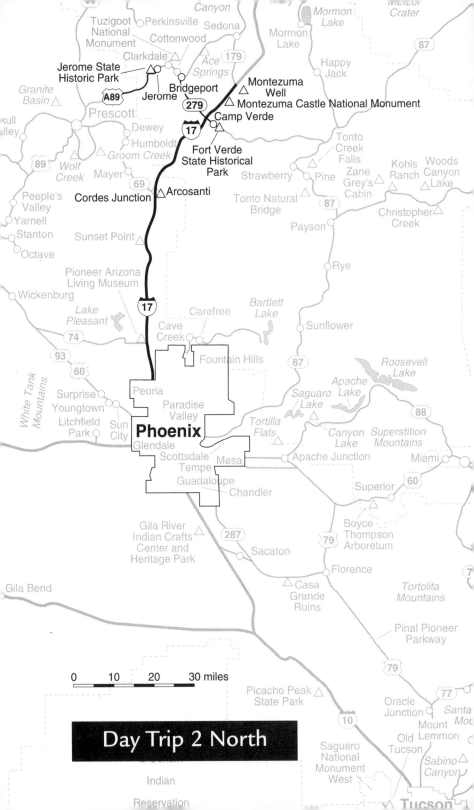

Day Trip 2 North

rant exists here, it's closed Mondays and Tuesdays. A shaded picnic area is always open. Call ahead for museum hours. Fee. (602) 465-1052.

Sunset Point. Follow the signs back to I-17 north. You may want to stop for a breathtaking view at this unique roadside rest stop, winner of an architectural award for excellence. Along with a sweeping panorama, you'll find a map, clean restrooms, and picnic tables.

CORDES JUNCTION

Back on I-17 north, continue to the Cordes Junction exit and Arcosanti, where you can visit a unique construction site.

WHERE TO GO

Arcosanti. I-17 at Cordes Junction, Mayer. Turn right at Cordes Junction Road and left at the stop sign. Follow a dirt road about 3 miles to Arcosanti—architect Paolo Soleri's vision of the future. Called the boldest experiment in urban living in the country, this energy-efficient town, which integrates architecture and ecology, has been under construction since 1970.

Soleri coined the word "arcology" to express his vision of a community in which people can live and work in harmony with the environment. In designing this prototype "city" under a single roof, Soleri combines an urban environment with a natural setting all within one structure. Ultimately, Soleri's plan utilizes both above- and underground space to concentrate human activity into an energy efficient environment while carefully leaving the vast surrounding acreage natural and undisturbed.

Arcosanti is being built by students and professionals who work and attend seminars on the site. Festivals and performances by visiting artists are scheduled during the year. Daily tours are available with a minimum of four people. Stop at the bakery and buy some of the excellent homemade breads and baked goods. Fee. (520) 632-7135.

WHERE TO EAT

The Cafe. The cafe at Arcosanti serves breakfast and lunch and features homemade foods prepared without preservatives or additives. A kids' menu is available. The cafe is not fancy, but the food is hearty and healthful. $-$$; (CC). (520) 632-7135.

CAMP VERDE

As you follow I-17 north, it plunges into a long downgrade that reveals the Verde Valley in all its splendor. Camp Verde is located near the geographical center of the state. Settled in 1864, it is the oldest town in the Verde Valley, literally growing up around what is now Fort Verde State Historical Park. If you've not been this way before, pull off at the marked scenic viewpoints and enjoy grand vistas along the way to this historic area.

WHERE TO GO

Fort Verde State Historical Park. Lane Street, Camp Verde. Take the first Camp Verde exit, 285, follow that road into Camp Verde, and turn right onto Lane Street. Visit the ten-acre Fort Verde Historical Park and see where Gen. George Crook accepted the surrender of Apache Chief Chalipun and 300 of his warriors in 1873. Crook left a distinctive mark on Arizona. In addition to his meeting with the Apache chief, Chalipun, the general had a rough wagon road cut up and along the Mogollon rim in 1884 to shorten the distance between Fort Apache and Fort Verde. Even today, that area is referred to as Crook's Trail.

Fort Verde was a major base for General Crook's scouts, soldiers, and pack mules during the Indian campaigns of the 1870s. As you walk along the dusty street of Officers' Row, you'll return to territorial days and better understand what it was like for the officers and their families who lived at Fort Verde during this period in history.

Tour the officers' quarters overlooking the parade ground, which are furnished in authentic 1880s military style. As you continue walking through the park, you may wonder at the Post Surgeon's spacious accommodations. In those days, patients were treated and surgery performed in the doctor's residence, while the post hospital was used only for quarantine and convalescence. Fee. (520) 567-3275.

MONTEZUMA CASTLE NATIONAL MONUMENT

To travel further back in time, follow Montezuma Castle Road 5 miles north from Camp Verde to Montezuma Castle National Monument. The ancient five-story Indian dwelling is carved out of a great limestone cliff. Although Indians lived in the valley as early as A.D. 600, it's believed that Sinagua farmers began building this dwelling sometime during the twelfth century A.D. When it was completed about three centuries later, the dwelling contained nineteen rooms, many of them suitable for living space.

The name Montezuma Castle is a misnomer. Montezuma, the Aztec king, never slept here. In fact, he was never here at all. When pioneers discovered the cliff dwelling, they mistook it for an ancient Aztec settlement and named it Montezuma Castle. Although the historical inaccuracy was determined later, the name stuck.

Stop at the visitors center first before taking the self-guided tour. Take time to view the hand-fitted stone walls and foot-thick sycamore ceiling beams; let your imagination fly.

There is a fee that also covers Montezuma Well. The picnic grounds offer lots of shady spots for lunch. (520) 567-3322.

MONTEZUMA WELL

Back on I-17 north, continue a few miles to the McGuireville exit. Follow the side road to Montezuma Well, but be ready for a bumpy, rough ride. This limestone sink was formed centuries ago by a collapsed cavern. Springs feed it continuously, and both the Hohokam Indians (who settled the Phoenix area in pre-Columbian times) and the Sinagua used the well for crop irrigation.

Just below the well are cliff dwellings built by the Sinagua Indians who were the northern neighbors of the Hohokam Indians who once inhabited the Salt River Valley. The Sinaguans left no written records, so their culture is interpreted only from archaeological evidence and the study of the Hopi who are believed to be their descendants. A hiking trail follows the rim of the sinkhole and then descends to the water's edge where more Sinaguan ruins can be seen. The rim trail is well marked with informational markers that describe native plants. The trail ultimately leads to the creek where the water from the well emerges through an underground passageway. The water, which maintains a constant temperature of 76 degrees, flows through irrigation ditches built by the Sinaguan hundreds of years ago. These canals are still in use today.

This area contains a Hohokam pit house, built around A.D. 1100, and Sinaguan dwellings. It's estimated that around 150 to 200 Sinaguans lived here between A.D. 1125 and A.D. 1400, when apparently they were forced out by a drought. Montezuma Well is free; the Montezuma Castle is $1 per person. (520) 567–3322.

JEROME

This area is as rich in lore as it was in ore. Although the steep ascent into Jerome is not for the faint of heart, the climb is replete with expansive views of the broad Verde Valley. In the distance you can see the Red Rocks of Sedona and even the far-off San Francisco Peaks in Flagstaff.

This is an unforgettable "living" ghost town that is perched atop Mingus Mountain (7,743 feet). Underneath the town, more than 100 miles of subterranean tunnels and shafts honeycomb the mountain where miners tore out a billion dollars in copper and other ore during the wild heyday of 1876. Back then Jerome lured men in search of luck and women in search of men. Gold and silver flowed and people poured in, building glorious residences fit for an eastern city.

Today all that remains of its former glory teeters on the precipitous slopes of Cleopatra Hill. The twisted, narrow streets, reminiscent of Europe, inspire even the most unimaginative photographer, so bring your camera and lots of film.

To get to Jerome from Montezuma Well, backtrack to I–77 South and A–279. From Montezuma Castle, pick up A–279 at I–17 and head northwest for 12 to 15 miles toward Jerome. Just north of Bridgeport, A–279 joins US–89; follow US–89A into Jerome.

WHERE TO GO

Gold King Mine and Museum. Located 1 mile northwest of Jerome on Perkinsville Road. Mining enthusiasts will enjoy seeing miners cages and artifacts displayed as well as an outdoor exhibit of a turn-of-the-century mining camp. Open daily. Fee. No phone available.

Jerome State Park. UVX Road. Originally the home of mining pioneer James S. Douglas, the state park features an extensive display of mining equipment. Museum lovers should follow UVX Road to the park where exhibits recounting the story of this once-flourishing copper mining community are displayed. As you browse through the mansion of "Rawhide" Jimmy, as he was known, you'll gain a sense of the personalities, places, and technology that forged this period of Arizona history. You'll need to retrace your steps to US–89A when you leave here. Open daily. Fee. (520) 634–5381.

Main Street. Jerome. US–89A becomes Main Street as it continues into Jerome. Park anywhere and walk around to get a sense of this special community. Now a popular tourist stop, Jerome almost became a ghost town; however, it's safe to assume that the ghosts now have left for quieter spots. Revived during the 1960s when hippies discovered it was both cheap and charming, today Jerome is a haven for people who eschew the urban scene.

As you walk around, you may want to stop in the shops, galleries, and restaurants that flourish in this area. Don't expect any uptown flash. Jerome is long on quaintness and short on commercial appeal. It's worth your time to spend a few minutes in the Jerome Historical Society on the corner of Main and Jerome streets to learn more about the town. You may contact the Jerome Historical Society at P.O. Box 156, Jerome, 86331, or call (520) 634–5477 in advance to request a town map and more information. While you are at the historical society, visit the Mine Museum in the building to see artifacts and exhibits illustrating Jerome's past glory.

Jerome attracts an eclectic mix of people, everyone from bikers to retirees. But up here everyone is mellow.

In the past ten years this town has become a center for arts and crafts, especially pottery. Items are fairly priced, and help is routinely friendly. You can discover some good bargains—especially during the annual arts and crafts show, which is held over the Fourth of July weekend.

Don't miss the Mining Museum Gift Shop as well as "Made in Jerome," which specializes in pottery, and "Nellie Bly's," a jewelry shop that features a wonderful variety of kaleidoscopes.

Stop in at the Chamber of Commerce and ask for a copy of the art registry, which describes the many art galleries in town. Pick up a directory to lodging and eating and the self-guided walking tour brochure.

WHERE TO EAT

The House of Joy. Hull Avenue, 1 block below Main Street. A converted bordello with lots of red velvet, gas lamps, and an upstairs that once catered to "business," this restaurant offers homemade gourmet food and old-time Jerome atmosphere. Open Saturdays and Sundays only. Dinner. Reservations are required. Call far ahead—a month isn't too long—after 9:00 A.M. Saturdays and Sundays. $$. (520) 634-5339.

WHERE TO STAY

Like many other small Arizona towns, Jerome is experiencing a growth of bed-and-breakfast establishments. Recommended are:

The Cottage Inn. 747 East Avenue. Turn right after the state park, third house on the right. This B&B can accommodate four guests in two antiques-decorated rooms with a sitting room. The owners serve a full breakfast. For reservations, write P.O. Box 823, Jerome, 86331. $$; (CC). (520) 634-0701.

The Rosegarden Bed & Breakfast. 3 Juarez Street. Call or write for directions. Juarez Street is directly opposite the Old Haven Methodist Church. This charming B&B accommodates a group of four, traveling together. Guests have the entire first floor of the home. There's a gorgeous view, an outer sitting room, and two rock walls as the house is built right into the corner of a mountain. An elaborate and elegant breakfast is served complete with cut glass and sterling silver. No check-in time, and breakfast is served at the guests' convenience. For reservations, write P.O. Box 313, Jerome, 86331. $$. (520) 634-3270.

Ghost City Inn. 541 Main Street. Originally built in 1898, the Ghost City Inn Bed & Breakfast, offers 5 theme rooms with shared bath, and the Cleopatra Hill Room with a private bath. Gourmet breakfast and afternoon tea and cookies, a spacious veranda with never-ending views, and turndown service complete with chocolate await visitors. $$; (CC). (520)-63GHOST.

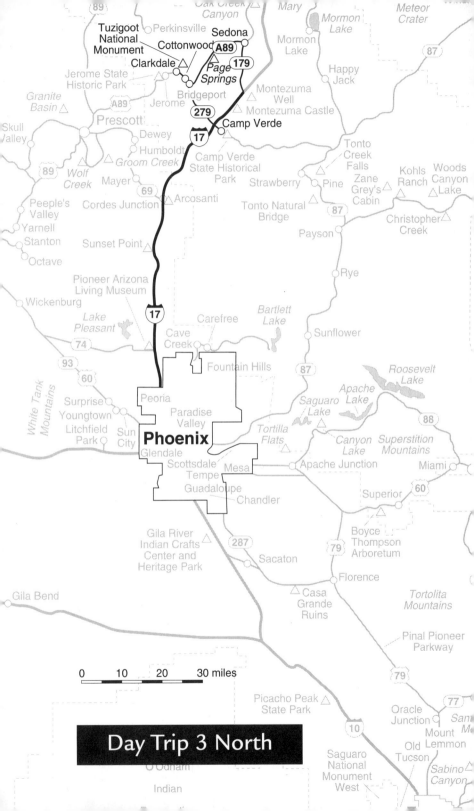

Day Trip 3 North

Begin the day with a visit to a prehistoric Indian ruin and complete it with a breathtakingly scenic ride through the Verde Valley. Arizona is proud to have several excursion trains running in the state. What's special about the Verde Valley train is it traverses an area that is not accessible to vehicular traffic. The cars are modern, but the scenery is ageless. For maximum beauty, take this trip during the spring or autumn when the verdant valley is dressed in its seasonal finest.

COTTONWOOD

From Phoenix, head north on I-17 to the Camp Verde junction. Follow A-279 northwest to Cottonwood.

According to legend, Cottonwood is named for the cottonwood trees that grew in a circle near what is now the center of town. Arizona historian Marshall Trimble disagrees. He attributes the name to the large stands of cottonwood trees that grew along the Verde River.

Regardless, visitors to the Historic Old Town of Cottonwood will find that cottonwoods are still as plentiful as the western flavor. Here you can walk on high sidewalks and see false front buildings. But don't let those "old tyme" places fool you. This town is growing as a retirement center and is home base for Alfredo's Wife, a popular clothing and gift manufacturer.

WHERE TO GO

Alfredo's Wife. 417 Willard Street. As you approach Cottonwood, this factory and outlet store is on the corner where US–89A and Willard Street meet. If you love whimsical, hand-appliquéd clothing, this outlet is a must. Everything is designed by one designer, and yes, there really is an Alfredo. Alfredo's wife's signature is a small mouse. All clothing and gift items are handmade by a cadre of women who stitch the designs in the Cottonwood workshop. (520) 634-5808.

CLARKDALE

Continue on A–279 to Clarkdale, which was once the smelting town for the mines in Jerome. Today Clarkdale is the departure point for Tuzigoot National Monument, the wilderness of Sycamore Canyon, and the Verde River Canyon Railroad.

Tuzigoot National Monument. If you are up for more Indian ruins, don't veer west onto US–89A, but continue north on A–279 to see another Sinaguan village. This ancient ruin is located between Cottonwood and Clarkdale and was forgotten until the 1930s when a team of archaeologists from the University of Arizona began excavating and exploring it. Their work was amply rewarded. They deduced that the original pueblo was two stories high and had seventy-seven ground-floor rooms. Built between A.D. 1125 and A.D. 1400, this ruin offers yet another intimate view of the ancient people who roamed, hunted, and farmed here. The pueblo is situated on a 120-foot-high ridge presenting a panoramic view of the Jerome-Clarkdale area. No doubt the Sinaguas stood there, centuries ago, and marveled at the undisturbed view.

Spend some time to walk along the trail at Tuzigoot. If you are fascinated by these people, don't leave without visiting the museum. Open daily. Fee. (520) 634-5564.

The museum displays rare turquoise mosaics, beads and bracelets made of shells, painted pottery, and a variety of grave offerings, items the native people left in graves to carry into the afterlife.

The Verde Canyon Railroad and Railroad Inn. The Verde Canyon Train travels through the Verde River Canyon, one of the richest riparian habitats in the Southwest. The train started service in November 1990. The modern diesel winds through extraordinary scenery. Sharp-eyed travelers at appropriate times of the year can spot eagles soaring, and everyone can enjoy white-water rapids and the majesty of the Promethean cliffs.

Trains have been running in this area since well before World War I. This particular train was called the "Verde Mix" because it carried people and coal and was bankrolled originally by U.S. Senator William Clark. Clarkdale was named for his family. Clark ran his own 73-foot Pullman Palace luxury car on the tracks.

Today, it's possible to duplicate Senator Clark's extravagance as railroad cars can be rented for private parties. The approximate cost for a first-class, private railroad trip is $50.00 per person. Wildflowers may be viewed from mid-March through May, and there are open-air gondola cars for outdoor viewing and photography.

The train leaves from 300 North Broadway, which is about 16 miles west of I-17, via exit 287. The 20-mile trip is scheduled every day but Tuesday, departing at 11:00 A.M. and returning at 3:10 P.M. Summer starlight rides are also offered. The train winds through Verde Canyon adjacent to the Sycamore Wilderness Area and passes a continuously changing landscape — from prickly pear in the desert to hardwood trees. A naturalist on board provides narration. The 40-mile round trip follows the river past red sandstone formations reminiscent of those seen in nearby Sedona. As Sinagua Indians once lived in this area, the thousand-year-old Sinagua ruins can be seen in the cliffs high above the water. At one point the train slows to go over S.O.B. Trestle, named for the foreman who ordered his crew to build this edifice. First class passengers receive hors d'oeuvres and cocktail service; coach passengers can purchase drinks and snacks. Overnight packages are available. Along the way, it passes a bald eagle nest, Indian ruins, and sandstone cliffs and goes through a 680-foot man-made tunnel. For information on schedules and fares and tour packages, call Sedona SuperRate at (520) 639-0010 or (800) 858-7245.

PAGE SPRINGS

From the Cottonwood and Clarkdale area, saddle up for a true west adventure by following US-89A to the Page Springs-McGuireville exit.

Page Springs Bar & Restaurant. 1975 Page Springs Road. A twenty-minute drive from Jerome on 89A, heading toward Sedona.

Take the Page Springs-McGuireville exit and proceed for about 21 miles until you see the restaurant on your left. Page Springs is situated along Oak Creek and is shaded by big sycamore trees. If you are lucky to get a window seat, you can watch the ducks paddling in the creek. Food is down-home American cooking with all-you-can-eat specials on barbecue ribs and prime beef. $-$$. For information, write HC 66, Box 2204, Cornville, 86325. (520) 634-9954.

Sedona
Oak Creek Canyon

SEDONA

This is one of the most popular day trips for visitors and residents alike. Desert dwellers love the lush green of Oak Creek Canyon and one never tires of the Red Rocks or the startling view as the highway plunges into the heart of this magnificent country. Dedicated shoppers enjoy poking around the intriguing boutiques and art galleries in Sedona and the village of Oak Creek. Outdoor buffs have a veritable banquet to choose from—everything from water sports to Indian ruins to hiking, to running or jogging up Schnebley Hill for the more hardy.

Although you can approach Sedona in a couple of ways, I-17 north to A-179 is a popular route. At the junction of A-179 and US-89A, head north on A-179 and continue toward Sedona. The trip is an easy, nonstop, two-hour drive from Phoenix. Along the way, you get a full dose of Sedona's famous Red Rocks, one of the reasons for the town's popularity. Although recently man has made his mark here with condominiums, shopping centers, and elegant homes, the Red Rocks still dominate the landscape. At an elevation of 4,300 feet, Sedona's weather is usually delightful. Although snow occasionally falls in winter, and summer temperatures can peak from warm to hot, the climate generally is ideal. You can easily spend a day (not to mention money) exploring indoors as Sedona offers a full complement of culture and recreation. Outdoor enthusiasts will find plenty to do as well. The area is rich with campgrounds and Indian

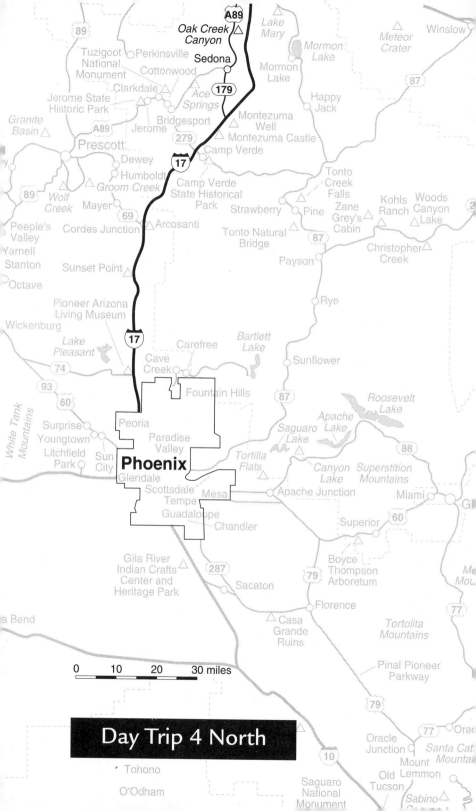

Day Trip 4 North

ruins. Hatcheries keep the fishing good. Between the glorious apricot-to-peach-to-purple sunsets and the burnished Red Rocks, Sedona is awash with color.

WHERE TO GO

Chapel of the Holy Cross. Heading toward Sedona on A-179, you pass the Village of Oak Creek. Continue on A-179 for approximately 5 miles. In the distance, on your right, you will see the Chapel of the Holy Cross against the Red Rocks. Turn right on Chapel Road, which leads to the church. The road is well marked with three signs announcing the turnoff. This is an inspirational and architectural treat. It is open daily to the public free of charge. (520) 282-4069.

Tlaquepaque. Continue north on A-179. As it bends right before crossing Oak Creek, make a sharp left turn. The entrances are immediately on your left. The cobblestone driveways are marked by rustic-looking stone gates that are almost hidden beneath the tall trees.

Tlaquepaque (Ta-la-kee-pah-kee) is a shopping center worth your time. Named for a suburb of Guadalajara, Mexico, this is a favorite gathering place for locals and tourists. Indulge yourself in the boutiques featuring everything from superb pottery, elegant glass, clothing, and gifts to art and sculpture. You can also feed your body, as well as your soul, at a number of excellent dining establishments.

As you walk through Tlaquepaque, notice the bell tower, which is a Sedona landmark. Peek inside the tiny chapel near the central plaza. Just as each Spanish and Mexican village has a church, Tlaquepaque has its chapel, which holds approximately twenty people and is used for private weddings and other ceremonies. For more information, contact Tlaquepaque, P.O. Box 1868, Sedona, 86336. (520) 282-4838.

The Red Rocks. There's no better way to see the red rocks of Sedona than by going off-road. There are about a half-dozen companies in Sedona that provide escorted tours. Here's a recommended favorite.

Sedona's famous **Pink Jeep Tours** and **Sedona Adventures** offers adventure for everyone who is daring enough to ride off the road in a Pink Jeep or open Land Cruiser, and up the hills and over the creeks to gain this special view of the majestic Sedona landscape. Pink Jeep Tours takes you through the Broken Arrow off-road areas, and Sedona Adventures explores the more remote Diamondback Gulch and includes some easy to moderate scenic hikes. You may call ahead to reserve space on one of the seven jeeps. Take anywhere from a one-and-a-half to a three-hour tour, or sign up for a rollicking all-day trip. Sunrise or sunset tours are particularly spectacular, and custom tours or barbeques can be arranged. This excursion is recommended for all ages, but be prepared for some wild driving and even wilder views. For more information about times and prices, write Pink Jeep Tours, P.O. Box 1447, Sedona, 86336. Fee. (520) 282-5000 or Pink Jeep Tours' Sedona Adventures at (800) 888-9494.

Honancki Ruins tours. Run by the Pink Jeep Tours operation, this tour gives you a chance to be escorted on an archaeological expedition of Indian ruins. Travel by jeep to back-country, unexcavated, unreconstructed cliff dwellings, which you'll explore, room by room. For more information on these tours, write to Pink Jeep Tours' Ancient Expeditions, P.O. Box 1447, Sedona, 86336, or phone (520) 282-2137.

Red Rock State Park. Follow US-89A 3 miles. Turn off onto Lower Red Rock Loop Road. Nestled on lower Oak Creek near Sedona, this 286-acre park was planned as an environmental center. A naturalist program offers tours that introduce you to the plants and animals in this special riparian setting. Approximately $11^4/10$ miles of Oak Creek wind through the park, and more than 135 species of birds and 450 species of plants and grasses have been identified here. First stop should be the visitors center. Then head off on any of the several trails. If you visit in winter, take a jacket or sweater. Free. (520) 282-6907.

Sedona Arts Center. US-89A at Barn Road. This center offers theater productions, visual arts exhibitions, and other art exhibits as well as concerts and festivals. Free entrance to the Exhibition Hall; art themes change monthly. (520) 282-3809.

Slide Rock State Park. On US-89A about 4 or 5 miles past up-town Sedona. Developed around a natural water slide that has been smoothed over by centuries of water (not to mention blue-jeaned derrieres), this park is a favorite spot for kids of all ages. Years ago, this was a casual experience. Today, the park is well maintained and organized. There's a fee for parking, but sliding in Oak Creek is still free. Those less adventurous will enjoy the verdant scene and the grassy picnic grounds.

Red Rock Crossing. Touted as the best all-around hiking trail in the Sedona-Oak Creek area, this trail is good for adults of all ages and fitness levels, kids and pets. To reach this hiking area, take A-89A west from Sedona to Upper Red Rock Loop Road. Go south on Red Rock Loop and look for signs to direct you to Red Rock Crossing. Parking costs $3. The hike begins by walking on a sidewalk that goes through a meadow surrounded by cottonwood trees. The sidewalk ends at Oak Creek. From there the hike continues along a gravel trail for approximately 20 minutes to the base of Cathedral Rock. The tricky part of this hike involves walking across some logs at the deeper parts of the creek.

Schnebly Hill. One of the most well-known hiking and mountain biking routes in Sedona, this is a 23-mile round trip through mind-boggling Sedona scenery. The road begins a half-mile south of the intersection of highways 89-A and SR-179 in town. The dirt road leads west from SR-179. Hikers and cyclists will see the ruins of the old Foxboro Lake Resort about halfway through the trip. The old carriage house stands on the left side of the road with the main building and swimming pool at the meadow's edge to the right. This is not a good ride after rain or snow, so it's a good idea to check with the Coconino National Forest Office for road conditions.

WHERE TO EAT

L'Auberge de Sedona. 301 L'Auberge Lane, Sedona. On US-89A, one block north of A-179. L'Auberge is gourmet without being stuffy. It offers an impressive menu from hors d'oeuvres to a six-course dinner. An outstanding selection of entrees and superb preparation and presentation have garnered raves, including being honored by the Chefs in America organization as one of "America's Finest Restaurants." Call for reservations. $$-$$$ (breakfast less); (CC). (520) 282-1661.

Enchantment Resort. Boyton Canyon. 525 Boyton Canyon Road, Sedona, 86336. Serving breakfast, lunch, and dinner and a champagne brunch on Sundays from 11:30 A.M. to 2:30 P.M. Jackets are required for men for dinner. $$-$$$; (CC). Reservations are recommended for dinner and Sunday brunch. (520) 282-2900.

Garland's Oak Creek Lodge. P.O. Box 152, Sedona, 86336. Coming north from Sedona, go 8 miles on US–89A and see the sign for Garland's on your left. Cross the creek and you're at one of Oak Creek Canyon's most charming settings. Call ahead for reservations for breakfast or dinner and sample some super home-cooked meals. $$$; (CC). (520) 282-3343.

Heartline Cafe. 1610 West US–89A. At the Y in the road, turn left and continue approximately a mile. It's on the right-hand side as you go toward West Sedona. The menu varies but the food is always fresh and delicious. For health-conscious eaters, there is a spa menu. Pastas and pizzas are excellent. Request to eat on the patio. $$–$$$; (CC). (520) 282–0785.

Rene at Tlaquepaque. This authentic French restaurant features great French bread and superb cuisine. The house specialty is an excellent rack of lamb. Don't be turned away by the French ambience. Inside, you'll find elegantly casual surroundings. You can come as you are, dressed for sightseeing. $$–$$$; (CC). (520) 282-9225.

WHERE TO STAY

L'Auberge de Sedona. 301 L'Auberge Lane, Sedona. On US–89A, one block north of A–179. This informal yet elegant French-style country inn is fast becoming well known throughout the country. The grounds alone are worth a visit. Its rosemary-scented pathways, shade trees, picnic tables, and stepping stones create a magical ambience for the various pine cottages nestled among the cottonwood trees. Beds are handcrafted and canopied. Love seats are overstuffed. Televisions and telephones are nowhere to be seen. $$$; (CC). Reservations: (800) 272-6777.

Enchantment Resort. Boyton Canyon. 525 Boyton Canyon Road, Sedona, 86336. Heading west on US–89A, turn right on Dry Creek Road and continue approximately 3 miles. Here you'll come to a T in the road. Turn left where you see the sign for Boyton Canyon. Go 2 miles farther. You'll come to a second T in the road. Turn right and follow the signs toward Boyton Canyon. This spectacular resort is carved into the most gorgeous setting in all of Sedona and is definitely worth the trip. The guard will direct you to the clubhouse, set high into Boyton Canyon. Indulge in tennis, swimming, golf, and hiking. $$$; (CC). For reservations: in Arizona, (800) 843–1691; out of state, (800) 826–4180.

Garland's Oak Creek Lodge. P.O. Box 152, Sedona, 86336. Coming north from Sedona, go 8 miles on US-89A and see the sign for Garland's on your left. Cross the creek and you're at one of Oak Creek Canyon and Arizona's best-kept treasures. This is a homey nine-acre resort set just across Oak Creek. Rooms are individual, freestanding log cabins and have no locks. Twelve of fifteen units have fireplaces, and all are charming. Although Garland's traditionally fills up on weekends—up to a year in advance—you are encouraged to call at the last minute, as cancellations do occur. A two-night stay is required, and breakfast and dinner are included. Open April 1 through November 15. $$$; (CC). (520) 282–3343.

Graham Bed & Breakfast Inn. 150 Canyon Circle Drive, Sedona, 85351. This elegant bed and breakfast is owned by Carol and Roger Redenbaugh. In addition to home-cooked breakfasts prepared by the hosts, guests enjoy designer touches in the individual suites and special amenities like a double Jacuzzi. This award-winning Mobil four-star inn also boasts a lushly landscaped pool area. $$$; (CC). (520) 284–1425.

Territorial House Bed & Breakfast. 65 Piki Drive. Hosts John and Linda Steele offer a choice of four rooms which include full breakfast and afternoon refreshments. The Red Rock Crossing room features a romantic king-size four poster canopy bed, oval marble whirlpool tub, separate glass shower and private deck. Grasshopper Flats features a queen-size barnwood bed as well as old west movies made in Sedona. Indian Garden is a pueblo-style room with a second floor balcony that comes equipped with a telescope for viewing the stars. Schnebly Station is a western 2 bedroom suite that is perfect for families or couples traveling together. $$; (CC). (520) 204–2737 or (800) 801–2737.

OAK CREEK CANYON

Oak Creek Canyon is just north of Sedona on US-89A. Don't see one without seeing the other. Oak Creek glimmers in autumn, sparkles cool and clear in summer, and occasionally is tinged with winter snow. The drive through Oak Creek Canyon is steep enough to satisfy a roller-coaster lover, but once on the canyon floor, you may park your car and walk around the area. Plan to take this drive north-to-south for the most breathtaking views.

For many sightseers, the drive through Oak Creek Canyon is experience enough. More ambitious types should take a casual stroll through the wooded area along the creek. Serious hikers may prefer more rugged challenges, so if you don't mind getting wet (you'll need to wade across the creek), there are more rigorous routes described in several books on outdoor Arizona available at local bookstores.

West Fork of Oak Creek Canyon. Continue on US–89A about 10 miles north of Sedona between milepost 384 and 385. Watch for two large posts with a heavy chain on the west side of the road about 100 feet north of a Dos Pinos sign. The trail begins as an asphalt path. You'll pass the ruins of the old Mayhew Lodge and then emerge into a riparian wonderland of red cliffs and pungent leaves. The trail crosses Oak Creek several times, so be prepared to balance on slippery rocks or wade across. Although this is a very popular hike, the trail offers a special slice of Arizona: peaceful, green, and wet! The deeper you go into the canyon, the more verdant the scene and, during autumn, more brilliantly colored. Free.

Often called "the city of seven wonders," Flagstaff is approximately two-and-a-half hours north of Phoenix, an easy day trip by Arizona standards. The scenic highway dips through the Verde Valley, climbs over the Mogollon Rim, or "the Rim" as it's better known, and ultimately reaches this 7,000-foot-high city. This is a trip of strong natural contrast: you travel from prickly pears to pines. If you take this drive in winter, you can swim in your heated Phoenix pool in the morning, ski all afternoon in Flagstaff, and return home to Phoenix that night!

Trivia lovers may enjoy knowing that most stories concerning the origin of the name Flagstaff involved some person lopping off branches of a lone pine and running a flag up the pole. Fortunately, someone thought "Flag-staff" had a better ring to it than "Flag-pole." In any event, it is documented that to celebrate the naming, a centennial flag was flown from a tall pine tree on July 4, 1876.

Today, this city is the seat of Coconino County, second-largest county in the country, and home to Northern Arizona University. The northern hub of the state, Flagstaff is a bustling little city, bisected by railroad tracks, surrounded by pines, and dominated by the 12,670-foot Mount Humphreys Peak, the tallest mountain in the state. The downtown has recently undergone a wonderful restoration. You'll find outdoor cafes and some fun shops here, everything from a terrific bookstore to outdoor stores. Surrounded by verdant splendor, the town is ringed with appealing new sections featuring reddish wood tones and rustic, ski-lodge motifs. During ski season, Flagstaff's Snow Bowl hums with the whoosh of downhill skiers

Day Trip 5 North

coursing down Mount Humphreys. Throughout the year, the city is home to a hardy breed of students and outdoor types. If you love plaid flannel shirts, this may be your place. With Flagstaff as your jumping-off point, the whole of northern Arizona opens up and a wonderland of day trips opens to you. (Read about these in the section titled Day Trips from Flagstaff.) In the meantime, here's a sampling of the sights to see when you visit this hub of northern Arizona.

WHERE TO GO

Arboretum at Flagstaff. On Woody Mountain Road off US-66, about 4 miles west of town. The center is located in a beautiful wooded area. At an elevation of 7,150 feet, it is the highest botanic garden in the United States doing horticultural research. The display gardens offer landscaping ideas for the arid West, but even non-gardeners will enjoy this quiet respite. Here are Arizona plants and flowers, many of which are rare and specially bred for this climate. For information, write P.O. Box 670, Flagstaff, 86002. Fee. (520) 774-1441.

Coconino Center for the Arts. 2300 North Fort Valley Road. On A-180 (Fort Valley Road). This regional art center offers a variety of arts programming including exhibits, musical performances, workshops, and demonstrations as well as a folk art program. Gallery shows of national importance are mounted. The Center offers "Trappings of the American West" every May and June, which brings together fine art and crafts that reflect the life of the American cowboy. Closed Mondays during the winter months. Free. (520) 779-6912.

Elden Pueblo. On US-89 north of I-40, just south of Winona Road on the northern edge of Flagstaff. Archaeology buffs will appreciate this masonry ruin. Largely unexcavated, it is believed to be a sixty- or seventy-room pueblo that dates from around A.D. 1100 and is considered an ancestral site by the Hopi. Continually under excavation, this pueblo was discovered in 1926 and is believed to lie on top of a pit house village. To join in the thrill of uncovering an ancient site, call the Coconino National Forest for public "dig days." These are held in the summer and provide opportunities for hands-on excavation. Free. (520) 523-9642.

Lava River Cave. Nine miles north of Flagstaff on US-180. Turn west (left) on FR-245 and continue 3 miles to FR-171. Turn south 1 mile to where FR-171A turns left. Continue a short distance to the mile-long lava tube cave. This primitive cave was formed 700,000 years ago by molten rock that erupted from a volcanic vent in nearby Hart Prairie. If you look at the floor, you can see wave-like undulations that are the remains of frozen ripples in the last trickle of molten rock that flowed from this cave. Inside, the temperature is forty-two degrees—even in summer—so dress warm. In winter, the cave can only be accessed by skiing to it. Bring flashlights because the interior is dark, slippery, and rugged. Free. For information, call the Public Affairs office at (520) 527-3490.

Lowell Observatory. 1400 West Mars Hill Road. Travel west on Santa Fe Avenue; following the street to the end, climb Mars Hill. Dr. Percival Lowell built the wooden, world-famous observatory in 1894. The planet Pluto was discovered here in 1930, and today the observatory continues to be a center of important scientific work. Interesting and informative guided tours are available daily. If you visit during the summer, plan on spending Friday night here when the observatory is open free to the public. Fee. (520) 774-3358.

Meteor Crater Museum of Astrogeology. (See Day Trip 1, East from Flagstaff.)

The Museum of Northern Arizona. 3101 North Fort Valley Road, Flagstaff. Three miles north of Flagstaff on US-180 at Fort Valley Road. From downtown Flagstaff, follow the signs to the Grand Canyon via US-180. A small jewel for those people interested in knowing about northern Arizona—especially the Navajo and Hopi cultures—the museum offers an outstanding rug display and gift shop. This museum is a "must" for visitors who are unfamiliar with northern Arizona as it provides a superb introduction to the Kaibab Plateau, the area which is home to the Grand Canyon. The museum has excellent interpretive exhibits for children as well as adults, as well as one of the best bookstores in the state. During the summer, several tribes showcase traditional arts and activities on the beautiful museum grounds. Route 4, Box 720, Flagstaff, 86001. Open daily. Fee. (520) 774-5211.

Pioneer Historical Museum. 2340 North Fort Valley Road. From downtown Flagstaff, follow the signs to the Grand Canyon via US-180. The museum is 2 miles north of town (just a mile before you get to the Museum of Northern Arizona). Operated by the Pioneer Historical Society, the facility is devoted to preserving Arizona's pioneer heritage. All kinds of artifacts depicting pioneer life are on display here to help you understand what it was like for those people who settled the area. Donation suggested. Closed Sundays. Box 1968, Flagstaff, 86001. For information, call the Arizona Historical Society at (520) 774-6272.

Sunset Crater Volcano National Monument. (See Day Trip 1, North from Flagstaff.)

Walnut Canyon National Monument. Off I-40 east, 7^1/2 miles east of Flagstaff at the Walnut Canyon turnoff. A beautifully preserved Sinaguan cliff dwelling, Walnut Canyon whispers of bygone centuries. This is one of the most beautiful spots in Flagstaff and is a great destination for people of all ages. Almost always peaceful and sylvan, Walnut Canyon offers well-marked trails as well as more rugged adventures. Stop first at the visitors center and decide whether to travel into this time warp by strolling on Rim Walk Trail or hiking down Island Trail, a 185-foot descent. Both provide a splendid view of the 300 small cliff dwellings that are found within this 400-foot deep canyon. If you choose the more strenuous path, prepare to take your time: it takes twice the effort to ascend as it does to descend. Fee. (520) 526-3367.

Flagstaff Snow Bowl. (Twenty-eight-mile round-trip.) Take A-180 (Humphreys Street) north 7 miles. Turn right at Snow Bowl Road and continue climbing up that dirt road another 7 miles to the end of the path, where you'll see the lodge. Indoor types can eat at the Snow Bowl snack shop and imbibe at the bar. Weather permitting, the top of the Snow Bowl is great for a panoramic view or picnic. A ski lift runs up Mount Humphreys, Arizona's highest peak, which towers over the San Francisco Mountain range. It's open in summer until mid-July and on weekends and holidays.

The view is dazzling. You go almost to the top of Mt. Agassiz to an elevation of 11,500 feet in thirty minutes. If you do this in the summer, take a jacket, as it's cool. As you ride you can see the Grand Canyon's North Rim more than 80 miles away as well as the dormant volcano field that surrounds the city. Kendrick Peak, Wild Bill, and Wing Mountain are prominent landmarks. You'll enjoy views of Mt. Humphreys, Hart Prairie, and ponderosa pines. The skyride is usually open only on weekends.

Once at the top, you can hike on any of a variety of interpretive trails with good descriptions of the vegetation and historical significance of the area. (520) 779-1951.

Riordan Mansion. 1300 Riordan State Historic Park. The mansion was built in 1904 for Timothy and Michael Riordan, who established the logging industry in Flagstaff. The interior has over 13,000 square feet with forty rooms, stained glass windows, and unique window transparencies created by the renowned turn-of-the-century photographer, Jack Hillers.

Don't miss the visitors center, which maintains an exhibit area and informative slide program. You can also bring a picnic and eat in the park. Guided tours are available. Call for hours. Fee. (520) 779-4395.

Historic walking tour. From the Riordan Mansion, continue north on Milton. From the arrival of the first railroad in 1882 throughout the postwar expansion after 1945, this was the business center for most of northern Arizona. The downtown has been restored and features many shops and galleries offering a fine array of Southwestern arts and crafts, specialty items, and clothing.

SCENIC DRIVE

Around the Peaks Loop. This loop takes you all the way around Arizona's highest mountain, winding through pine forest, aspen groves, open prairies, and rustic homesteads. You can do this drive any time when snow doesn't close the road. In spring you'll enjoy a carpet of wildflowers; in autumn the trees blaze gold. Along the way you can get out of the car and hike or camp.

To enjoy this loop, drive northeast on US-89 from Flagstaff for 14 miles. Turn west 12 miles to FR-151. Then go south 8 miles to US-180. It's 9.5 miles back to Flagstaff.

The entire loop is 44 miles and roads are suitable for cars. Plan on spending about two hours enjoying the magnificent scenery.

WHERE TO EAT

You can't tell this from the highway, but Flagstaff is a full-service restaurant town. Everything is here from Oriental to Thai, barbecue to coffee shops, natural to elegant continental dining. Here are some favorites. Ask the Flagstaff Convention and Visitor Bureau for a brochure with a complete listing. Stop in at 101 Route 66, Flagstaff, 86001, or call (520) 774-4505.

Charly's Restaurant and Pub. 23 North Leroux Street, in the old Weatherford Hotel in downtown Flagstaff. Built in 1898 by John Weatherford, a Flagstaff merchant, the Victorian-style structure is one of the best examples of red-sandstone architecture in Flagstaff. Fun and funky, it is great for lunch or dinner, and Sunday brunch is special. Enjoy outstanding soups; there's lovely music while you dine. Open daily. $$; (CC). (520) 779-1919.

Cafe Espress. 16 North San Francisco Street. Indulge in lots of good natural food, homemade baked pastries, and a variety of coffees. $-$$; (CC). (520) 774-0541.

Chez Marc Bistro. 503 North Humphreys Street. Dine inside in a restored house or outside on the patio. Nouvelle French. $$-$$$; (CC). (520) 774-1343.

Cottage Place. 126 West Cottage Street, in the old town area south of the railroad tracks. This famous landmark restaurant is in an old Flagstaff house. Service is gracious. The food is worth the wait. $$-$$$; (CC). (520) 774-8431.

El Charro Cafe. 409 South San Francisco Street. This family-owned restaurant offers authentic Mexican food. On Saturday night, the family mariachi band performs. $; (CC). (520) 779-0552.

Gretels Blackforesthouse. 605 West Riordan Road. Just off Milton, close to the NAU campus. This restaurant is hidden away in a little house that has survived neighborhood development. Family owned and operated, it serves wonderful German food. $$; (CC). (520) 773-1551.

Kelly's Christmas Tree Restaurant. 5200 East Cortland Boulevard. Christmas happens all year long here. Continental dining is featured. The scallops are outstanding. Feast on homemade rolls and desserts and dine at a leisurely pace. $$-$$$; (CC). (520) 526-0776.

Main Street Bar & Grill. 14 South San Francisco Street, south of the tracks. This is a neat little place with great food. Barbecue is a specialty. Homemade soups and desserts are served up along with live entertainment. $; (CC). (520) 774-1519.

Black Bart's Steak House. 2760 East Butler Avenue. This is a good family place featuring steaks and chicken, cowboy beans and biscuits. See the old-time review put on by the waiters and waitresses. You'll pay extra for the show but it's worth it. $$; (CC). (520) 779-3142.

Macy's. 14 South Beaver (on the south side of the Santa Fe Railroad tracks). This funky coffeehouse is a local favorite. In addition to serving breakfasts (they have great teas, coffees, baked goods, etc.), Macy's also serves excellent lunches and dinners. $-$$; no (CC). (520) 774-2243.

Mama Luisa Italian Restaurant. 2710 North Steves Boulevard. Tiny but terrific. Italian food here is excellent. $-$$$; (CC). (520) 526-6809.

Pasto. 19 East Aspen Avenue. Excellent Italian food in downtown. Flagstaff has a small but charming historic downtown that makes this special. $$; (CC). (520) 779-1937.

Horsemen Lodge and Restaurant. 8500 North 89. Old West atmosphere is set against a background of the San Francisco peaks. Steaks and other western casual fare are served in a rustic atmosphere. $$; (CC). (520) 526-2655.

WHERE TO STAY

All kinds of accommodations await tourists. Choose from bed and breakfasts and rustic cabins to modern motels and resorts. Check with the Flagstaff Convention and Visitor Bureau, 211 West Aspen Avenue, Flagstaff, 86001, or call (520) 779-7611 for a complete listing of hotels, motels, and other accommodations. Here are three to start you off.

Best Western Woodlands Plaza, 1560 East Santa Fe Avenue. This is an elegant resort hotel that offers luxury at surprisingly reasonable prices. It won a Three Diamond Award and has a heated swimming pool. Nonsmoking rooms are available and fine dining is nearby. $$; (CC). (520) 774-7168, or Best Western reservations at (800) 528-1234.

Quality Suites. 2000 South Milton Road. You will find very comfortable rooms with VCRs. The owner started the "no smoking" room concept. Breakfast is included. $$; (CC). (520) 774-4333 or (800) 228-5151.

Little America. Butler Avenue and I-40. This is a large

(248-room) facility. The rooms are big and well appointed, and the bathrooms are luxurious and equipped with telephones. You have several dining rooms to choose from. $$; (CC). (520) 779-2741 or (800) 528-1234.

Bed & Breakfasts

These are all in beautiful old homes and are privately owned and run. Each one serves outstanding breakfasts.

Birch Tree Inn. 524 West Birch Avenue. This is a lovely place with amenities including a pool table. Nonsmoking only. $$; (CC). (520) 774-1042.

Dierker House. 423 West Cherry. Just three rooms are available in this wonderful old house, but each room is furnished with lovely antiques. The owner cooks a fabulous breakfast and keeps fresh cookies out for munchy attacks. $$. (520) 774-3249.

Inn at 410. 410 North Lereoux. Nine suites are decorated to perfection. Some are singles; some are suites. Each has its own bathroom, and the breakfast is superb. $$$; (CC). (520) 774-0088.

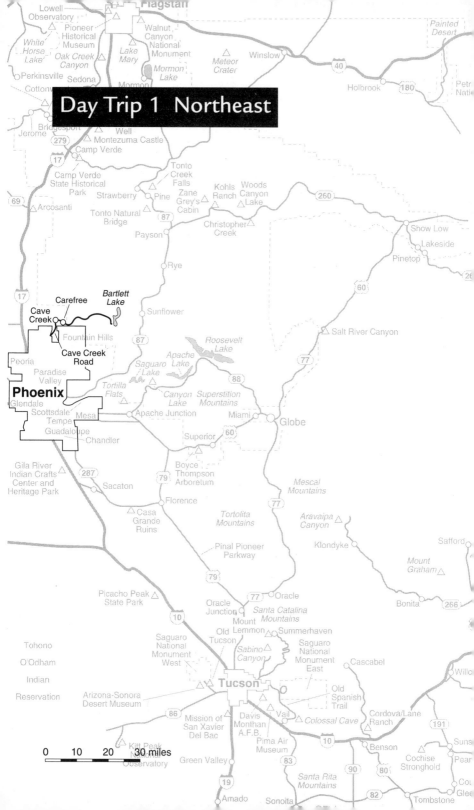

CAVE CREEK

This day trip begins at Cave Creek and offers a peek into the not-so-distant past. Along the way, you see the Phoenix urban area at its most posh. Comfortable distances and good shopping make this a relaxing, easy trip. Although the desert northeast of Phoenix is rapidly being developed, the vast Tonto National Forest is just an arrowhead's throw away. If you are concerned that this close-in desert is fast disappearing, remember that Arizona is only 18 percent privately owned. Since most of the land belongs to the state and federal governments, hopefully much of it will be saved for posterity.

Cave Creek is a funky little old town that has resisted urban flash, unlike its sister city, Carefree, which was built to attract the well-heeled. A mining camp in the 1880s and a ranching community after the mines gave out, today Cave Creek offers city dwellers an alternative to urban life.

When Tonto National Forest was established here in 1903, the first tourists started to arrive. Bartlett Dam, built in 1935, brought more people. The terrain adjacent to Tonto National Forest is dotted with lakes and punctuated by mountains and provides an array of outdoor recreation opportunities. There is an abundance of wild game in the area including deer, wild pig, mountain lion, duck, quail, and dove, so opportunities abound for hiking, fishing, horseback riding, and rockhounding.

47

Keep your eye out for antiques shops. There are some intriguing places to browse. To get to Cave Creek, follow I-17 to the Carefree Highway eastbound. Turn east. It becomes Desert Foothills Drive. Individuals who cared about the desert made the 101 signs identifying the desert plants along the road. As you maneuver along the dips, take time to notice these identifying markers and learn about the unusual environment.

WHERE TO GO

Cave Creek Museum. 6140 Skyline Drive, Cave Creek. Open October to May, the living history of the desert foothills area is presented in this small museum through displays of pioneer living, ranching, mining, and old guns. Exhibits also describe the cultures of the Hohokam, Yavapai, and Apache. Free. (602) 488-2764.

WHERE TO EAT

The Horny Toad. 6738 East Cave Creek Road. This is a *gen-u-ine western joint*. Fried chicken (lots of it) is a specialty and the hamburgers are great. Lunch and dinner served daily. $$; (CC). (602) 488-9542.

Satisfied Frog. 6245 East Cave Creek Road. Just up the street from the Horny Toad, this restaurant serves equally delicious food. Lunch and dinner, featuring western fare, are served daily. Plan to kick up your heels Friday and Saturday when the "Frog" rocks with country music. Don't miss the honky-tonk piano and the popcorn wagon. Cool off by strolling through the western "town," filled with western souvenir shops. $$; (CC). (602) 488-3317.

El Encanto Mexican Cafe. 6248 East Cave Creek Road. Right across the street from the Satisfied Frog, this comfortable hacienda-style restaurant satisfies that urge to binge on burritos. Request a table on the outside patio and overlook a lagoon where you can watch the ducks and sip a frosty margarita. Great respite after a busy day of sightseeing in the desert. $-$$; (CC). (602) 488-0024.

CAREFREE

Another 1950s Arizona phenomenon, Carefree was a real estate developer's dream planned to lure those who have the means and the time to enjoy their leisure. Continue east on Cave Creek Road a mile or so and you're there. The street names say it all—Easy Street, Nonchalant Avenue, Ho and Hum streets, Rocking Chair Road. Carefree is an elegant little community of large homes, green golf courses, and busy boutiques set like jewels into rocky bezels.

WHERE TO GO

El Pedregal. Heading north on Scottsdale Road from Scottsdale, continue north toward Carefree. You'll see the bright colors of this Moroccan-inspired, fiesta-style center in the distance on the east side of the road. Park and have fun! Wander through the various boutiques, stop at the yogurt shop for outstanding frozen yogurt, and spend time at the numerous art galleries. This area is becoming a second destination (besides downtown Scottsdale) for viewing art. You'll find fine restaurants and, on Thursday evenings during the summer, free concerts held on center stage. Open daily.

The Sundial. Go east on Cave Creek Road to Sunshine Way and turn right. You'll see the sundial right ahead of you. This is the largest sundial in the western hemisphere and a Carefree landmark.

The Spanish Village. Carefree. Follow Tom Darlington Drive (Scottsdale Road) south to the signs for shopping. Here you'll find narrow streets trimmed with wrought iron and lined with gift shops and restaurants.

The Boulders Resort & Club. In Carefree. Head south on Tom Darlington Drive (Scottsdale Road) and turn left just prior to the pile of boulders. Follow the signs to The Boulders Resort & Club. This top-class resort is consistently rated as one of the best resorts in the country in terms of service, amenities, and natural beauty. The free-form architecture and desert setting are amazing and offer one of the most elegant experiences during almost any time of year.

WHERE TO STAY

The Boulders Resort & Club. In Carefree. Head south on Tom Dar-lington Drive (Scottsdale Road) and turn left just prior to the pile of boulders. Follow the signs to The Boulders Resort & Club. Breakfast, lunch, and dinner are available at the resort and the club, which is one of Arizona's finest and most posh resorts. If service and superb amenities appeal to you, if you love golf and want to see the desert in its most pristine state of elegance, The Boulders is for you. Room prices include all meals. Golf is extra. $$$; (CC). (602) 488-9009.

BARTLETT LAKE

Bartlett Lake. Continue east on Cave Creek Road about 6 miles. You'll see a fork in the road and a sign to Bartlett Dam Road. Follow the road to the right. It's unimproved, which means dirt, but if you want an adventurous drive, it's for you. The last miles are the roughest. As your teeth jounce inside your mouth, you may wonder why this section of the road isn't paved. You'll understand when you reach this relatively quiet and undisturbed body of water. Boaters and fishermen love keeping Bartlett Lake somewhat inaccessible. It gives them acres of skiable water, virtually untouched by too many other human feet. If you decide to make this trip, know at the outset that the lake is the attraction. Except for a ranger station, there are no facilities here. That's the allure—rustic beauty unmarred by con-cession stands.

To return to Phoenix, retrace your steps. Follow Bartlett Lake Road to Cave Creek Road and turn south on Scottsdale Road to Scottsdale. From there, it's an easy trip back to Phoenix via Lincoln Drive and Camelback, Indian School, or Thomas roads.

NORTHEAST DAY TRIP 2

Payson · Tonto Natural Bridge
Kohl's Ranch
Worth More Time:
Christopher Creek and Woods
Canyon Lake

PAYSON

Beginning with Payson, this excursion features a scenic Arizona highway, elegant in every season. You'll cross the Fort McDowell Indian Reservation, enter the Tonto National Forest, climb through the Mazatal Mountains, and ultimately experience the carved cliffs and dramatic landscape of the Mogollon Rim country. This is an excellent summer getaway and a "must see" in the autumn. In winter, you'll see cars loaded with ski equipment as families head for the Sunrise ski area. Your main destination is Payson, considered the "Festival Capital" of Arizona. Payson can thank Zane Grey and Grizzly Adams for some of its fame, but nobody can beat Mother Nature for good press.

To reach Payson, head northeast on the Beeline Highway (A-87)—it's right near the border of Scottsdale and Mesa on your map. After crossing the Indian reservation, you'll enter the Tonto National Forest. The road will begin to twist and turn, and you'll pass Sunflower and Rye. Thirteen miles later, you'll reach Payson. Located in the exact center of the state in the world's largest stand of ponderosa pine, Payson sits at 5,000 feet and is a sportsman's paradise.

Founded in 1881 as a gold mining camp, Payson counts tourism as its number one industry. Payson hosts myriad festivals. Stop in at the Chamber of Commerce, at Beeline Highway and Main Street, to pick up maps and information on what's doing.

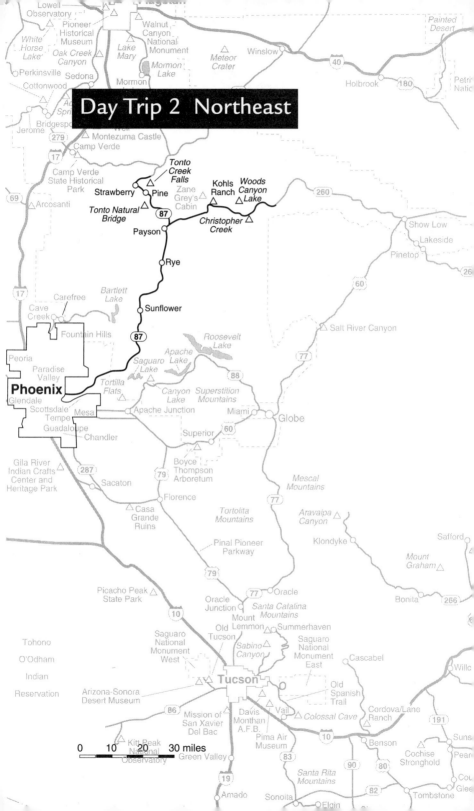

WHERE TO GO

The Swiss Village. A–87 on the north side of Payson. Friendly people, gingerbread architecture, a good doughnut shop, and lots of gift shops make this a good shopping and refreshment stop.

    Museum of the Forest. 1001 West Main Street, Payson. This three-building complex, operated by the Northern County Historical Society, offers a reception area, gift shop, archaeology library, two-story exhibit building (handicapped accessible), meeting room, and outdoor picnic area. Exhibits depict northern Gila County history, pioneer families, and archaeology. Free. (520) 474–3483.

    Zane Grey Museum and Counseller Art. 408 West Main Street, Suite 8, Payson. The original Zane Grey cabin was destroyed by fire. This museum contains photos, books, memorabilia, letters, and free video viewings of Zane Grey's life and times. Free. (520) 474–6243.

TONTO NATURAL BRIDGE

About 12 miles north of Payson on A–87, the world's largest travertine natural bridge arches 183 feet above the stream bed. Measuring 150 to 400 feet in width, it is composed of travertine, white limestone, and red coral deposits. The area is laced with ancient Indian caves. This facility is privately owned. The walk down (and back up) to Tonto Natural Bridge is steep and rocky. If you aren't in good shape, you may want to reconsider. Do wear rubber-soled shoes. *Be forewarned,* but also know that the view is well worth the trek. Once you are down at the bridge, obey *all* signs and watch your step.

    This is a small place by Arizona standards but one which rewards the visitor with amazing views. At the bottom of this deep ravine filled with pine and sycamore trees, is a cathedral-size chamber, 183 feet high which has been carved out by a flowing creek. The natural area contains a small waterfall that cascades from the roof of the chamber and creates rainbows across the face of the rock. Natural Bridge is the newest of Arizona's 26 state parks and is quite undiscovered by state and national park standards. The 160-acre park has recently undergone a $5 million renovation which has paved the road, built parking lots and renovated the lodge that was built in 1927.

    The access road inclines sharply down and ends at the lodge which is nestled in the wooded valley. To reach the trailhead, park your vehicle and continue to the top of the broad bridge. From here you can look down to the deep gorge below. Turn left and navigate an incredibly steep trail with carved-in-stone steps and metal-cable railings. It is a fun but challenging trek. The Parks Department has created an alternate route down with a gentler incline and easier footing.

Both trails go down 180 feet to the bed of Pine Creek. The trails end at the wooden platform built over the creek. Wooden steps down from the platform lead to the chamber. While the footing is slippery in some places, once past the falling water, the shaded chamber is dry and peaceful. This is a good place to sit and enjoy the mystery of this special place. Hikers can continue on, following a set of arrows designed by the Parks Department to keep hikers on the trail. The hike leads upstream past a variety of fantastic sculptures carved by erosion and tumbling rocks. Numerous caves are hidden within the walls. The trail leads to the other side of the bridge along a wooded stream bed for about a half mile. At one point, it leads across the top of another waterfall.

Tonto Natural Bridge was discovered by a prospector, David Gowan, who found the hidden gorge in 1877 while being chased by Apaches. He hid in one of the caves for two nights. Later, he convinced his nephew in Scotland to bring his family to Arizona and live on the property. The nephew, David Gowan Goodfellow, built the lodge and the bridge and opened it to tourists in 1908. The lodge is not open for overnight guests as it needs more renovation to meet health codes. Fee.

WHERE TO GO

Tonto Creek Falls. A half mile above the junction of Tonto and Horton creeks, 10 miles north of Payson, is the site of this natural waterfall. The area around Payson is studded with sylvan splendor, so stop for a cool respite in a busy day of sightseeing.

KOHL'S RANCH

Known for its rustic elegance, **Kohl's Ranch** is a favorite with locals and visitors. Turn right onto A-260 at the junction of A-87 and A-260 and continue 17 miles to the ranch. Be sure to call ahead for breakfast, lunch, or dinner at this longtime Payson landmark. While you're there, enjoy Tonto Creek, which runs through the property. If you have time for a quiet retreat at this rustic lodge, burrow in for a weekend in one of the cabins that dot the property. $$$; (CC). Use the toll free number from Phoenix: (602) 271-9731; in Payson, (520) 478-4211.

WORTH MORE TIME: CHRISTOPHER CREEK AND WOODS CANYON LAKE

Hikers and outdoor types will want to continue east another hour on A-260 to see Christopher Creek and Woods Canyon Lake. Both destinations offer excellent opportunities for camping, fishing, boating, and hiking.

Or you may prefer to head north on A-87 another 15 to 20 miles to see the town of Strawberry and, just 3 miles away, its neighbor, Pine. Both communities are nestled in spectacular woodsy settings and offer travelers a taste of rural, rustic Arizona at its best. Although Strawberry has the oldest standing schoolhouse in the state, most tourists come for the views rather than specific sights. If you decide to visit the area, Strawberry and Pine are geared to handle visitors.

From Payson, take A-87 south for a direct return to Phoenix. Or branch off on A-188 toward Punkin Center and Roosevelt Lake and return on the Apache Trail (A-88) past Tortilla Flat, and on into Mesa, Tempe, and Phoenix. This is a secondary road and part of it is unpaved. The Apache Trail is renowned for its gorgeous scenery. However, if you come back this way, you're in for some steep climbing and curvy driving on a gravel road. (Refer to Day Trip 1, East from Phoenix, for more information about the area.)

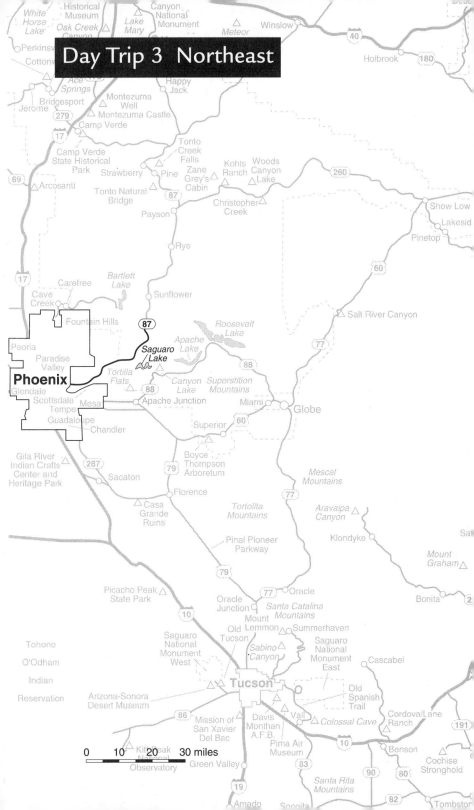

SALT RIVER RECREATION CENTER AND SAGUARO LAKE

For a real change of pace, take a short drive and a long float down the river. Drive north on A–87 to the Saguaro (Sa-wa-ro) Lake cutoff (Bush Highway). Follow the signs past the entrance to Saguaro Lake and the Salt River Recreation Center.

Saguaro Lake was formed by Stewart Mountain Dam and is one of the several lakes built for water reclamation purposes. You can find out all about tubing at the central office, including where to get in and out on the Salt River. Tubing is fast becoming Arizona's state sport, as a visit to the Blue Point area of the Salt River will attest on any hot day.

Follow the signs to the recreation area's parking lot. Here you'll find a place to rent inner tubes and a bus that takes you to the "put in" spot. Getting into the river involves a slippery descent. While you're tubing, pay attention to signs so you know when to get off the Salt River. At the designated spot, there will be a bus to take you back to the parking lot where you left your car. If you miss the "get off," you'll have to hike back to the bus stop.

Wear shorts or a bathing suit and tennies; pack beverages and an inner tube (or rent one there). Bring sunscreen, friends, rope, a Styrofoam cooler you can lash to an extra tube, and a hat or visor if the day is extremely warm. Be prepared for some gentle, but exciting, rapids. While the water is rarely deep, tubers can get into trouble if they don't pay attention to the rocks and snags. Tubing is a great way to spend a day from May through September. To check on river conditions, call (602) 984-3305.

If getting wet and wild doesn't appeal to you, follow the signs to Saguaro Lake for a more peaceful view of water life.

WHERE TO GO

Fort McDowell Casino. On the Fort McDowell Indian Reservation. On A-87 (known as the Beeline Highway). Going northeast from Fountain Hills, northeast of Scottsdale, you'll see signs announcing the casino before you approach the Saguaro Lake cut-off (Bush Highway). Like other reservations, the Ft. McDowell tribe has discovered a steady source of income. Games run every day and night and the crowds pour in. Although this is no competition for Las Vegas or even Laughlin, Nevada (just across the Colorado River from Arizona), this casino is very popular. (602) 837-1424.

Saguaro Lake. Eight miles north of Shea Boulevard on SR-88 at the Saguaro Lake Marina. Saguaro Lake is a popular summer destination for all water sports. For a less rugged experience, take a ride on the *Desert Belle,* an 86-foot sternwheeler. Day tours are offered for one-hour narrated cruises. Fee. (602) 671-0000.

Precision Boating. Rent a boat to fully enjoy a day on the lake. Call the Arizona Marine Office, (602) 986-0969.

Saguaro Lake Excursion. Cruise the lake on a paddle boat. Fee. For schedule information, call (602) 837-3060.

Usery Mountain Park. At Bush Highway and Usery Pass Road. Continue on Bush Highway to Usery Pass Road. Turn left onto Usery Pass Road and follow it for 2 or 3 miles to this elegant mountain park. Spend time hiking the well-marked nature trails, or riding (if you trailer in your own horses). This is one of the nicest mountain parks "out in the tules."

WHERE TO EAT

Lake Shore Inn Restaurant. At the Saguaro Lake Marina. A full-service menu features down-home fare. Come for biscuits and gravy at breakfast, barbecued chicken and sandwiches at lunch, and steaks and seafood at dinner. Call for hours. $$; (CC). (602) 984-5311.

WHERE TO STAY

Saguaro Lake Guest Ranch, 13020 Bush Highway, Mesa, 85205. Follow Shea Boulevard to A–88. Continue to the Saguaro Lake turnoff and follow signs. Privately owned and operated since the 1930s, this rustic ranch is nestled beneath towering red cliffs that border the Salt River. The drive to the ranch is worth the time just for the view. If you take a raft trip with the Cimarron River Company, which floats the river here, guides will point out the eagles' nests high on the cliffs. Float trips offer all the fun of white-water rafting without the fear of rapids. This section of the Salt is scenic and serene and wildlife abounds. Cardinals and Baltimore orioles can be seen flitting through the trees in the spring.

The twenty-five cabins are comfortable, clean, and air conditioned. Many hold four people comfortably. The lodge includes a large room dominated by a huge river-rock fireplace, piano, and bookshelves stuffed with books. The dining room is equally spacious. There's even a small swimming pool to cool you off on a hot spring day.

Call ahead to reserve a cottage for an overnight or make reservations for lunch or dinner as part of a day's outing.

From the ranch you can also take two- and three-hour trail rides offering gorgeous views of Four Peaks, Saguaro Lake, and the desert. $$; (CC). Closed from late May to September except for special groups. (602) 984–2194.

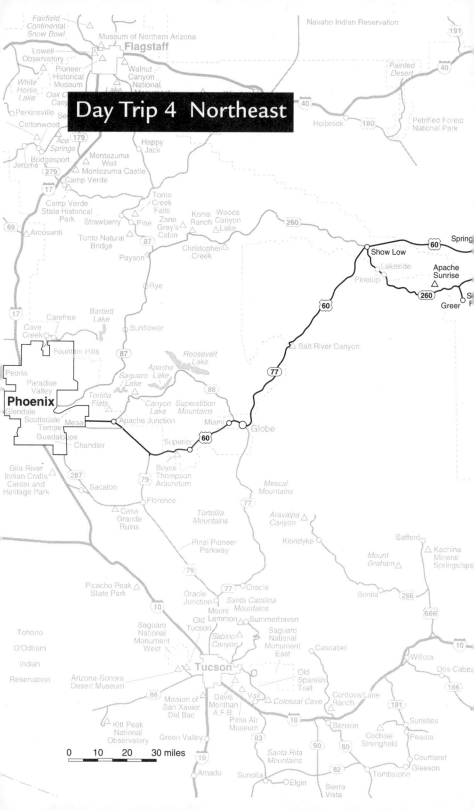

Day Trip 4 Northeast

Day trips 4 and 5 are "Arizona style," which means long hauls for a single-day adventure. If, though, you have the stamina—or better yet, a night to stay over—these places have much to offer, including activities not found anywhere else in the state.

SPRINGERVILLE AND CASA MALPAIS PUEBLO

Head northeast from Phoenix on US-60, 220 miles to Springerville, home of Casa Malpais Pueblo. Springerville is a small town (approximately 2,000 people) set amid great beauty.

Casa Malpais. On US-60. A National Historic Landmark, this was once the site of a thriving city that was occupied for about 200 years and then mysteriously abandoned in about A.D. 1400.

The museum opened in 1991, although the first professional anthropologist, Frank Cushing, visited the area in 1883. While the area is miles away from the Colorado or New Mexico border, the pottery found here is similar to that found in the Four Corners region.

The "House of the Badlands," or Casa Malpais, overlooks the Little Colorado River's Round Valley. From the site, there is a breathtaking view of the White Mountains, which lie to the south.

What makes this archaeological site so special is that the museum and field laboratories are open to the public for visitation. Guided tours are available for a fee, and participatory workshops are given in both education and excavation. Call for tour information. Museum entrance is free. (520) 333-5375.

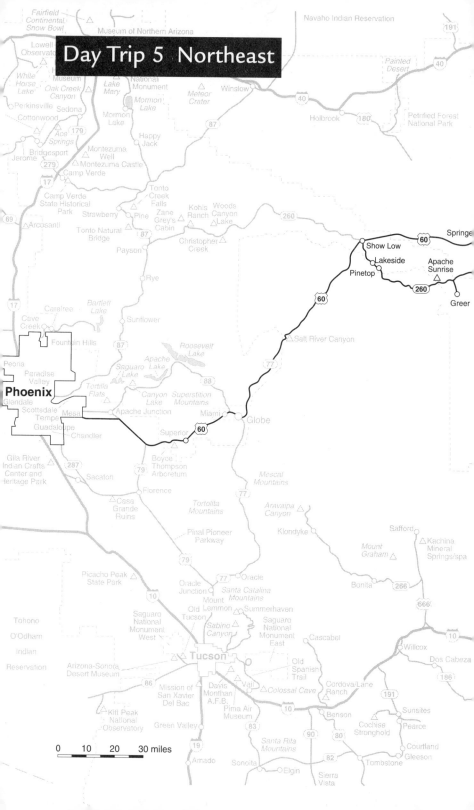

GREER

From Springerville, head southwest for 13 miles to Greer. You'll pass by South Fork Canyon before finding this small mountain village 5 miles south of A-260. Greer is perched at 8,525 feet, which makes it an ideal destination all year around. The area is a sportsman's paradise offering fishing, backpacking, ice skating, sleigh rides, and downhill and cross-country skiing. In cooperation with the U.S. Forestry Service, Greer has developed 35 miles of cross-country ski trails.

WHERE TO STAY

RED SETTER INN. 8 Main Street, Greer, 85927 or P.O. Box 133, Greer, 85927. From Phoenix, take US-60 to Globe. Continue on 60 to Show Low. Then take A-260 east to Greer Junction, A-373. The inn is at the end of A-373. This no-smoking and no-kids upscale bed and breakfast can accommodate 18 to 20 guests who enjoy seeing the great outdoors from relaxing Adirondack chairs. Formal landscape is kept to a minimum. Each room opens onto a small private deck or large common deck and Room 4 comes equipped with a telescope! Common rooms provide guests with more places to read and relax and the innkeepers offer guests plenty of books and magazines. The Red Setter Inn was voted Arizona's Best Bed and Breakfast by the *Arizona Republic* in 1996. The inn does not have a liquor license and a minimum of two nights is required during the weekends. Included in all room rates is a full cooked breakfast and a sack picnic lunch for guests who stay two nights or longer. $$; (CC). (520) 735-7441.

SOUTH FORK

WHERE TO STAY

Sierra Springs Ranch. Located in Arizona's White Mountains, Sierra Springs Ranch was once a high-country working cattle ranch. With five unique, luxurious cottages located on 76 acres, the ranch can accommodate up to fourteen people. Each cottage boasts its own individual decor and the lodge offers a full exercise and fitness center as well as a game room. To reach the property, turn on Bucksprings Road (1 mile from Pinetop), drive $^6/_{10}$ mile, and turn left on SkyHi Road. Drive 2 miles to Sierra Springs Ranch. $$-$$$; (CC). For information write to: P.O. Box 32100, Pinetop, 85935. For reservations call (520) 369-3900.

South Fork Guest Ranch. Located between Springerville and Sunrise, right off A-260, 5 miles east of the Greer Junction, this family-owned guest ranch sits on the banks of the Little Colorado River and the South Fork Creek. You may roam through thirty-eight wooded acres as you picnic or participate in lots of recreation opportunities. There are seventeen units, many featuring multiple bedrooms. All cottages are equipped with dishes, silverware, pots, pans, linens, coffeepot, and toaster. During the winter, there's a minimum stay of two nights; in summer, four nights. The ranch's restaurant, Ms. Elle's, provides fine dining in the pines for those times you don't want to cook. $$-$$$; (CC). Write for information: Box 627, Springerville, 85938. Call for reservations at (520) 333-4455.

SUNRISE

Sunrise Park Resort. P.O. Box 217, McNary, 85930. This is a fully developed downhill ski area with a lodge, restaurant, and ski school located on the White Mountain Apache Indian Reservation. The mountains offer a variety of challenges, and the snow is often excellent. Open all year long, in the summer, the area is a center for hiking and mountain biking as well as fishing and sailing on Sunrise Lake. Horseback riding, in-line skating, archery tournaments, and volley-ball are also scheduled. In the winter, call for snow conditions and reservations. (800) 772-SNOW. Sunrise Sport Center (520) 735-7335.

To return to Phoenix continue east on A-260 to Show Low and the junction of US-60. Follow US-60 east to Phoenix.

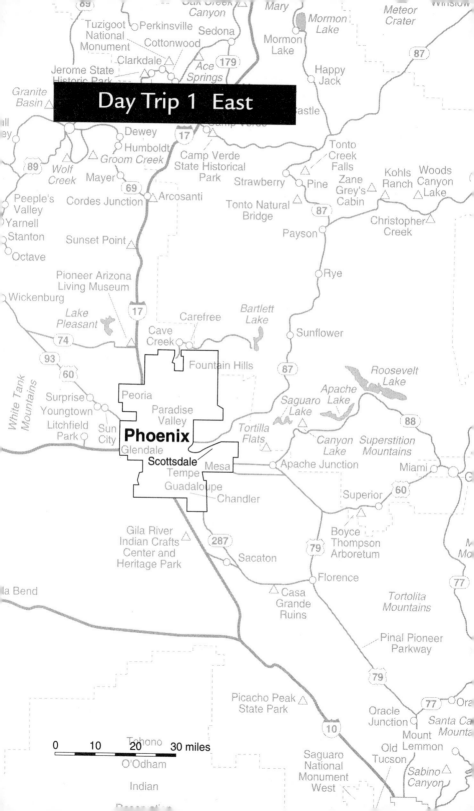

Day Trip 1 East

EAST

DAY TRIP 1

Scottsdale

Worth More Time:
Salt River Pima-Maricopa
Indian Community

SCOTTSDALE

No trip around Phoenix is complete without a day in Scottsdale. Famous as "The West's Most Western Town," Scottsdale is the shopping and art hub of the Valley of the Sun. It's difficult to believe that only a few decades ago Scottsdale Road was unpaved and cowboys rode into town on Saturday night to whoop it up. Today it's a gathering spot for art aficionados, dedicated shoppers, and gourmets.

Follow Glendale Avenue east to Scottsdale. East of Sixteenth Street, Glendale becomes Lincoln Drive. Continue east on Lincoln Drive and, as you near Twenty-fourth Street and Lincoln, look to your left. There's Squaw Peak, one of Phoenix's in-town mountain parks. Fit Phoenicians routinely climb Squaw Peak—some do this daily. If you have time and good walking shoes, turn toward the mountain at the sign to the park and explore a bit.

Continue on Lincoln Drive to Scottsdale Road. You'll pass through the town of Paradise Valley (not to be confused with the Paradise Valley area of Phoenix). This is a wealthy residential community of one-acre-plus home sites and a few well-manicured resorts. Paradise Valley is nestled between Mummy Mountain to the north and Camelback Mountain to the south.

Turn south onto Scottsdale Road and head into town for shopping and browsing. Later, you'll drive north to see other attractions. Scottsdale prides itself on its thriving downtown, outstanding art galleries, and variety of fine restaurants. During the tourist season (October through April) be prepared for traffic.

Scottsdale is named for General Winfield Scott, and, although it has only come of age as a city, the town has long been a favorite vacation spot. Turn-of-the-century residents used to rent out rooms and screened sleeping porches to visitors who passed through. Scottsdale's civic history is punctuated with innovation and creativity. City fathers got on the urban redevelopment bandwagon early and turned a run-down section of downtown into a showcase for business and government. They were also instrumental in developing the flood-prone Indian Bend Wash into a series of green city parks and lakes. Today this beautiful, nationally acclaimed park runs the entire length of town along Hayden Boulevard. Every day of the year you can find activity there—from roller skating, fishing, and soccer to volleyball, baseball, and jogging.

WHERE TO GO

Fifth Avenue. As you head south on Scottsdale Road, turn west onto Fifth Avenue (there's a light). Drive slowly and look for a free parking space anywhere along the street. The city also maintains several free lots. This shopping area is replete with unusual boutiques and gift shops. Fifth Avenue ultimately meets Indian School Road, a main east-west thoroughfare. Best advice is to bring plenty of cash and be ready to browse.

Craftsman's Court. Running south from Fifth Avenue, one block west of Scottsdale Road. If you don't know it's there, you can miss this charming section. Walk down this narrow short street to discover specialty shops and a quaint patio setting.

Marshall Way. Intersects with Fifth Avenue, one block west of Craftsman's Court. Marshall Way is also a unique street. Some places to visit here include:

Seeger's Gallery. 7122 Stetson Drive. By appointment only. Make an appointment to see the "Seeger People." Dick Seeger, a longtime Scottsdale artist, has been doing unusual work with plastics for years. He combines his photographic and artistic skills to come up with one-of-a-kind portraits. (602) 949–1130.

Joanne Rapp's The Hand and the Spirit Crafts Gallery. 4222 North Marshall Way. More a mini-museum than a crafts gallery, The Hand and the Spirit features nationally recognized craftspeople. Shows are held for artists. If you enjoy seeing the best in sophisticated contemporary crafts, this is the place for you. (602) 949-1262.

The Lovena Ohl Gallery. 4251 North Marshall Way. This gallery features the finest in Native American art and craft with work by contemporary masters. Lovena Ohl was an Arizona tradition. Years before Indian jewelry and artwork became fashionable, she sought out young, unknown artists on the reservation and brought their work to the attention of discriminating collectors. The gallery, now run by her nephew, features the work of such acclaimed artists as Larry Golsh, Harvey Begay, Tony Da, and James Little. (602) 945-8212.

Minds Eye Contemporary Crafts. 4200 North Marshall Way. Outstanding Arizona and Southwestern craftspeople are featured in a dazzling display of different styles, textures, and designs. (602) 941-2494.

IMAX Theater. Scottsdale Road and Fifth Avenue. Acclaimed as the finest motion picture system in the world today, the theater's state-of-the-art design and equipment include a screen five stories high and a 14,000-watt, four-way, six-channel digital sound system. Fee. For current listings and prices, call (602) 945-4629.

Lisa Sette Gallery. 4142 North Marshall Way. The most "New York" space in Scottsdale, this gallery features very fine and very contemporary art and photographs. Museum quality shows are mounted. Owner Lisa Sette is knowledgeable and approachable. (602) 990-7342.

Main Street

During your stroll through the Fifth Avenue area, be sure to wander along Stetson Drive, 70th Street (recently renamed Goldwater Boulevard), and Sixth Avenue as well. Once you have covered Fifth Avenue, you're ready to move on to Main Street. Main Street is lined with western and traditional art galleries, and this area, more than any other in Scottsdale, reflects the city's emphasis on the arts. More than ninety galleries serve a town of 130,000, and you quickly realize that painting, sculpture, and crafts are big business here.

To reach Main Street, drive east on Fifth Avenue to Scottsdale Road. Turn south on Scottsdale Road and turn west at Main Street. Later you'll turn east to visit Old Town Scottsdale and its western shops.

WHERE TO GO

You'll notice immediately that Scottsdale's Old Town area projects an "Old West" image. The pedestrian crossing areas are set off in simulated brick, and the sidewalks along Main Street are shaded by wooden-shingled porticos extending from the buildings. These serve a practical, as well as an aesthetic purpose. During the hot summer months, when temperatures climb upward to 110 degrees, the roofs afford essential shade.

Park free anywhere on Main Street. If you arrive in Scottsdale during the tourist season (October through April), do attend one of the Thursday evening art walks. Every Thursday night during the fall, winter, and spring months, galleries host open houses and openings.

Art enthusiasts will discover that Main Street represents a good mix of styles and schools. Many collectors visit Scottsdale because of its fine western galleries. There are many fine contemporary, Native American, and graphic art galleries for artifacts, home accessories, and antiques.

As you cross Scottsdale Road, heading east on Main Street, another world opens—one dedicated to the Old West. Park on Main Street east of Scottsdale Road, walk east to Brown Street, and then turn north. This area is a mecca for tourists; shops range from junk to funk—with some fine jewelry and clothing shops featuring western wear tossed in for good measure.

Stroll north on Brown Street toward Indian School Road for more shopping or browsing at Pima Plaza. Located on First Avenue between Scottsdale Road and Brown, Pima Plaza has restaurants, art galleries, and unusual shops, including one completely devoted to music boxes.

Civic Center Mall

The Civic Center Mall area backs up to Old Town. Once a run-down section of Scottsdale, it is now a source of pride. The government complex includes the Scottsdale City Hall, City Court, Library, and Center for the Arts, all designed by local architect Bennie Gonzales. The rolling lawns of the mall also act as an outdoor art museum for an impressive collection of contemporary sculpture.

WHERE TO GO

Historic Old Town Walking Tour. At the Little Red Schoolhouse on Civic Center Mall, you can pick up a self-guided walking tour guide that will take you to fourteen destinations including the Center for the Arts and the Scottsdale Library. The Little Red Schoolhouse is almost in the center of the original Scottsdale town site. It was built in 1909 at a cost of $4,500 and had two classrooms for grades one through eight.

From the 1920s until the 1960s, the area around the schoolhouse contained a barrio, or neighborhood, that began when Mexican laborers and their families arrived to work in the cotton fields that surrounded Scottsdale.

Walking west to Brown Street, you can see the next points of interest at the corner of Brown and Main streets. **Bischoff's Shades of the West** is a western collectible store today, but in 1897 it was the site of the first general store. By the 1940s it was an arts and crafts center called Arizona Craftsmen. **Affordable Elegance/Cactus Cones** still has a portion of the original adobe wall visible. Walking south on Brown Avenue, you see **Our Lady of Perpetual Help Catholic Church,** which today is the home of the Scottsdale Symphony. Built in 1933 by volunteer labor and donated materials, it consists of 14,000 adobe blocks, each weighing fifty pounds.

Continuing south on Brown to **Cavaliers's Blacksmith Shop** brings you to what was the edge of town. The original building was tin. The Cavaliers still own and operate it and, along with conventional smithing, produce ornamental wrought-iron items.

Heading east on Second Street brings you to **Los Olivos** restaurant, established by the Corral family fifty years ago. It was named for the olive trees that lined the street. The olive trees were planted in 1895 by Gen. Winfield Scott, the founder of the town. From here the tour continues to the **Scottsdale Center for the Arts, Library,** and **Scottsdale Historical Museum**.

Scottsdale Historical Museum. 7333 Scottsdale Mall. In the area of Brown Street and Main Street, this museum includes photographs, furniture, and other items depicting Scottsdale's early days. Free.

The Scottsdale Library. 3839 Civic Center Plaza. Stop in to enjoy the architecture and ambience. Visit the Arizona room as well. Here you'll see displays featuring items from Arizona history—from rare books to silver saddles.

This is worth a trip just to enjoy the architecture of the new wing. Note the dove of peace that "floats" high above the entrance. The image is naturally projected by sunlight. Also marvel at the magnificent quill pen which hovers above the inkwell.

The Scottsdale Center for the Arts. 7383 Scottsdale Mall. This facility boasts a theater for the performing arts and visual arts gallery. Both the theater and gallery feature outstanding, nationally known artists. In addition, the Scottsdale Arts Center Association sponsors special events during the year, including an outdoor crafts show. There's also a unique gallery shop for browsing. Admission to the Center is free but performances and exhibits often have fees. The gift shop of this performing and visual arts center is one of the best secrets of the city. Shop for unusual objets d'art, jewelry, books and other unique items all very well priced. Check with the box office for schedules. (602) 994-ARTS.

Trailside Galleries. 7330 Scottsdale Mall. Western art lovers will find much to enjoy at this gallery where a variety of works by important artists is featured. There's also a fine print gallery. (602) 945-7751.

Fashion Square Area

For more shop-til-you-drop, head for Fashion Square at Scottsdale Road and Camelback. What used to be two malls is now a mega-mall that ranks as the largest in the valley. Wander through several department stores and browse through row upon row of boutiques. Dine at fine and casual restaurants.

The Borgata

For a taste of Rodeo Drive, Arizona style, continue north on Scottsdale Road to one traffic light north of McDonald Drive. You'll see what looks like a fortress on the left. This is the Borgata. (When it was new, locals called it "Fort Ostentatious," but since then it has won the hearts and minds of all.) It was designed to resemble an ancient Italian village. Why Italy in the midst of Arizona? Who knows? As you stroll through the interior brick courtyard, you'll find a clutch of Arizona's—and the world's—most chic shops. Friday afternoons through May, there's a fun farmer's market with live music.

Complete the day with a visit to The Cosanti Foundation and Taliesin West, north on Scottsdale Road. Finish up with some Arizona mountain scenery on your way to Fountain Hills, a scenic planned community, where you'll see the world's tallest fountain.

North Scottsdale

These destinations are north of Shea Boulevard and east of Scottsdale Road.

The Desert Center at Pinnacle Peak. 8711 Pinnacle Peak Road. Travel north on Pima Road to Pinnacle Peak Road. Turn west (left) to the Desert Center at Pinnacle Peak, which is located in a quaint Mexican-style village center. The center specializes in bringing the essence of the Sonoran Desert to life through hands-on scientific experiences. Ethnobotany, archaeology, and ancient Indian skills are featured for groups. Desert aficionados will want to do a morning or afternoon at The Desert Center. Tours are available by reservation. The scenery, in North Scottsdale under the nose of Pinnacle Peak, is straight out of a western film. Call for information about hours. Free. (But donations preferred.) (602) 948-0232.

The Fleischer Museum. 17207 North Perimeter Drive. Take Pima Road north, crossing Frank Lloyd Wright Boulevard (Bell Road). Take the first left past Frank Lloyd Wright. Continue a half mile to Perimeter Drive. Turn right to find this impressive-looking museum. More than 200 paintings by more than eighty artists create a comprehensive study of the California School of American Impressionism, which flourished from the late 1800s to 1940. Free. (602) 585-3108.

Out of Africa. Fountain Hills. Follow Shea Boulevard east to Beeline Highway. Turn left on Bee Line and follow that highway for 2 miles. Watch carefully for the turn-off to the Fort McDowell Indian Reservation and follow the OUT OF AFRICA sign, which you'll see on your right. Here you'll find a rustic but unique demonstration of the relationship that can exist between big cats and people. The cats—lions, tigers, leopards, etc.—are in habitats; the people are walking all around them. The owners of Out of Africa put on "shows," which are really lectures about the cats' behavior. While both adults and young children will enjoy this outing, be prepared to sit and watch for an hour and a half at least. Snacks and drinks are available. This "bare bones" operation, although not a park in any of the usual senses, nevertheless offers a fascinating insight into these magnificent creatures. Often visitors can pet lion cubs and get to know the cats personally. The idea for Out of Africa began with psychological research on big cats. Call ahead for show times and tours. Open all year. Fee. (602) 837-7677.

WHERE TO GO

The Cosanti Foundation. 6433 Doubletree Ranch Road, Paradise Valley. As you leave the Borgata, go north on Scottsdale Road to Doubletree Ranch Road at the fourth stoplight. Turn west and watch for the sign to The Cosanti Foundation on the south side of the street. Wander through Paolo Soleri's enchanted studio. You'll be fascinated by the Soleri wind chimes. Made and sold on the premises, they make wonderful Arizona keepsakes. You also can ask to see the scale model for Arcosanti, the prototype community that Soleri is building in the desert north of Phoenix. Donation suggested. (602) 948-6145.

Taliesin West. Taliesin West, Scottsdale, 85259. Scottsdale Road to Shea Boulevard. Turn east on Shea for about 4 miles and make a left at Via Linda. Go approximately 0.4 mile and turn left at North 108th Street. Follow that to Taliesin West.

Taliesin West is the headquarters for Taliesin Associated Architects and an architectural school teaching the design principles and philosophy of the late Frank Lloyd Wright, one of America's most respected architects. Wright died in 1959, but his belief that environment and structure should blend into a total harmony continues to influence architects throughout the world. Call for information on night nature walk tours.

"Under construction" since the 1930s, Taliesin West has been built and maintained by professionals and students who live and work there. (The original Taliesin was built in Wisconsin in the early 1900s.) The structures serve as a living testimony to Wright's enduring genius.

The compound is constructed of native Arizona materials. The main building is positioned and designed to take full advantage of the warm winter sun. Hour-long tours given by Taliesin staff and students are available daily. These talks are exceptionally informative. Closed during the summer. Call for information. Fee. (602) 860-8810.

Rawhide. 23023 North Scottsdale Road. On Scottsdale Road, 4 miles north of Bell Road. Privately owned, this authentic 1880s town is a great stop for families. It has shops, a museum, ice cream parlor, stage coach ride, and much more. If you visit during July and August, wear a hat because the "town" is hot and dusty. You'll get a real appreciation for the Arizona pioneers. They did it all without the benefit of nearby ice cream parlors and cold beer! See the Conestoga wagon and hear the story of what it was like to come west. The Native American Village requires an admission fee but inside you'll find authentic Native American dancers and artists selling handmade jewelry and other crafts. The Village was built by Native Americans using only materials available to their ancestors. It is staffed by 30 Indians who represent seven different tribes. Children are admitted free without a ticket. Admission is free, but fees are charged for various rides and activities. (602) 502-1880.

WHERE TO EAT

While Scottsdale is renowned for restaurants, these special places serve up unique Arizona atmosphere.

El Chorro Lodge. 5550 East Lincoln Drive, across from Marriott's Mountain Shadows Resort. A "must" for visitors and a long-time favorite of locals, El Chorro offers a large patio for outside dining. During the cooler months, this patio is perfumed with mesquite smoke that drifts from the big outdoor fireplace. Inside El Chorro, diners have their choice of rooms that meander through the old lodge. Owners Evie and Joe Miller pride themselves on the fine home-cooked menu. El Chorro "sticky buns," made with pure butter, grace each table. $$$; (CC). (602) 948-5170.

Handlebar-J. 7116 East Becker Lane. One block northwest of Shea Boulevard off Scottsdale Road. Good for steaks and ribs and live country music, this is a place locals frequent to eat and dance country western. Tourists should try the house special drink. $$; (CC). (602) 948-0110.

Rancho Pinot Grill. 6208 North Scottsdale Road, located on the west side of Scottsdale Road in a corner shopping mall just south of Lincoln Drive and immediately north of the Borgata shopping center. This is an informal gourmet dining experience that features dishes prepared with fresh, local ingredients. The sophisticated dining area is decorated with cowboy memorabilia. A long wooden bar is a great place to wait for your table, sipping a glass of wine from their outstanding collection of wines. This is a local favorite so call for reservations. $$$; (CC). (602) 468-9463.

Rawhide. 23023 North Scottsdale Road. Head north on Scottsdale Road, 4 miles north of Bell Road. Steaks, chicken, and ribs are served in a western dance hall atmosphere. This is especially recommended for families since young children are welcome. *Hint:* You can also enjoy the ambience by visiting the saloon where you'll find live country-western music served by waitresses in full Gay 90s regalia. $$; (CC). (602) 502-5600.

Pinnacle Peak Patio. 8655 East Via De Ventura. Take Scottsdale Road north to Pinnacle Peak Road; turn east on Pinnacle Peak to where it dead-ends into Via De Ventura. Go north on Via De Ventura. You can't miss the huge rambling complex, which is famous for mesquite broiled steaks, as well as for cutting off the neckties of unsuspecting "dudes" who come into a cowboy place too dressed up. There is indoor seating for 2,400 and outdoor accommodations for nearly 6,000. If you take an unsuspecting friend, make sure he wears an old tie, because Pinnacle Peak Patio is merciless. (After the tie is cut, it is displayed along with the owner's business card.) Stay for dancing to live cowboy music, or walk off your dinner by strolling around the grounds or browsing in the shops. $$; (CC). Open daily. (602) 585-1599.

WHERE TO STAY

Scottsdale is a mecca of resorts. Here are a few favorites.

Hyatt Regency Scottsdale at Gainey Ranch. 7500 East Double Tree Ranch Road. Contemporary architecture, great golf, tennis, and a pool featuring a sand beach are part of the charm here. You can ride a gondola on the lake and have dinner at one of the hotel restaurants. $$$; (CC). (602) 991-3388.

Hermosa Inn. 5532 North Palo Cristi Road, Paradise Valley. Take

40th Street to Stanford Drive, turn west, following Stanford to Palo Cristi (36th Street). You'll see the sign on the northwest corner of the intersection. This is an old small resort that was recently "saved" by a local developer with an eye for history. The low-slung buildings are surrounded by green lawns. The rooms are spacious and well designed. The dining room is cozy and delightful with a great bar area for relaxing. Homey but chic, this small hotel has been a local favorite since it was reopened. $$$; (CC). (602) 955–8614.

Gardiner's Resort on Camelback. 5700 East MacDonald. This is one of the best places in the world to play tennis. Casitas are luxurious and large, the food is superb, and the service outstanding. Tennis instruction can't be topped. This small, elegant property is a jewel hidden on Camelback Mountain. Each casita is nestled into the mountain face. While the place can be sold out, the ambience is always serene and quiet—except for the lob of tennis balls on the many courts. Closed mid-June through mid-August. $$$; (CC). (602) 948–2100.

Marriott's Mountain Shadows Resort. 5641 East Lincoln Drive. One of the old grand resorts in the area, it boasts fabulous gardens and a lovely pool. There's a challenging 18-hole, par-3 course on the grounds. Tennis and health club facilities are also available. Restaurants are excellent. $$$; (CC). (602) 948–7111.

Marriott's Camelback Inn Resort Spa and Golf Club. 5402 East Lincoln Drive. The Camelback Inn has maintained its four star, five diamond rating since the awards were introduced. It features sprawling grounds, elegant pools, and one of the most complete and beautiful spas in the Valley. Casitas are private and tucked away under the shadow of Mummy Mountain. $$$; (CC). (602) 948–1700.

The Phoenician. 6000 East Camelback Road. The newest and most lavish resort in the Valley, it features rolling golf courses, a jungle swimming pool setting, and a nature trail with more than one hundred kinds of cactus along the way. Rooms are oversized; suites are vast. Sunday brunch is the best in the Valley. $$$; (CC). (602) 941–8200.

Scottsdale Plaza Resort. 7200 North Scottsdale Road. Five pools are located on this spacious property. There's shuttle service to nearby shopping. The upscale Seville shopping center is across the street. Remington's, the property's restaurant, is excellent and offers continental dining and live music. $$$; (CC). (602) 948–5000.

The Scottsdale Princess. 7575 East Princess Drive. Grand and impressive, this Moorish-style resort features world-class golf and tennis, patios that go on forever, and sumptuous dining. Best shops are Saguaro & Son gallery and Frilly Chilies, for women's apparel. $$$; (CC). (602) 585-4848.

WORTH MORE TIME: Salt River Pima-Maricopa Indian Community

The Salt River Pima-Maricopa Indian Community is surrounded by Scottsdale, Tempe, Mesa, and Fountain Hills. Established in 1879, it is home to two tribes, the Pima and the Maricopa Indians. About 6,000 people live at this Community which covers just over 52,000 acres.

Visitors are welcome to visit the Hoo-hoogam Ki Museum, located at 10,000 East Osborn Road to learn about the heritage and culture of these two tribes. The word "Hoo-hoogam Ki" means "House of those who have gone," and refers to the Pima's ancestors, the Hohokam Indians, who were the original residents of the Salt River Valley.

The small museum is constructed of adobe and desert plants and contains interpretive exhibits that describe these tribes' heritage. Baskets, pottery, photographs and other historic articles are on display and community members are often at the museum demonstrating their skills as potters and basket weavers.

An added treat is the outside dining room located at the back of the museum. Here is a walk-up order window and some picnic tables grouped under a thatched *ramada*. The ladies of the Community cook authentic Indian fry bread, burritos and other favorites. The dining cafe serves breakfast and lunch and is open to the public.

This urban tribe owns several business enterprises such as the Pavilions Shopping Mall at Indian Bend Road and Pima Road, which is the largest retail outlet built on Native American land, and Miss Karen's Yogurt.

Visitors are always welcome at powwows which are held in April, September and November. For information, call the Hoo-hoogam Ki Museum (602) 874-8190. For general information about the Community, contact Tribal Administration at (602) 874-8000.

DAY

EAST

Tempe · Mesa
Apache Junction
Tortilla Flat · The Lakes

TRIP 2

TEMPE

The East Valley is booming. Just twenty years ago, most of eastern metropolitan Phoenix was open space. Snowbirds, or winter visitors, as they are more politely called, flocked to the East Valley in cold weather. Farms flourished and although small towns hinted that one day they would become urban centers, such amazing growth seemed light-years away. Cotton was king, but much of that is history now. As you drive out of Mesa toward Tortilla Flat you'll pass through an unrelenting wave of development for the first few miles.

New homes and businesses sprout faster than any crop here. Consequently, as you leave the urban area behind and continue along the famous Apache Trail, you'll marvel at the wild natural beauty so near the city. When your day is done, you'll even know the answer to those ubiquitous bumper stickers that ask: "Where the Hell is Tortilla Flat?"

Tempe once was a sleepy little college town. No more. Today it is the home of one of the nation's largest universities—Arizona State. Originally called "Hayden's Ferry," Tempe has a history that's liberally sprinkled with famous Arizona names. The town owes its past, present, and future to Judge Trumbell Hayden, a miller, educator, and all-around promoter, who established a ferry across the Salt River in 1872. The community, which quickly followed, became known as Tempe by 1877. Almost immediately, Judge Hayden began lobbying the territorial government to establish a teacher's college in Tempe. That tiny college grew up to be Arizona State University (ASU).

79

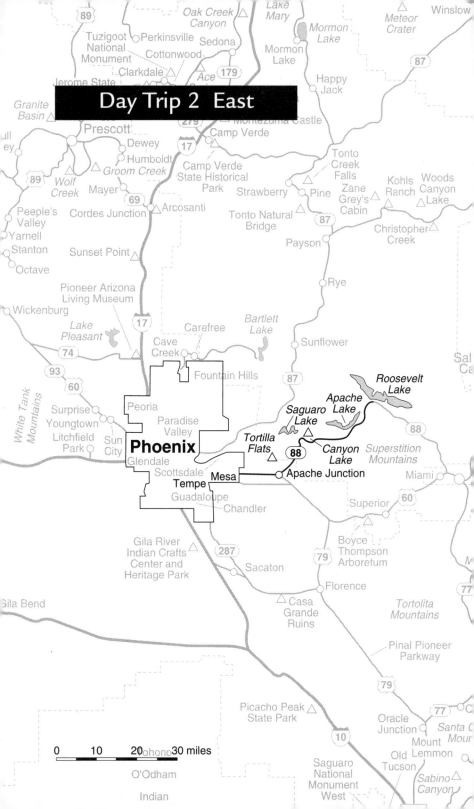

Today Tempe continues to be a pioneer community. The city is building one of the initial demonstration projects for a redeveloped Salt River, the Rio Salado project. Twice a year the town hosts a superb crafts festival along Mill Avenue. And, of course, it continues to be proud of its home-town school, ASU.

If you want to see the campus, park in one of the visitors' lots and walk around the palm-lined malls. When school's in session, parking is tight—you'll understand why parking is the bane of the 1990s college student's existence.

To get a sense of Tempe's past and future, drive through the quaint downtown. Follow Mill Avenue south past Gammage Center for the Performing Arts. You may wish to make a quick jog east to see Tempe City Hall at 31 East Fifth Street. Turn east off Mill Avenue onto East Fifth for a short half block to get a glimpse of this unusual contemporary structure. Designed in the shape of an inverted pyramid, the glass and steel building shades itself from the glaring Arizona sun.

WHERE TO GO

Arizona State University Gammage Center for the Performing Arts. On the corner of Mill Avenue and Apache Boulevard. This was the last public building Frank Lloyd Wright designed. Although he did not live to see it completed, it's a hallmark of Wright's vision. Follow Scottsdale Road south into Tempe, where it becomes Rural Road. Turn west onto University Drive and south on Mill. You'll see the center's distinctive pink color and scalloped roof line just beyond the curve on Mill between University and Apache. The public may purchase tickets to events at Gammage. There's a full season of music, dance, theater, and lectures. To inquire about scheduled events, write to the Gammage Box Office, Arizona State University, Tempe, 85287. Half-hour tours of the building are available on a limited basis. Call for times and days. Free. (602) 965–5062.

If you want to spend more time on campus, pick up a map from an attendant at any of the visitors' parking lots. The map will direct you to other points of interest such as:

The J. Russell Nelson and Bonita Nelson Fine Arts Center. Tenth Street and Mill Avenue on campus. ASU boasts a magnificent visual-and-performing-arts complex by noted architect Antoine Predock. This Egyptian-inspired group of buildings is definitely worth your visit. Within the complex you'll find the University Art Museum, which has one of the finest American ceramics collections in the country. The various traveling shows as well as the permanent collection are all outstanding. The complex also includes the Paul V. Galvin Playhouse, the University Dance Laboratory, and other interior and exterior exhibition and performing space.

The Red River Opry. 730 North Mill Avenue. Situated in the environmental and historic tourism area called The Papago Trail, the Opry stages live variety shows that feature a blend of country music, comedy, and nostalgia. Great for families, the productions are staged in a state-of-the-art, 1,000-seat facility. Fee. Call for show information. (602) 829–OPRY.

MESA

To get to Mesa from Tempe, follow Apache Boulevard east. As it enters Mesa, Apache becomes Main Street. Once known primarily for its wide streets—wide enough for an ox team to turn around—Mesa is a fast-growing city that is proud of its excellent schools and churches. The Chamber of Commerce, 120 North Center, has information on the community center, historical and archaeological museum, little theaters, and youth museum. (602) 969–1307.

WHERE TO GO

The Arizona Museum for Youth. 35 North Robson Street. One of only two children's museums in the country that focuses on the fine arts, this is a special family place. The museum is owned by the City of Mesa and the Arizona Museum for Youth Friends Inc. It opened in 1981 in a temporary facility, moved to its permanent facility in 1986, and has been nationally honored in a *USA Today Weekend* magazine article as the "Most Outrageously Artful" children's museum in America.

The exterior of the brick building gives no hint of the exciting interior environment designed to titillate the imagination, stimulate the mind, and captivate the eye. Three exhibits are mounted annually, one for each of the fall, spring, and summer school semesters.

Artwork is installed at a child's-eye level, and traditional museum displays are interspersed with participatory activities to enhance and reinforce the visual experience.

School and community groups are led by trained museum staff in the mornings. The public can enjoy the museum at its leisure or take escorted tours. In addition to the exhibits, the museum holds workshops and classes and puts on special events. Group tours are available Wednesday morning and afternoon. Fee. (602) 644-2468.

Champlin Fighter Museum. Located at Falcon Field on McKellips Road just east of Greenfield Road. If you want to see vintage aircraft, this is the place to go. The collection contains fighter aircraft from World War I through Vietnam. The collection is stored in two hangers which were part of a secret British Royal Air Force training ground built in the early stages of World War II before the U.S. entered the war. The World War I aircraft date almost to the beginning of aviation history and are works of remarkable craftsmanship. Since 1983 the Champlin Fighter Museum has been the home of the American Fighter Aces Association which is an exclusive association of top pilots. An "Ace" must be credited with downing five or more enemy aircraft in aerial combat. Fee. (620) 830-4541.

Mesa Southwest Museum. 53 North MacDonald. Located in the heart of downtown Mesa, the museum features regional artifacts and related art as well as traveling exhibits and art shows. Special children's activities and workshops are scheduled. You'll find the history of the Southwest from dinosaurs and ancient Indian civilizations to the settlement of the West. There are accessible, hands-on exhibits that families will enjoy visiting as well as outdoor displays, which include a one-room schoolhouse and gold-panning stream. Fee. (602) 644-2169.

The Mormon Temple. 525 East Main Street. This imposing structure serves as Arizona headquarters for the Church of Jesus Christ of Latter-day Saints. Although the sanctuary is open only to Mormons, the visitors center welcomes guests. There you may learn something about the Mormon faith and hear about the Mormon men and women who came west to establish homes, farms, and communities. Tours of the Temple grounds are conducted every half hour. Call for more information. (602) 964-7164.

Usery Mountain Recreation Area. Follow Usery Pass Road 12 miles northeast of Mesa to the main entrance. This 3,324-acre recreation area provides trails for hiking and horseback riding, camping and picnic areas, and an archery range. Eleven hiking trails are lush with desert vegetation and are of varied difficulty. The most popular are Wind Cave Trail and Pass Mountain Trail. Open daily. Fee. (602) 984-0032.

WHERE TO EAT

Rockin' R Ranch. 6136 East Baseline Road. Mosey on over to Arizona's Wild West town. The specialty is chuck wagon suppers and the Cowboy Steakhouse serves huge steaks as well as fish, ribs and chicken. Kids enjoy the western town complete with petting zoo. Enjoy horse-drawn wagon rides, pan for gold, and see mountain men and gunfights and entertainment by the Rockin' R Wranglers. Good family entertainment. Reservations are requested and private steak fries can be arranged. Open Saturdays only in the summer, call for information and reservations $$-$$$; (CC). (602) 832-1539.

APACHE JUNCTION

Continue east on US-60/US-89 to Apache Junction, which calls itself "the gateway to the Superstition Mountains." This range has fascinated people for almost a century, ever since the German immigrant Jacob Waltz arrived in Arizona in 1863 to prospect for gold. According to legend, Waltz found, or possibly stole, one of the very rich Peralta gold mines deep in the Superstitions. Try as he did, however, he never again was able to find the mine and prove his claim.

Because people mistakenly thought that the immigrant was from Holland, as Waltz continued his search, the story grew about the "Dutchman's Lost Mine." In time, the unproven claim became known as "The Lost Dutchman's Lost Mine," a misstatement that no one has bothered to correct.

Apache Junction itself is a sprawling conglomeration of commercial property and mobile homes set against the spectacular Superstition range. Drive through Apache Junction and continue on A-88 to begin the Apache Trail, a section of Arizona that quite impressed President Theodore Roosevelt. Observing that it combined the grandeur of the Alps, the glory of the Rockies, and the magnificence of the Grand Canyon, he called it "the most awe-inspiring and most sublimely beautiful panorama Nature has ever created." Teddy Roosevelt predicted in 1911 that the Salt River Valley would boom and attract people from throughout the country.

WHERE TO EAT

The Mining Camp Restaurant and Trading Post. 6100 East Mining Camp Road, Apache Junction. Turn left onto A-88 at Apache Junction and continue north for 4 miles.

This landmark restaurant is built of rough sawn ponderosa pine that was hauled from Payson. A replica of the old mining camp cook shanty sits at the base of the Superstition Mountains. The interior has also been copied with amazing authenticity. A trading post sells authentic Indian relics, legendary maps and photos of early mining days. Food is served family style and is all you can eat, offering never-ending amounts of hearty western food amidst a rustic gold-mining atmosphere. Dinner only. $$; (CC). (602) 982-3181.

TORTILLA FLAT

Travel 18 miles northeast on A-88 to reach Tortilla Flat, one of the last true outposts of the West. Here visitors will find a rustic dining room featuring hamburgers and chili, a weatherbeaten-looking small hotel, and a public restroom. This is a fun place to stop.

Although tiny by anyone's standards, Tortilla Flat is the last town between Apache Junction and Roosevelt Dam. A few miles east of Tortilla Flat, the Apache Trail turns into a rough, gravel road. If you decide to continue east to Roosevelt Lake, prepare yourself for a rugged and even hair-raising trip.

A-88 is one of the most crooked roads in the nation. It was named for the Apache Indians who helped build it and was constructed to haul materials for Theodore Roosevelt Dam. The route snakes through some of the prettiest mountains and desert in the Phoenix area. Along the way is Tortilla Flat, the only surviving stagecoach stop on the route. The buildings were destroyed by fire some years ago but have since been rebuilt. Today you can stop at the general store, cafe, and post office. The prickly pear cactus ice cream and the chili are specialties.

WHERE TO GO

Goldfield Ghost Town. 4650 North Mammoth Mine Road. Three and a half miles north of Apache Junction on A–88. This is an authentic ghost town where you can go on a mine tour and pan for gold. There are specialty shops and antiques, a museum, and a unique steak house with spectacular views of the Superstition Mountains. (602) 983-0333.

THE LAKES

If you're ready for more scenery, follow the Apache Trail on A–88 east 28 miles through the chain of man-made lakes on the Salt River that includes Canyon Lake, Apache Lake, and Roosevelt Lake, which is much larger than the other two. Roosevelt Lake is located on the gravel road after the pavement ends. The unpaved stretch is notable, not only for its rough surface, but also for its steep descent into Fish Creek Canyon. Adventurous tourists are advised to make this trip by traveling east, not west, in order to easily see approaching automobiles.

The Apache Trail is a trip of unforgettable beauty in all seasons. The trip winds through scenic desert mountain vistas, climbs in hairpin turns and finally plunges into Fish Creek Canyon. Because of the condition of the road, it is slow-going in places. But that only gives travelers more time to enjoy the breathtaking views of desert lakes, saguaros and mountain landscapes.

Fish, water ski, relax, swim, or just enjoy the desert lake views. Each lake offers services for travelers.

WHERE TO GO

Canyon Lake. Follow A–87 16 miles north of Apache Junction to the Canyon Lake Marina. Like all Arizona lakes, Canyon Lake is a hotbed of summertime activity from power boating to water skiing to jet skis. Those who prefer to have a less strenuous experience will enjoy *The Dolly,* a 103-foot stern-wheeler. The day cruise takes $1^1/2$ hours and is narrated. Lunch is available, and box lunches may also be purchased. Romantics may prefer the dinner cruises, which are priced according to the changing menu. Call ahead for reservations and menu information. $$; fee for the cruises. (602) 827–9144.

Apache Lake. You'll find a full-service resort and marina with houseboat rentals, boats for fishing, and tackle. Check with the Apache Lake Resort for more information. (520) 467–2511.

Roosevelt Lake. Roosevelt Lake is your ultimate destination and is well worth the trip which traverses paved and unpaved roads that snake through some of the best desert scenery in central Arizona. Although the road through Fish Canyon is not paved, it is graded. The Apache Trail is a magnificent drive at all times of the year but especially beautiful in the spring and fall. A year-round haven for unwinding, Roosevelt Lake is popular among skiers, bass fishermen, and campers. There's a full-service marina. The Visitors Center is definitely worth a visit as it tells the story of how Roosevelt Dam was constructed through models, exhibits and outstanding photographs. The Visitor Center also affords a magnificent view of the panorama of Roosevelt Dam, one of the major masonry dams in the world. (520) 467–2245.

Roosevelt Dam. Roosevelt Dam remains one of the most important reclamation projects in the U.S. Without its ability to stop flooding and provide a well-managed source of water, the Phoenix metropolitan area would not have developed as it has. In addition to providing water and protecting from flooding, the dam creates a sight of amazing beauty.

Tonto Basin Ranger Station and Visitor Center. Located at Roosevelt Lake, this new visitor center tells the story of Roosevelt Dam through models and exhibits. A good bookstore provides you with additional information about the dam and this riparian area. If you are interested in camping, the center has current information on Roosevelt Lake's modern campgrounds. Some even have solar heated showers. Open daily. Fee. (520) 467–3200.

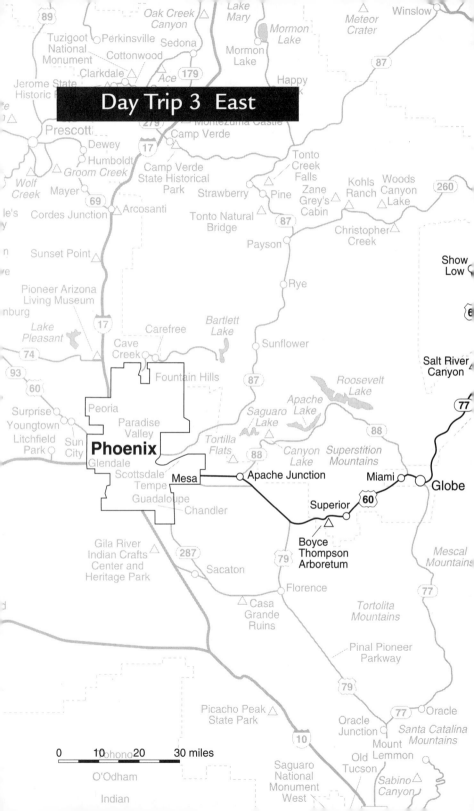

Day Trip 3 East

89

Oak Creek
Canyon

Lake
Mary

Meteor
Crater

Winslow

Tuzigoot
National
Monument

Perkinsville
Cottonwood

Sedona

Mormon
Lake

Mormon
Lake

87

Clarkdale

Ace

179

Jerome State
Historic

Prescott

Dewey

Humboldt

Camp Verde

17

Camp Verde
State Historical
Park

Montezuma Castle

Happy

Tonto
Creek
Falls

Tonto Creek
Falls

Kohls
Ranch

Woods
Canyon
Lake

260

Groom Creek

Strawberry

Pine

Zane
Grey's
Cabin

Wolf
Creek

Mayer

69

Arcosanti

Tonto Natural
Bridge

87

Christopher
Creek

le's

Cordes Junction

Payson

Show
Low

n

Sunset Point

Rye

6

ve

Pioneer Arizona
Living Museum

nburg

Lake
Pleasant

17

Carefree

Bartlett
Lake

Sunflower

Salt River
Canyon

74

Cave
Creek

Fountain Hills

87

Roosevelt
Lake

77

93

60

Peoria

Apache
Lake

Surprise

Youngtown

Paradise
Valley

Saguaro
Lake

Litchfield
Park

Sun
City

Phoenix

Tortilla
Flats

88

Canyon
Lake

Superstition
Mountains

88

Glendale

Scottsdale

Mesa

Apache Junction

Miami

Globe

Tempe

Guadalupe

Superior

60

Chandler

Boyce
Thompson
Arboretum

Gila River
Indian Crafts
Center and
Heritage Park

287

Sacaton

79

Mescal
Mountains

Florence

77

Casa
Grande
Ruins

Tortolita
Mountains

Pinal Pioneer
Parkway

79

Picacho Peak
State Park

Oracle
Junction

77

Oracle

Santa Catalina
Mountains

Mount
Lemmon

10

Tohono

Old
Tucson

0   10   20   30 miles

O'Odham

Saguaro
National
Monument
West

Sabino
Canyon

Indian

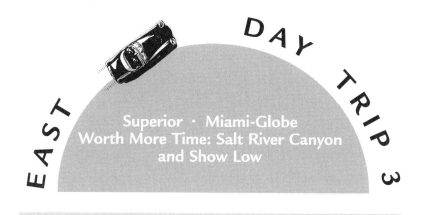

Superior · Miami-Globe
Worth More Time: Salt River Canyon
and Show Low

SUPERIOR

Pick up this trip in Apache Junction and travel southeast on US-60/US-89 toward Superior. The approximately 50-mile drive from Mesa to Superior takes you deep into copper-mining country. Arizona owes its history to the mines and the railroads, for the presence of precious minerals—gold, silver, and copper—lured people west. The railroads opened the land so that men could carry those treasures out and, in the process, made the territory accessible to settlers.

The main street of this small town follows Queen Creek, which is nestled among the copper-stained mountains. In 1875 this was a bustling silver- and gold-mining center. Today its future hangs on a precarious copper thread.

WHERE TO GO

Boyce Thompson Southwestern Arboretum. US-60/US-89 just a few miles west of Superior. As you drive toward Superior on US-60/US-89, turn right at the sign and follow the driveway into the arboretum. This vast (1,076-acre) living museum was the dream of William Boyce Thompson, a mining magnate and philanthropist. He endowed not only this site, but also a sister institution, The Boyce Thompson Institute for Plant Research on the Cornell University campus in Ithaca, New York. The Arizona arboretum is all the more intriguing because of its Sonoran desert location.

89

This is one of the most special spots in Arizona. The grounds are well marked and, in most places, are wheelchair accessible. The long loop trail will take you an hour to two hours depending upon how long you stay at each designated stop along the way. There are myriad side loops to follow depending upon your interest and the season.

If you have never meandered through a shady and fragrant eucalyptus grove, stared at the myriad twisted arms of a 200-year-old giant Saguaro cactus, or tried to figure out how the bizarre Boojum tree grows, you've missed some of the desert's best pleasures. Begin your tour at the visitors center and get acquainted with this living garden before heading out on the well-marked trails. They begin with some "easy-does-it" walks and graduate to more challenging terrain.

One fascinating section is devoted to Old World trees, including the pomegranate, Chinese pistachio, and olive, that are of major economic importance in various parts of the world. You will be amazed to learn how many different trees can grow in the Arizona desert. Open daily except Christmas. Fee. (520) 689-2723.

MIAMI-GLOBE

Continue on US-60/US-89 east to Miami and Globe. As you enter Miami, look for the sign noting the site of the Bloody Tanks Massacre of Apaches. Proceed east to Globe, the seat of Gila County and a center for cattle and mining. Globe began as a mining town in 1886, but now it is the trading center for the San Carlos Apache Indian Reservation and a favorite headquarters for wild pig *(javelina)* hunting. Apart from the natural setting, the main attraction here is mining, although in recent years the town has become a focus for historical renovation. A historic home tour is held each February in which the whole town participates. Pick up a self-guided walking and driving tour map at the Chamber of Commerce. Stop in at the Globe-Miami Chamber of Commerce, 1360 North Broad Street, Highway 60, Globe, 85501, or call (520) 425-4495 for information on the area.

As in many Arizona small towns, public buildings often do not have street addresses. However, Arizonans are a friendly bunch so you can always ask directions. You should include the **Gila County**

Historical Museum on US–60/US–89 in your tour. This small museum holds a treasure trove of pioneer and mining artifacts collected throughout the region. It's open daily and is free. No phone.

You can see local and regional artists represented at the restored old courthouse, now the **Cobre Valley Center for the Arts,** at Broad and Oak streets. This museum is open daily and is free. Then, too, the area is laced with fascinating Pueblo Indian ruins. Ask about them at the Chamber of Commerce.

Group tours of the open pit mine and smelter operations are available. If you want to learn more about mining on your own, however, pick up A–77 at Globe and head south to Winkleman and Hayden, two small copper-mining communities that are 1 mile apart. Here you can hook into Day Trip 1, Southeast from Phoenix by circling through San Manuel to Oracle Junction. At Oracle Junction follow US–89 for a 42-mile drive north to Florence. You can also continue on A–287 from Horace to A–87 back through Chandler to Mesa. This is a 246-mile drive, and much of it traverses old stagecoach routes that are surrounded by massive copper-stained mountains.

WHERE TO GO

Besh-Ba-Gowah Archaeological Park. Jess Hayes Road. Take Broad Street through Historic Downtown Globe for approximately 1.5 miles. You'll see the turnoff for the park. Besh-Ba-Gowah is the remains of a prehistoric village that overlooks Pinal Creek in the shadow of the Pinal Mountains. The walls and structure are made of rounded river cobble and mud, and the careful reconstruction lets you experience the plazas and living quarters as they must have been centuries ago. Artifacts, including a weaving loom, grinding stones, and even a large squash, are carefully positioned in some of the reconstructed rooms.

Besh-Ba-Gowah means "a place of metal" or "metal camp." This pueblo consists of more than 300 rooms and once housed 400 people. It was built and occupied from about A.D. 1225 to A.D. 1400 by the Salado Indians. These people were accomplished farmers and grew crops including corn, beans, and squash along the banks of Pinal Creek.

The community also functioned as a trading center. The Salado made pottery and traded widely. They also wove baskets of sotol and yucca fibers as well as fine cotton cloth, and they adorned themselves with bracelets and necklaces made of shells they acquired by trading their pottery and baskets.

Like many pueblos, it is suspected that drought drove the people out. Besh-Ba-Gowah lay abandoned for years but underwent excavation and stabilization in the 1980s. The park opened in 1988. There is an excellent, small museum on the grounds that displays artifacts relating to this site. Fee. (520) 425-0320.

Gila Pueblo. Gila Pueblo College, Six Shooter Canyon. Gila Pueblo is just a five-minute drive south of Globe past Besh-Ba-Gowah park. Owned and operated by Eastern Arizona College, it was originally excavated in the early 1920s by an amateur archaeologist who owned the property where the dig is located. At the height of its occupation, it contained more than 400 rooms, and approximately 1,500 people once lived here.

The inhabitants were skilled potters and weavers. Unlike other pueblos, Gila Pueblo was never abandoned. Instead, sometime around A.D. 1450, the entire community was destroyed by an act of war. Most of the people were murdered, and the village burned to the ground. Researchers suspect that the violence was perpetrated by the nearby Salado populations. Free. (520) 425-3151.

WHERE TO SHOP

Antiques & Collectibles. The Globe/Miami area is becoming a treasure trove for antiques lovers. *Johnny's Country Corner,* 383 South Hill, has an outstanding array of quilts and quilting supplies. Pick up a brochure from the Chamber of Commerce that details the antiques trail.

The Cobre Valley Center for the Arts. 101 North Broad Street. This cooperative is housed in the historic Gila County Courthouse, which has been renovated to its original splendor. The arts and crafts exhibited are by local artists. Free. (520) 425-0884.

McKusick Tile Studio. Route 1, Box 35-D. Call for directions. This is a unique family business located in the foothills of the Pinal Mountains, 4 miles south of Globe. Tiles are produced in ancient ways and designs are Southwest. If you want to visit on a weekend, please call ahead. (520) 425-5051.

WHERE TO STAY

Noftser Hill Inn. 425 North Street. Call for directions. This is a bed and breakfast housed in an old elementary school that sits on a hilltop overlooking Globe. Built in 1907, it was originally known as the North Globe Schoolhouse. Generations of successful Arizonans were educated here including Rose Mofford, former governor of Arizona. The owners, Pam and Frank Hulme, are renovating it with love, dedication, and great attention to detail. When completed, there will be eight rooms, some large enough to house a family comfortably. Breakfast is gourmet Southwest, and the company is delightful. $$. (520) 425-2260.

WORTH MORE TIME: SALT RIVER CANYON AND SHOW LOW

From the Miami-Globe area continue northeast on A-77/US-60 another 87 miles for a magnificent plunge through the wild beauty of the Salt River Canyon and a visit to the community of Show Low. You should plan to spend the night in Show Low or head southeast for approximately 5 miles on A-160 to Lakeside or Pinetop and stay there.

The Salt River Canyon begins about 30 miles northeast of Globe on A-77/US-60 and is often called "the mini Grand Canyon." Take this drive during the daytime so you can appreciate the spectacular sights. The highway twists and turns for 5 miles from the top of the canyon to its floor.

This is one of the most scenic stretches in all of Arizona. Along the way, you can pull off at several lookout points to admire the artistry wrought by millions of years of erosion. If you have packed a light lunch, picnic at one of the several shady spots provided at the bottom of the canyon. This area is well marked. Pull off, park, and walk down a flight of steps to the riverbank. Adventurous adults and children will want to explore the river, swim, or fish. If you travel 7 miles downstream on a dirt road, you'll see the amazing **Salt Banks**. The formations tower 1,000 feet above the river, looking like giant ocean waves frozen in time and about to crest.

When you're ready for the long climb out of the canyon, continue approximately 60 miles northeast on A-77/US-60 to Show Low. This small community is a hub of activity for the four million acres of the White Mountain Recreation Area, which include 500 miles of trout streams and fifty lakes. It is also home to **Sunrise Park,** the state's most complete ski center and resort.

Show Low enjoys a high, cool climate and a backdrop of exceptional forest land. Its name reputedly came from an incident involving C. E. Cooley, who had been a government scout with General George Crook. Cooley married the daughter of Chief Pedro of the White Mountain Apaches and, in 1875, established a home on what is now called Show Low Creek. His place became a favorite spot for travelers. Marion Clark was Cooley's partner, but at some point in the relationship, Clark decided to end their hotel venture. To settle on who should stay and who should leave, the two agreed to play a card game of Seven-Up. When the hand was dealt, Cooley lacked a single point to win. As they prepared to draw cards, Clark is reputed to have said, "If you can show low, you can win." Cooley tossed his hand down and said, "Show low it is." Clark moved up the creek to what is now Pinetop, and thanks to the deuce of clubs, Cooley stayed. More importantly, the name stuck.

Today Show Low is the trade and service center for southern Navajo County and portions of southern Apache County. Tourists use it as a jumping-off point for recreation in the White Mountains. You'll find modest facilities here, including motels, cabins, and campgrounds. For more information, contact the Show Low Chamber of Commerce, P.O. Box 1083, Show Low, 85901, or call (520) 537-2326.

SOUTHEAST DAY TRIP 1

Sacaton · Casa Grande
Florence

SACATON

Gila River Indian Crafts and Heritage Park. Sacaton. Follow I-10 east to exit 175, which leads to the center. If you have never visited an Indian reservation, this may appear a stark landscape. The word "sacaton" means "tall, rank herbage unfit for forage." Historian Marshall Trimble notes that the grass is good for forage, so maybe the meaning is that of another definition for "sacaton," which is "broad, flat land." The old Butterfield Stage Line ran through here in 1858 on its way from Tucson to Yuma. The **Gila River Indian Crafts Center** does a brisk business in authentic Indian jewelry of turquoise, silver, and beadwork; pottery from many different tribes; Seri wood carvings; Navajo rugs; and other gift items. In addition, there are an Indian art gallery, historical museum, park, and a coffee shop featuring piping-hot Indian fry bread. The center is open daily. (520) 963-3981.

CASA GRANDE

Casa Grande was traditionally an agricultural and manufacturing town that has now expanded into the retail industry with two major retail shopping outlet centers located conveniently along I-10. The community is located midway between Phoenix and Tucson. It was founded in 1879 and named for the famous Hohokam Indian Ruins,

95

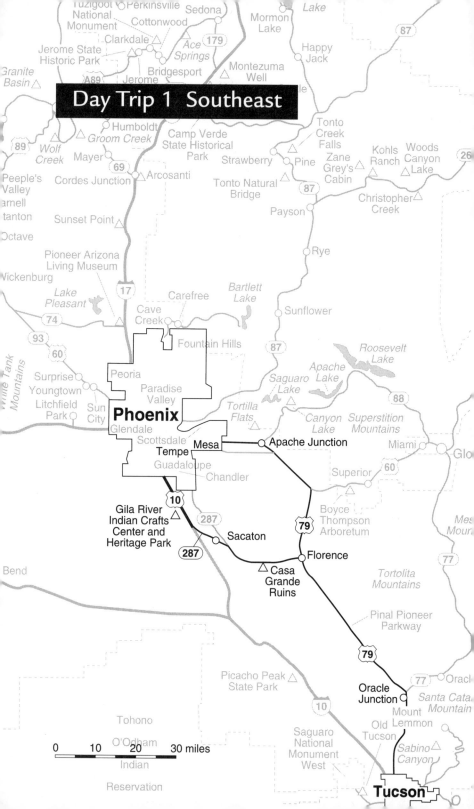

which are located 20 miles to the northeast. This is the largest community in Pinal County.

WHERE TO GO

Casa Grande Valley Historical Society. 110 West Florence Boulevard. Located in downtown Casa Grande, this museum presents many historical facts about the area. Exhibits focus on the history of the region from the arrival of the railroad in 1879 to the present. Agriculture, mining, and transportation are all represented. There is a landmark 1920s stone church and a one-room schoolhouse also on the grounds. Fee. Call for hours. (520) 836-2223.

FLORENCE

Continue east on A-287 to Florence, approximately 9 miles from Coolidge. Florence has two main claims to fame: its courthouse and the prison. The fifth-oldest city in the state, it was established in 1866 by a local Indian agent, Livi Ruggles. The community grew rapidly and became the county seat when Pinal County was chartered in 1875. In spite of its desert setting, Florence is an agricultural community. Local crops include cotton, cattle, sugar beets, grain, and grapes.

Poston Butte, named for Charles Poston, the "Father of Arizona," is a nearby landmark. A monument at the summit of the butte marks his grave. The town is also known as the "Cowboy Cradle of the Southwest." During the depression when jobs and money were scarce and the bottom fell out of the milk market, ranchers were planning to dump their milk rather than sell it at a loss. A local rancher, Charlie Whittlow, declared that he would give his milk free to the schoolchildren rather than waste it. Other communities soon picked up Whittlow's idea, and as a result, the national milk and free lunch program for schoolchildren was started in this country. An odd sidelight to this story is that while Whittlow was a rancher and *not* a cowboy, as a result of his actions, his home became known as "The Cowboy Cradle of the Southwest."

If you want to continue to Tucson (See Day Trip 2, Southeast from Phoenix), you may take US-79 south (Pinal Pioneer Parkway) for a 42-mile scenic stretch between Florence and Oracle Junction and then continue south to Tucson. This drive takes you through a unique natural garden where virtually every type of Arizona desert flora is displayed. Depending upon your time and botanical interest, you can explore easily accessible side roads along the way.

To return to Phoenix from Florence take US–79 north for 16 miles to its junction with US–60. Turn west and follow US–60/US–89 47 miles to Phoenix through Apache Junction, Mesa, and Tempe (Day Trip 2, East from Phoenix).

WHERE TO GO

McFarland Historical State Park. Corner of Main and Ruggles. This park features the first Pinal County Courthouse, an 1878 adobe structure. Inside are exhibits that describe how the building was used as a courthouse and later as a hospital. There is also a historical exhibit featuring Arizona notables Charles Poston, Levi Ruggles, and Pearl Hart. The career of Ernest West McFarland, who was a senator, governor, and justice, is also highlighted, and his personal and public collections are displayed in the archives. The first Saturday in March is Florence Founders' Day. Fee. (520) 868-5216.

Florence Visitor Center. 291 Bailey Street. Located in the heart of the historic district, visitors are asked to sign the official guest book here. This is the place to get maps and brochures about special events that take place during the year as well as inquire about the local businesses and restaurants. Open weekdays 9 A.M. to 4 P.M. (520) 868-4331.

Casa Grande Ruins
National Monument
Columbia University's Biosphere 2

CASA GRANDE RUINS NATIONAL MONUMENT

This day trip takes you "back to the future" with a full day of touring an ancient Indian ruin and then a space-age environment. From Phoenix, take I-10 east to exit 175 through Sacaton. From Sacaton take A-287 southwest for approximately 14 miles to Coolidge. As you approach Coolidge you will come to the Casa Grande Ruins National Monument, an eleven-room, eleven-family, 600-apartment building built by the ancient Hohokam and Pueblo Indian farmers. This structure was constructed of hardened mud blocks that are 5 feet long, 2 feet high, and 4 feet thick. Today it is protected by a giant steel "umbrella." While its original use is still debated, this is the only four-story Indian ruin structure found in the United States, and the only example in Arizona of a structure from the Classic Period (A.D. 1300–A.D. 1400).

Discovered in 1694 by Father Kino, the structure had already been burned when he came upon it. The Pima Indians had a custom of burning the inside of their buildings when they abandoned them. The ruins were explored in 1882 by Dr. J. Walter Fewks of the Smithsonian Institution. Dr. Fewks returned to do more exploration in 1906 and 1908.

As you wander through these imposing ruins, pay special attention to the calendar holes. Two small openings in the east and center rooms are placed so the sun's rays come through. The streak of light passing through both holes and lining up on a target occurs near the spring and fall equinoxes.

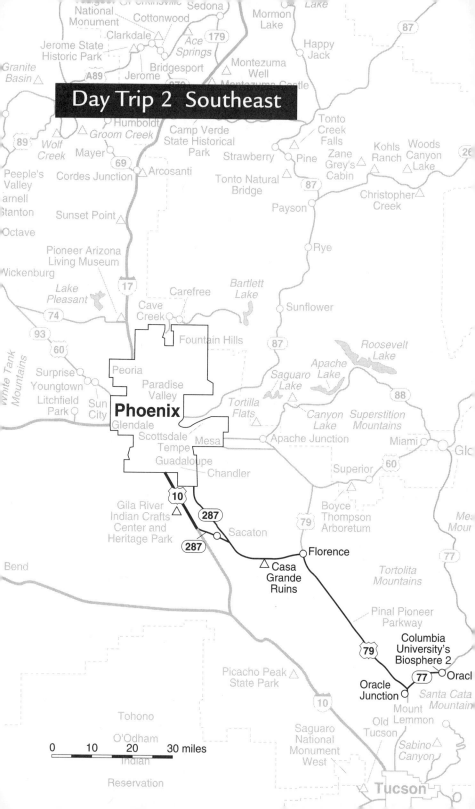

If you visit with smaller children, ask for the special trail guides that are available for youngsters. The guides are free, but a donation is always appreciated. Fee. (520) 723-3172.

COLUMBIA UNIVERSITY'S BIOSPHERE 2

From Casa Grande Ruins National Monument continue on A–287 west to Florence. Then travel south on US–79 to Oracle Junction and join A–77. Follow A–77 to mile marker 96.5 at Oracle and follow the signs to Biosphere 2 and SunSpace Ranch.

Columbia University has taken over Biosphere 2 and added a new educational and research dimension to this project. The University offers degree study programs and conferences on the site. The Earth Exploration Program joins Biosphere 2 Center scientists and Columbia University faculty and other leading educators and researchers with visitors to provide stimulating educational experiences at this self-contained, simulated "world."

This 2.5-acre enclosure is a microcosm of Earth, or Biosphere 1. The project has been under way since 1984 and is a human experiment in which four men and four women have periodically lived inside a sealed and recreated "earth environment" for extended periods of time.

Stocked with nearly 4,000 species of plants and animals, the project replicates seven life zones, or biomes, including a tropical rain forest, marshland, desert, savanna, mountains, and ocean.

Although it was controversial, Columbia University has "legitimized" Biosphere 2 in the eyes of educational and research interests. The original purpose of the project was to see if humans could live in a sealed environment and whether that environment could sustain itself. Columbia University's Biosphere 2 continues the research but emphasizes education. Exhibits demonstrate how man's actions and natural forces are changing the planet and its environment.

Columbia has also opened a portion of Biosphere 2 to visitors—Mission Crew living quarters and the Command and Control "Nerve Room." In addition, study courses are offered both on and off campus focusing on a variety of "earth friendly" topics. Courses are held throughout the year.

The Biosphere sits nestled on a ridge between two rocky outcroppings. It is a dramatic structure, almost like a futuristic ship landed from another galaxy, surrounded by several dome-like structures, which are the "lungs" of the project.

The informative tour takes visitors around the Biosphere and inside the newly opened area. The tour begins in the theater where visitors learn about the philosophy behind this experiment in which virtually everything is recyclable and nothing is disposable. It then continues around the grounds of the project to give visitors an understanding of this massive experiment. Fee. Ask for the monthly event calendar and tour times. (520) 896-6200 or (800) 828-2462.

WHERE TO EAT

The Cañada del Oro Restaurant. On the grounds of Biosphere 2 the restaurant features unique cuisine and panoramic views of the mountain and city. Indoor and outdoor seating is available all year round. The cafe serves Biospherean recipes as well as other fare. Visitors can buy a cookbook that contains recipes the Biosphereans used, "Eating In." $$; (CC). (520) 896-6222.

WHERE TO STAY

Columbia University's Biosphere Hotel and Conference Center Highway 77, Mile Marker 96.5, P.O. Box 689, Oracle, 85623. Oversized large rooms with views of the Catalina Mountains and Biosphere 2 await you. The atmosphere is serene, and the rooms are immaculate. Some have mini-bars. Overnight tour package includes tour, dinner, and breakfast. Call for rates. $$-$$$; (CC). (520) 896-6222.

PICACHO PEAK

Tucson is an easy two-hour trip from Phoenix on I-10. Along the way, you can stop at Picacho Peak State Park, or you may wish to drive straight through and spend the entire day in Tucson.

Picacho Peak State Park. Picacho Peak State Park is located 60 miles southeast of Phoenix just off I-10. From the ranger station, follow the Barrett Loop to the trailhead of Hunter Trail.

Located half way between Tucson and Phoenix, this landmark soars to 3,400 feet. Calloway Trail ($^7/_{10}$ mile) and a short nature loop ($^1/_2$ mile) offer pleasant excursions, but hotshot hikers should head for Hunter Trail and a steep $2^1/_{10}$-mile trek to the summit.

The ascent begins immediately on a clearly marked, difficult path. In forty-five minutes even the semi-fit can reach the saddle where a panoramic view of the Sonoran desert extends beyond the Picacho Mountains to the Catalinas near Tucson. In spring the desert floor may be carpeted with bright orange Mexican poppies, adding vibrant color to the stands of sun-bleached ocotillo and saguaro.

From the saddle the trail gets rough, plunging down 300 feet before climbing to the summit. Twelve sets of cable, anchored into bare rock, provide handholds. Hardy hikers will discover that the view from the top is glorious. Carry water, wear boots and gloves, and expect a rugged, three- to five-hour round-trip. Hikers should avoid the summit trail during June, July, and August.

Long a beacon for wayfarers, Pichacho Peak was known to prehistoric Hohokam Indians who traveled here on trade routes. Later

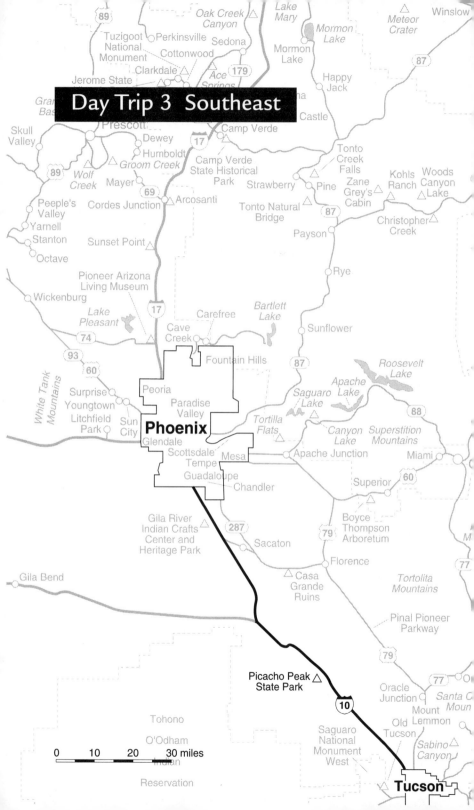

Pima Papago Indians and Spanish missionaries camped on this site. On April 15, 1862, two advance Union and Confederate units clashed near Picacho in the westernmost battle of the Civil War. Reports of casualties vary, but it's known that three Union soldiers were killed. A monument commemorates the skirmish, and the battle is reenacted every March.

A second memorial within the park honors the Mormon Battalion, which built the first wagon road across the Southwest in 1846. Fee. (520) 466–3183.

TUCSON

When you think of Tucson, think mountains. The oldest continually inhabited city in the country, Tucson is surrounded by the Santa Catalinas to the north, the Rincons to the east, the Santa Rita Mountains to the south, the Tucson Mountains to the west, and the Tortolita Mountains to the northwest. With an elevation of 2,410 feet above sea level (about 1,000 feet higher than Phoenix), the "Old Pueblo," as Tucson is called, has a drier and slightly cooler climate than its big sister 100 miles to the north.

Tucson wears its Hispanic heritage like an elegant mantilla. Mexico lies just 60 miles to the south, but the Mexican influence is only one force that helped shape this city. Four cultures co-exist here: Spanish, Mexican, Native American, and, of course, contemporary American.

This cultural blend adds an intellectual vitality to Tucson. Where Phoenix shines with glass and chrome, Tucson glows with pink adobe and wrought iron. Where Phoenix can be wide-open western, Tucson can slip back in time and roll its "R's." Whether you stroll through the Barrio, the old, mostly Mexican-American neighborhood, or walk along the "movie-set" campus of the University of Arizona (U. of A.), you'll be acutely aware of how this half-old, half-new city pursues its blended destiny.

WHERE TO GO

Metropolitan Tucson Convention and Visitors Bureau. La Placita Village at 120 West Broadway. Pick up additional information about the Old Pueblo to learn how the original walled Presidio of San Agustin del Tucson was built by the Spaniards in 1776. You can see a piece of that wall preserved under glass on the second floor of the old **Pima County Courthouse** at the corner of Washington Street and Main Avenue. You'll also learn about the four flags that have flown over Tucson. In 1776, the Spanish claimed it. Later, it belonged to Mexico. In 1853, Arizona was included in the Gadsden Purchase, and Tucson became part of the United States. Then, during the Civil War, the city became part of the Confederate territory.

There is recent history to discover as well, for Tucsonians were determined to rescue their decaying downtown. As you walk around the revitalized central city and drive through the omnipresent foothills, you'll be introduced to contemporary Tucson, a city for tomorrow. *Megatrends* author John Naisbitt singled out Tucson as one of the ten cities of great opportunity in the United States.

As the Pima County seat, this city of about 600,000 people serves as the economic hub for both southern Arizona and northern Mexico. As you shop and dine here, you will notice that many of the restaurants and retail outlets serve both Phoenix and Tucson. But despite the desert climate, open skies, and familiar names, you'll soon feel the difference in spirit between urban Phoenix and more laid-back Tucson, a difference that the smaller community celebrates.

Arizona Historical Society/Tucson. 949 East Second Street. This museum features changing and permanent exhibits that tell Arizona's history from Spanish Colonial times through the Territorial years. There's also a research library and gift shop, and docent-led tours are available by reservation. Free. (520) 628-5774.

Center for Creative Photography. On the University of Arizona campus. During the week, park in the garage at Speedway and Park on the northeast corner, and walk across the street to the Center. A collection of more than 50,000 photographs are housed in this striking, contemporary building. The archives of Ansel Adams are housed and displayed here. A research library is open to the public. Donations suggested. Free. (520) 621-7968.

John C. Fremont House. 151 South Granada Avenue. The Arizona Historical Society operates this home, which is a restored 1880s adobe. It was once rented by Territorial Governor Fremont. It was also the home of the pioneer Sosa and Carrillo families and contains nineteenth-century furnishings as well as a collection of American antiques. There is a unique "touch table" for children. Reservations are suggested. Free. (520) 622–0956.

International Wildlife Museum. 4800 West Gates Pass Road. Nearly 300 mammals and birds from six continents are realistically displayed in natural habitats with many excellent interactive exhibits that provide additional information. While the building looks like a misplaced castle-fortress in the desert, the collection is complete and well displayed. There are guided tours, wildlife films, videos, and restaurants. Fee. (520) 624–4024.

Playmaxx, Inc. 2900 North Country Club Road. This museum features a unique collection of yo-yos from 1930 through the future. Exhibits include a photo history, and factory tours are available. Free; donation requested. (520) 322–0100.

Tohono Chul Park. 7366 Paseo del Norte. This park is landscaped beautifully with natural vegetation and gardens that feature nature trails, demonstrations, and ethnobotanical gardens. There's also a geological re-creation of the nearby Catalina Mountains, a recirculating stream, *ramadas,* art gallery with good quality arts and crafts displayed, and exhibit hall. The gift shop is worth browsing through, and a tearoom is available for refreshments. This is a great destination for a breakfast or lunch respite. Free. (520) 742–6455.

Tucson Botanical Gardens, 2150 North Alvernon Way. Enjoy a collection of gardens that includes a historical Tucson area, arid landscaping, herbs, irises, tropical greenhouses, wildflowers, Native American crops, and vegetables. Fee. (520) 326–9255.

University of Arizona Museum of Art. On the campus of the U. of A. A permanent collection of art spans the Middle Ages through the twentieth century. There are changing exhibitions that feature student, faculty, and guest artists. Free. (520) 621–7567.

WHERE TO EAT

Tucson has wonderful restaurants serving all varieties of ethnic food. Mexican food is served Sonoran style and slightly spicier than the Phoenix version. Continental cuisine is as elegant as that found in any city three times its size. Here are some with special historic or cultural significance.

Arizona Inn. 2200 East Elm Street. Continental dining is graciously served at this landmark hotel. Located in the central city, the dining room is quiet and relaxing. Furnishings are all original and were made by the returning veterans of World War I. You can eat indoors or outdoors where you face the lovely gardens. The food is as terrific as the setting. $$–$$$; (CC). (520) 325–1541.

Janos. 150 North Main Avenue. Janos is acknowledged as one of the best chefs in Tucson. The setting alone is worth a visit. The restaurant is located in a historic 1885 adobe home in the Presidio section of downtown and meanders through high-ceilinged, elegant rooms. Service is friendly and warm, and the menu, which changes seasonally, is uniformly superb. Presentation is special, and reservations are required at this four-star, award-winning dining favorite. $$$; (CC). (520) 884–9426.

Karichimaka Restaurant. 5252 South Mission Road. When it opened in 1949, this restaurant, on the way to San Xavier Del Bac, was out in the country. The city has grown up but the location remains the same as does the cuisine, Sonoran-style Mexican food. $–$$; (CC). (520) 883–0311.

The Tack Room. 7300 East Vacor Ranch Trail. Tucson's only five-star restaurant, and a local favorite for years, this definitely is worth your time and money. The continental food is excellent, the atmosphere polished and genteel. Plan an entire evening enjoying the twinkling views of Tucson in the distance, impeccable service, and outstanding cuisine. $$$; (CC). (520) 722–2800.

Li'l Abners. 8501 North Silverbell Road. Li'l Abners claims it serves up "world famous" mesquite-broiled steaks and chicken. They are delicious. This location was a Butterfield Express stage stop during pioneer days. Today it offers dining, drinking, and dancing served up in a lush desert area. To get there, you'll head west on Ina Road to Silverbell. Turn north on Silverbell. $$–$$$; (CC). (520) 744–2800.

Pinnacle Peak. 6541 East Tanque Verde Road, in Trail Dust Town. Like the Phoenix edition, this is western living at its most casual—and dangerous if you wear a tie. Anyone who wears a tie in Pinnacle Peak risks its being cut off by the waitress or waiter in a public ceremony. The cut tie is displayed in the restaurant along with the wearer's business card. Cowboy steaks, ribs, and western pit beef in a skillet are specialties. After dinner walk around Trail Dust Town and enjoy the shops. Even if you don't buy anything, the walk will do you good after downing a gigantic steak. $$; (CC). (520) 296–0911.

WHERE TO STAY

Like Phoenix, Tucson is famous for its resorts. If you have a "hankerin" for a dude ranch, Tucson is bursting with them. There are more guest and dude ranches in southern Arizona than anywhere else in the country. If you prefer a quick overnight in a basic motel, you can find that, too. But if you want to stay in out-of-the-ordinary accommodations, read on. For a more complete list of accommodations, contact the Arizona Hotel & Motel Association, 2210 East Camelback, Suite 125B, Phoenix, 85016, or call (602) 553–8802.

Arizona Inn. 2200 East Elm Street. If you like historical Tucson at its most serene, you'll enjoy this world-famous hotel. There is no flash or glitz here, just unhurried, unchanged hospitality served up at its best. In the heart of town, the Arizona Inn has served an illustrious clientele over the years. Ask the staff about the celebrity guests who like the paneled, hacienda mood of this homey inn.

The Inn has eighty rooms, all individually decorated, and many have private patios. The atmosphere is 1930s with 1990s amenities. The library in the main sitting room is filled with books, the living room is stately but inviting, and the 60-foot heated pool is sheltered on all sides. The restaurant is one of the city's best and features continental cuisine. But while the main dining rooms are lovely, plan to have breakfast on the patio. Then be sure to stroll around the grounds to enjoy the gardens of this gracious hotel.

The history of the Arizona Inn is fascinating. Take time to read the small book placed in each room that tells its story. This is one of the best places to stay in the city if you enjoy a very civilized approach to vacationing. Even one evening here can do a lot to unwind a harried guest. Prices are reasonable in the winter and downright bargains in the summer. $$–$$$; (CC). (520) 325–1541 or (800) 421–1093.

Loews Ventana Canyon. 7000 North Resort Drive. Tucson's most elegant addition to the total resort scene has it all. Choose from golf, tennis, swimming pools, horseback riding, nature trails, superb restaurants, and health club facilities in an incomparably beautiful desert setting.

Golfers rave about the desert courses. The Gold Room presents ultra-sophisticated dining. But man-made attractions pale beside following the nature trail on the property, a gentle, easy, twenty-minute walk you can do in the daytime or evening. A gorgeous waterfall greets you at the end of your brief journey. $$$; (CC). (520) 299-2020 or (800) 522-5455.

The Westin La Paloma. 3800 East Sunrise. The hotel offers tennis, racquetball, volleyball, swimming, a Jack Nicklaus-designed golf course, and more. Rooms have balconies or patios, and child care can be arranged. Five restaurants serve everything from fresh seafood to gourmet meals, and hungry swimmers will appreciate simply swimming up to the poolside bar and grill to chow down. $$; (CC). (520) 742-6000.

GUEST RANCHES

The Tucson area has a number of excellent guest ranches within an hour or two of the city. For a complete listing, contact the Metropolitan Tucson Convention and Visitor Bureau at (520) 624-1817. Most guest ranches are small and accommodate no more than sixty guests. Some offer opportunities for "dudes"; others are for more rugged riders. Names to know include the **Lazy K Bar Guest Ranch,** 16 miles northwest of Tucson; **White Stallion Ranch,** 17 miles northwest of Tucson; and **Wild Horse Ranch,** in Tucson. All are close to the city.

Tanque Verde Guest Ranch. Route 8, Box 66, Tucson. This is a Tucson landmark, a year-round ranch featuring comfortable, western accommodations, one hundred horses, tennis courts, indoor health spa, and gourmet dining. You'll need to stay longer than overnight to get a flavor of all that this ranch has to offer. The ranch backs up to a national forest filled with saguaros. Riding trails wind through unspoiled desert. Tanque Verde runs an excellent riding school. Instruction is available, and all levels of riders can be accommodated. The breakfast trail ride is a special treat. Don't be surprised to hear many languages being spoken here as this is a favorite with international guests.

The atmosphere is western casual. The patios and dining areas are spacious. It's great in the winter, spring, and fall. Summer packages make this an affordable destination for families and international guests. $$$; (CC). (520) 296-6275.

Bed & Breakfasts

El Presidio Inn. 297 Main Avenue. This is an award-winning luxury B&B in a historic Victorian adobe mansion built in 1880. The garden is romantic and lush, and the appointments are superb. Located within walking distance of Tucson's historic downtown, guests enjoy a complete breakfast, evening treats, and elegant surroundings. $$–$$$. (520) 623-6151.

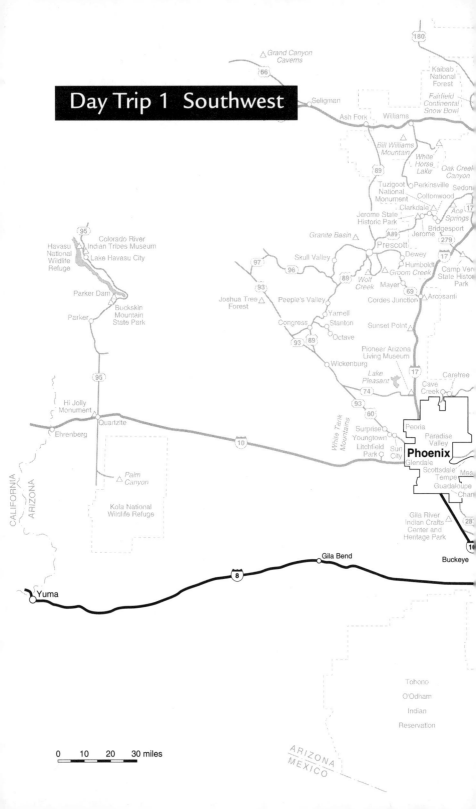

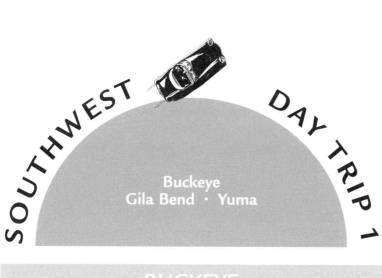

BUCKEYE

Eagle Mountain Ranch. 12100 South Dean Road, Rainbow Valley, 85326. Take I-10 West to exit 121, Jackrabbit Trail. Go south on Jackrabbit Trail to Narramore Road. Turn west to Dean Road and follow the signs to Eagle Mountain Ranch. This rustic, western stables and miniature western town is located 45 minutes west of Phoenix in the town of Rainbow Valley, just outside of Buckeye. Buckeye is an agricultural community that is testimony to what Phoenix looked like prior to the population boom following World War II.

Although now connected by freeway to the big city, Buckeye clings to its rural roots. The drive to the ranch is lined with cotton and cornfields, with mountains rising in the distance, unimpeded by intruding tall buildings. The sense of wide open space is so great, utility lines seem almost nonexistent.

Eagle Mountain Ranch is surrounded by the Estrella and White Tanks Mountains. It offers guests the opportunity to see the wide open real west from horseback (or hayride wagon) any day of the week. The ranch is adjacent to 300 square miles of open desert range and is punctuated by the Buckeye Hills which offer miles of varied riding trails.

Owners Dale and Pat Parker organize trail rides at the ranch complete with steak cookouts, campfires, and traditional cowboy breakfasts. Rides are organized for groups or individuals. The Parkers ask that individuals (as opposed to groups that book further in advance) call for reservations at least 24 hours in advance. They request a minimum of 2 people to book a ride. Eagle Mountain Ranch is open every day of the year.

Eagle Mountain Ranch was desert—claimed at the turn of the century by two horsebreakers and bought from them by the Parker family. After more than 35 years living an urban life as an engineer, Dale Parker decided to come back to a simpler way of life and returned to the family farm where he grew up raising cotton and cattle, to share this special lifestyle.

Recently the Parkers have begun constructing a small "western town" for their guests' enjoyment. The "town," designed and built by an ex-Hollywood stuntman friend, spreads under the shade of an enormous cottonwood tree. The area enables visitors to enjoy cookouts, breakfast or relaxing while visiting with Dale Parker who is a wealth of information about the geology and history of the area.

Eagle Mountain Ranch accommodates guests with short-to-overnight trail rides. Dale and Pat Parker have a standing contract with a wrangler who provides the horses. The two-hour ride—especially sunset rides during the summer months—is highly recommended. $$. (602) 386-2316.

WHERE TO EAT

La Placita. 242 Monroe, Buckeye. This newly remodeled authentic Mexican restaurant was designed by owner Joe Amabisco and serves authentic Mexican dishes made from recipes handed down through generations of Joe's family. Groups can ask about arranging a Mexican Fiesta. Open daily for lunch and dinner except Sunday. $-$$. (602) 386-3632.

After a day of the Old West, "riding the range" and indulging in homemade Mexican fare, day trippers can head east on I-10 to return to Phoenix, or stay the night in nearby Goodyear.

GILA BEND

Pick up this day trip following I-10 southeast out of Phoenix to its junction with I-8. Then go 62 miles west on I-8 to Gila Bend and continue 117 miles on I-10 to Yuma.

This is a long (approximately four-hour) trip; however, there are enough historical attractions to make it worthwhile. If you make this trip during the hot summer months, drive during the early morning or evening hours. Along the way, you'll see the surrealistic California sand dunes near Yuma.

Gila Bend is often called the fan belt capital of the world, not because fan belts are made here, but because there are probably more belts *replaced* here than any other place in the world.

Originally, the town grew up where the Gila River took a deep bend toward the south before heading west. The community prospered when the Butterfield Overland Stage scheduled stops here in the 1870s. Miners en route to California gold fields, mail-order brides, and eastern businessmen who were sizing up the future made themselves at home in Gila Bend for a night or two.

Then, in 1880, the train came near town, and the town gradually moved away from the river toward the tracks. Ultimately the river changed its course and moved north of town. All that's left of the river's influence is the city's name.

YUMA

Situated in the southwestern corner of the state, Yuma has an interesting heritage. History confirms that the area was visited as early as 1540 by the Spaniards. By the 1870s this community was the key southwestern city in the territory. First called Colorado City (for the river), then Arizona City (for the territory), and eventually Yuma City, the name finally was shortened to Yuma.

Yuma won a permanent place in Arizona Territory by 1870. Today the residents of this city rely on the same river waters to support agriculture, commerce, recreation, and the military. Located close to San Diego and Mexico, this small city attracts thousands of winter visitors to its sunny environs.

Today some historic buildings commemorate what was once the busy **Yuma Crossing.** The Colorado and Gila rivers once converged here before the Gila changed its course. Eighty years before the Pilgrims landed, beginning in 1540, Spanish explorers rode through this land in search of the Seven Cities of Gold.

As time passed, countless trails met at this junction. Kit Carson guided American troops. The Mormon Battalion trudged through, carving the first road from Santa Fe to San Diego, and during the gold rush days, more than 30,000 people seeking their fortunes trekked across the river here on their way to California.

In the 1850s, the shallow draft steamboat opened the Colorado River to shipping, and Yuma became a major riverport of entry for Arizona. The Fort Yuma Quartermaster Depot swarmed with the bustle of a military supply hub. During the 1860s, 1870s, and 1880s, during the height of the Apache Wars, the Yuma Quartermaster Depot supplied military posts throughout the region. Then the train arrived in 1877, and the depot was abandoned in 1883.

WHERE TO GO

U.S. Army Quartermasters Depot/Arizona State Park. Second Avenue behind City Hall. The Depot was established in 1864 and served the entire Southwest as a matériel transfer and distribution point for troops stationed at the military outposts throughout the Arizona Territory. The Depot saw much activity during the 1870s and 1880s during the height of the Apache Wars. It was abandoned in 1883 after trains arrived here in 1877. Both the Quartermaster's office and the stone Water Reservoir have been restored to their original condition.

Yuma Old Territorial Prison. Giss Parkway and Prison Hill Road, right off I-8 near the Colorado River. Now a state park, the prison operated from 1876 to 1909 and had a miserable reputation. Western bad men (and women) used it as their address—folks such as Buckskin Frank Leslie and "Heartless" Pearl Hart. Museum exhibits document the story of the prison cells, which are authentically furnished, and add a hands-on sense of reality. You can also take a ranger-guided tour of the facility. Fee. (520) 783–4771.

Century House Museum. 240 South Madison Avenue. This was the home of pioneer merchant E. F. Sanguinetti and is one of Yuma's most historic buildings. Now a regional museum of the Arizona Historical Society, it holds historical documents, photographs, and artifacts. Walk through the gardens and aviaries on the grounds. Free. (520) 782–1841.

Quechan Indian Museum. Across the Colorado·River from Yuma at Fort Yuma on Indian Hill Road, this museum is located near the territorial prison. Fort Yuma, one of the oldest military posts in Arizona, is now headquarters for the Quechan tribe. Inside you'll see exhibits of tribal artifacts. Fee. (619) 572-0661.

Yuma Art Center. 281 Gila Street. Located in a restored Southern Pacific Railroad depot, the center presents exhibitions of contemporary Arizona and Indian artists. Fee. (520) 783-2314.

Pick up a self-guided tour pamphlet from the Chamber of Commerce, 377 Main Street, for more to see in Yuma. (520) 782-2567.

Peanut Patch. 4233 East County Thirteenth Street. This store was opened in 1977 on the Didier Family Farm and sells some of the finest peanut products in the West. Nuts are grown on the farm and sold at the store on the property. Tours of the plant are available. Free. (520) 726-6292.

Yuma County Live Steamers. Eighth Street and Levee. From October through June train buffs can ride back through time on the historic Yuma Valley Railroad. The train travels along the banks of the Colorado River through the Cocopah Indian Reservation. Passengers ride aboard a 1922 Pullman Coach pulled by a first-generation 1941 diesel locomotive. A local historian tells stories, which adds to the fun. Lunch and dinner rides are scheduled, but the train has been known to run sporadically. Fee. Call for more information and reservations. (520) 783-3456.

Yuma River Tours. 1920 Arizona Avenue. Don't see Yuma without taking a river tour. The boats travel past ruins and petroglyphs, ferry crossings and homesteads. You'll see steamboat landings and mining camps and visit a wildlife refuge, one of the few untouched refuges in the entire country. This is a special experience that shouldn't be missed. Fee. (520) 783-4400.

WHERE TO EAT

Chretins. 485 South Fifteenth Avenue. This family-owned Mexican restaurant is huge, old, and funky. Expect to wait if you arrive on a weekend during the winter, but the Mexican menu is homemade. The atmosphere is old Yuma with a touch of Mexico. $$; (CC). (520) 782-1291.

La Fonda Tortilla Factory. 1095 South Third Avenue. This place serves excellent Mexican food. The service is slow, but the tortillas are delicious. $$; (CC). (520) 783-6902.

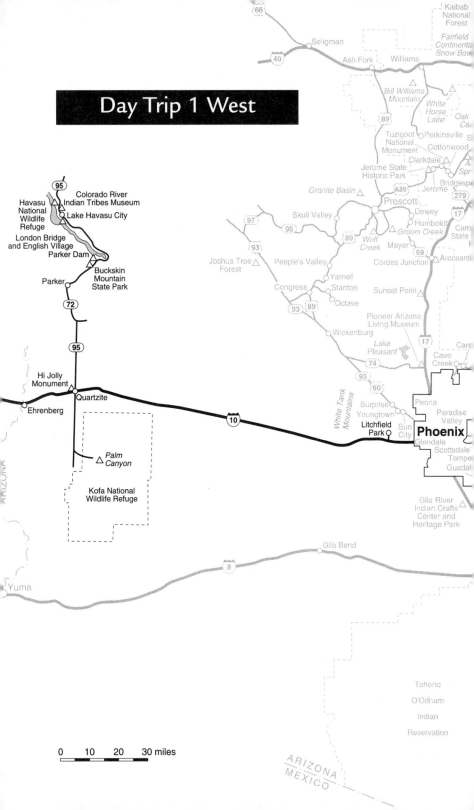

Day Trip 1 West

QUARTZSITE

To visit the main destination of this day trip, Lake Havasu City, you'll drive four and one-half to five hours—one way. Obviously this trip is best done as an overnight in Lake Havasu City. Head west out of Phoenix on I-10 past Litchfield Park. Eventually, after 112 miles, I-10 intersects with A-95 to Quartzsite.

Situated in the Mohave Desert, Quartzsite is best known for its great numbers of "snow birds" (winter visitors, as they are called) who flock to this community each year in vast numbers, pulling mobile homes with them. Visitors appreciate the sunshine and inexpensive, quiet living Quartzsite affords. The town hosts an annual rock and mineral show in February that attracts more than 850,000 people.

WHERE TO GO

Hi Jolly Monument. Quartzsite, in the Quartzsite City Cemetery. Go west on the main street from the center of town about a quarter mile and follow the signs to the road leading to the city cemetery. Here you will see an unusual reminder of a pioneer experiment.

In the 1850s the U.S. War Department decided to introduce camels into the desert. The Hi Jolly Monument honors Hadji Ali, one of the Arab camel drivers who was brought here to drive the beasts.

119

The experiment was successful, but the cavalry members disliked riding the disagreeable, smelly animals and wanted to disband the camel corps. The official report stated that the beasts got sore feet from walking over the desert, when in actuality the cavalry got sore from riding the camels!

When the camel experiment ended, most of the other drivers went home, but Hadji Ali, or Hi Jolly as he was called, stayed to become a prospector. He is buried in the city cemetery.

Nineteen miles west of Quartzsite is Ehrenberg, a haven for rock hunters looking for agates, limonite cubes, and quartz—all abundant in the area.

PALM CANYON

Hikers will want to detour south for about 20 miles on A-95 to the Kofa National Wildlife Refuge. Watch for the sign 18.7 miles south of Quartzsite that reads: PALM CANYON AND KOFA GAME RANGE (It's an old sign; it should say PALM CANYON AND KOFA NATIONAL WILDLIFE REFUGE.). Turn east and follow the gravel road leading to the canyon. You must drive slowly for about 9 miles. There's a parking area at the end of this road. You can hike a quarter mile through the towering narrow canyon on a trail to Palm Canyon. This secluded spot, nestled in the Kofa Mountains, is home to Arizona's only native stand of palm trees.

Don't attempt to visit Palm Canyon during the hot summer months. Temperatures soar; and you'll sizzle. Hiking is at its best during the spring and autumn. The best time to visit is from the end of October through April. Free. (520) 783-7861.

PARKER

Retrace your route by driving north on A-95 to its intersection with A-72. Follow A-72 northwest to Parker, which is 35 miles north of Quartzsite. If you have time to explore, stop at the Parker Chamber of Commerce, 1217 California Avenue, (520) 669-2174, to pick up information. You will find a variety of events during the year, including several boat races, so check to see what's going on.

Parker is a river town—part California beach, part Arizona river rat—and exists for power and water sports. Late summer can be brutal. August temperatures climb to 120 degrees, sometimes for a week at a time.

Each year the community hosts an international inner tube race in mid-June. It attracts hundreds of dedicated tubers who travel along the 7 miles in a variety of outlandish outfits.

WHERE TO GO

Buckskin Mountain State Park. Twenty miles north of Parker on A-95. Situated along a grassy, shady section of the riverbank, this park offers a quiet respite in often-raucous Parker. Enjoy the many campsites and hiking trails. There is a concession operation, but you might prefer to bring a picnic lunch. Fee. (520) 667-3231.

Colorado River Indian Tribes Museum. Corner of Agency and Mohave roads in Parker. This newly renovated museum displays the world's largest collection of Chemehuevi Indian basketry. In addition, visitors will enjoy seeing Mohave pottery and exhibits that interpret the four tribes in the area: Mohave, Chemehuevi, Hopi, and Navajo. The only museum in La Paz County, it stresses both historical and cultural exhibits. Inquire here about how to see the Blythe Intaglios, ancient Mohave figures that are etched in the nearby desert. For more information, write to the Colorado River Indian Tribes Museum, Route 1, Box 23-B, Parker, 85344. A donation is suggested. (520) 669-9211.

Parker Dam. On A-95 in Parker Dam, California, 17 miles north of Parker, Arizona. Continue on A-95 through Parker and turn right at Agency Road. There's a stoplight. Continue on that road to the dam. As you cross the river onto the dam, you'll enter California; the Colorado River is the state boundary.

Parker Dam was built on the Colorado in 1934 and is one of the deepest dams in the world. You'll see only about one-third of the structure; the rest is under the water's surface. With a height of 320 feet and base thickness of 100 feet, it's an imposing edifice. Behind it is Lake Havasu, which contains 648,000 acre-feet of water. (An acre-foot is the amount of water it takes to cover one acre to a depth of one foot.)

You can take a self-guided tour of the dam, which includes stops from the top of the dam to the generating station below the water. Taped speeches describe what you're seeing. If you've never visited a desert dam and you have a spare half hour, treat yourself to the experience and marvel at the technology. Free. For more information, contact the Parker Chamber of Commerce in Arizona, (520) 669–2174.

LAKE HAVASU CITY

From the dam, drive north for an hour on A–95, which winds along the riverbank to Lake Havasu City. This area, like neighboring Parker, is best known for water-based recreation. You can make the Phoenix-Lake Havasu City trip in a day, but then it's more of a marathon than a day trip. It is better to plan this trip as an overnight, or even two overnights, so you have time to enjoy the area.

Lake Havasu City, established in 1963, was designed as a self-sufficient, planned community for several thousand residents. Although somewhat isolated from the rest of the state, it continues to attract newcomers and is growing into an attractive community for people who love a quiet, water-recreation lifestyle. Don't expect to see any "big city" stuff here. Come to relax, not for fine dining. Lake Havasu City is strictly small-town.

Geologically, the area around Lake Havasu and Lake Havasu City is a gold mine. Within a 10-mile radius are specimens of volcanic rock, geodes, jasper, obsidian, turquoise, and agate. Indian relics and abandoned mines also make this trip worthwhile for adventurous backpackers. If colored chips interest you more than pretty rocks, you're just 150 miles from Las Vegas and less than an hour from Laughlin, Nevada, across the Colorado River.

Make the Lake Havasu area Chamber of Commerce, 1930 Mesquite, Suite 3, your first stop in town. As you enter Lake Havasu City, you'll come to a stoplight. Head away from the lake and drive to the top of the hill. Turn left and then take the first immediate left into the parking lot. The chamber is located in the two-story building. Ask for a visitor's packet and dining guide. (520) 453–3444.

WHERE TO GO

Blue River Safari. Plan to take this guided boat trip while you're in Lake Havasu City to learn about the lake and the **Havasu National Wildlife Refuge,** which is located along the north shore of Lake

Havasu, a few miles north of town. This wildlife preserve is home to a number of birds and small game. Fee. (520) 453-5848.

The Dixie Bell. Anchored at the dock near London Bridge. Lake Havasu is a dream come true for water sports fans. Nearly every form of boating is available from canoeing and water skiing to jet skiing to riding paddle wheelers. *The Dixie Bell* is a replica of an Old South stern-wheeler. It's the largest boat of its nature on the Colorado River and maintains a regular cruise schedule. The tour is narrated and takes one hour and twenty minutes. Fee. For information, call (520) 453-6776 or (520) 855-0888.

Lake Havasu and Lake Havasu State Park. This lake, which was formed when Parker Dam was built on the Colorado River, is 45 miles long and attracts fishermen, boaters, water and jet skiers, and nature lovers. From town, follow Lincoln Bridge Road, which sweeps along the western boundary of Lake Havasu City. As you drive, you'll see signs for many public beaches that are state owned and operated. All types of facilities are offered—from camping to resort living.

You can rent a houseboat, jet skis, or speedboat and cruise the blue lake expanse, or you can just drive to a beach, roll up your pants legs, and wade around to your heart's content. The beachfront is rocky, so those with tender toes should take tennis shoes.

The 13,000-acre park, which was developed along the 23 miles of shoreline surrounding Lake Havasu, contains beaches and campgrounds.

Three beaches are especially popular. **Pittsburg Point,** at Lake Havasu City, is across from the London Bridge and has a variety of concession facilities. Follow McCulloch Boulevard across the bridge and continue on McCulloch as it loops around and becomes Beachcomber Boulevard. **Windsor Beach,** north of the London Bridge on the mainland, is a good day facility and has boat-launching ramps. From McCulloch Boulevard turn north onto London Bridge Road and go north to Windsor Beach. **Cattail Cove,** 15 miles south of Lake Havasu City on A-95, has concession campgrounds and is easily accessible to the lake. Fee. For more information, call Lake Havasu State Park. (520) 855-7851.

London Bridge. At McCulloch Boulevard and A-95, spanning Thompson Bay. Gimmicky? Of course. But there is a thrill to walking, bicycling, or driving over The London Bridge, as incongruous as it seems suspended over the Colorado River in Arizona.

How did it get there? In 1967 the City of London decided that the London Bridge was too small for the current volume of traffic, so after 136 years of use, the bridge was offered for sale. Robert P. Mc-Culloch, Sr., the founder of Lake Havasu City, purchased it, had it dismantled in England with every block numbered, and shipped it to the United States. Three years later, the reconstruction was finished at a total cost of $7.5 million. It was a publicity stunt of grand proportions that instantly put Lake Havasu City on the map. The London Bridge formally opened in Arizona in October 1971 to the delight of everyone who sees it.

The English Village. This is the area around the bridge that sports a full-sized village featuring gift shops and restaurants. Somehow, under the shadow of the London Bridge, it doesn't seem incongruous in its Arizona desert setting. Wander around or stop to eat at one of the restaurants or cafes.

NORTHWEST DAY TRIP 1

Glendale · Peoria
Sun Cities · Wickenburg
Joshua Forest Parkway
Ghost Towns of Congress, Stanton,
and Octave · Lake Pleasant

GLENDALE

Unlike most Arizona drives, this excursion is not scenic at first. But take heart—the gorgeous desert foothills await. Along the way you'll pass through urbanizing Phoenix, visit the world's largest retirement community, and get a taste of the Old West. Be prepared for city driving and long, open stretches. You'll cross the Agua Fria River (which may or may not have water in it depending upon the season) and view the White Tank Mountains in the distance.

Drive northwest on Grand Avenue (US–60) from Phoenix through Glendale, once called "The City of Perpetual Harvest." Established in 1885 as a church community, Glendale soon became a farming town. Today it is one of the largest shipping points for fresh garden vegetables in the country.

Glendale in recent years has found its niche as a center for antiques and quaint shops. Although it is Arizona's fourth-largest city, it purposefully looks back to the days when life was simpler and people were friendlier. Tourists are discovering Glendale's historic downtown which looks like a turn-of-the-century village. Antiques buffs appreciate finding the state's greatest concentration of antiques shops as well as a fine assortment of craft galleries, restaurants and tea rooms. Of special interest is the candy factory which is open to tours. Free trolley rides loop through downtown and Catlin Court. The third Thursday of every month in November and December more than 40 antiques stores and galleries host the Antique Walk until 9 P.M.

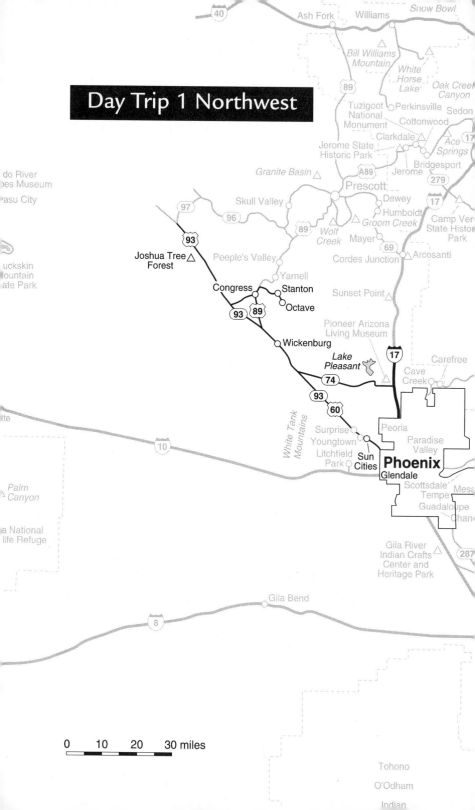

Day Trip 1 Northwest

WHERE TO GO

Catlin Court Historical District. 5890 West Palmaire Avenue, Glendale. Located near the heart of Glendale, Catlin Court is bordered by white picket fences and brick-trimmed sidewalks. Here are gazebos and gaslights and gardens as well as historic craftsman bungalows which have been beautifully restored. Catlin Court contains tearooms where visitors can turn back the clock to more gracious times and rows of antiques shops and craft boutiques. For information, call (602) 435-2559.

Cerreta Candy Company. 5345 West Glendale Avenue, Glendale. This family-owned business makes candy for Disneyland, Magic Mountain and Knotts Berry Farms among others. Free tours of the factory are offered. The wrapped candies are terrific. Free. For tours, call (602) 930-1000.

Sahuaro Ranch Park. Located on 59th Avenue north of Olive. Sahuaro Ranch includes a 16-acre park and preserves one of the Phoenix area's finest and oldest homesteads. The ranch has seven original buildings, a lavish rose garden and more than 100 peacocks that roam the grounds. When you enter the park you will see the main house and buildings. Continue on, and you will see the public park area, complete with *ramadas* and playgrounds. It is listed on the National Register of Historic Places. To reserve a special *ramada,* call the City Parks and Recreation department at 930-2820. Tours of the main house begin in mid-October through May weekends from 1:00–4:00 P.M. Tours are held every 30–45 minutes. For more information, or to book *ramadas* for large parties or weddings, call the Glendale Historical Society at (602) 435-0072.

PEORIA

Although not a garden spot of the Southwest, Peoria offers one attraction especially for children.

The Wildlife World Zoo. Three miles west of Litchfield Road on Northern Avenue. Follow Grand Avenue (US-60) and turn right on Litchfield Road. At Northern Avenue, turn right again. The zoo is 4 miles west on Northern. Walk through an aviary with over thirty species of tropical birds and see the largest collection of marsupials (kangaroos and wallabies) in the country, all five types of the world's ostriches, and America's most complete pheasant display. Fee. (602) 935-WILD.

SUN CITIES

Back on Grand Avenue (US-60) continue northwest through Young-town to Del Webb's Sun City and Sun City West. These retirement cities are about 20 miles from downtown Phoenix. You'll know you're near when you see more electric golf carts than cars on the streets! Established in 1954, Youngtown was the first retirement community in the United States and continues to attract retirees. However, that town has been eclipsed in size by the Del Webb developments, which were begun in 1960. Today Sun City and Sun City West comprise the world's largest retirement communities. Even if you aren't thinking of giving up the office for golf, they are worth a visit.

At Sun City West, your driving tour includes Sundome Plaza, the vast Sundome Center for the Performing Arts, sports pavilion, Johnson Library, and other points of interest. For information, call (602) 584-3118, or visit the development office, 13323 Meeker Boulevard.

WICKENBURG

Leaving the golf cart set behind, follow A-93 north to Wickenburg for a taste of the old and new West. As you proceed, you'll enter rolling foothills dotted with saguaros, ocotillos, and mesquite.

Wickenburg is located approximately 54 miles northwest of Phoenix and sits at the foot of the Bradshaw Mountains on the banks of the Hassayampa (Hah-sa-yampa) River. Legend has it that anyone who drinks from the Hassayampa never tells the truth again. As you approach the Hassayampa you may wonder how anyone ever drinks out of the river anyway, since usually it is a wide, dry, sandy riverbed. But look again. The green, lush area around it demonstrates the power of a desert river. Even a sporadic flow of water creates fertile soil out of dusty ground and a stretch of the river flows underground.

Wickenburg was established by Henry Wickenburg, who searched for an elusive vein of gold for ten years. There are numerous stories about how he finally found that treasure. Some may be more truthful, but this legend is the best: When the failed prospector landed in what is now called Wickenburg, he was discouraged and alone. His partner had no faith in him, and to make matters worse, Wickenburg's balky burro refused to move. Looking up, the prospector saw a vulture circle, land, and eye the stubborn beast. In utter disgust, Wickenburg picked up a rock to throw at the bird. When the rock dropped, it split in half and revealed gold.

Regardless of the veracity of that tale, Wickenburg did stumble over the richest gold lode in Arizona and named it the Vulture Mine. Although his claim has long been exhausted and is no longer even open for tours, the town of Wickenburg retains its rustic gold rush image.

WHERE TO GO

Frontier Street. This area is preserved as it was in the 1800s with a fine railway station, a former hotel, and other buildings. Follow US–60 west as it crosses the Hassayampa River. Frontier intersects with US–60. Wander at will.

Desert Caballeros Western Museum. 21 North Frontier Street. Turn left onto Frontier from US–60. Parking is next to the railroad tracks. Staffed and built by dedicated volunteers, this museum contains works by well-known western artists, including Frederic Remington and George Phippen. In addition to the art gallery, visit the Hall of History, period rooms, mineral room, and Mexican room. This museum is one of the state's lesser known gems as the collection and the facility are both outstanding. The museum can be toured in an hour and is very much worth the trip. Free for children under 6. (520) 684-2272.

Old 761. At Apache and Tegner streets behind the Town Hall. From the museum, follow Frontier Street northwest to Apache Street. Turn right on Apache to just north of Tegner Street. Here you will see the original steam engine and tender that chugged along the tracks from Chicago to the West.

Jail Tree. Tegner and Center streets. From Old 761, follow Apache Street south. Turn left onto Tegner Street. You'll come upon a large 200-year-old mesquite tree. Since Wickenburg didn't have a jail, the law used this tree to tether rowdies who caused trouble. You can see the leg irons, still attached to the tree, which accomplished the task.

Law-abiding citizens can stop, clamp on the irons, and have their pictures taken.

Hassayampa River Preserve. On US–60, 3 miles southeast of Wickenburg. The preserve entrance is on the west side of the highway near mile marker 114. Although the Hassayampa River flows underground for most of its length, it comes to the surface near Wickenburg. Owned by the Nature Conservancy, the area has been restored to its natural state as a shady, life-filled riparian area. Today the Hassayampa Preserve consists of 5 miles of one of Arizona's last and finest Sonoran Desert streamside habitats.

The preserve and headquarters were once parts of the Frederick Brill Ranch, now listed on Arizona's State Register of Historic Places. The four-room adobe core, which serves as the Visitor Center, was built in the 1860s by Brill, a Prussian immigrant who raised cattle and operated a stagecoach way station. An entrepreneur, Brill planted fruit orchards and operated the first carp farm in the state near Palm Lake.

When the Nature Conservancy purchased the property in December 1986, much of the land had been overgrazed and returned to desert. With care, it has become an invaluable biologic riparian resource.

Trails are easily accessible and not strenuous. A 1-mile nature trail leads through the leafy, gladed area next to the river. There's a less scenic but shorter loop trail around Palm Lake. On both trails it is important that all visitors respect the fragile ecosystem of the preserve. The revegetation has been one of the miracles of Mother Nature, and the Conservancy wants to protect it for generations to come.

In addition to the self-guided walks, naturalists lead hikes on a seasonal schedule. These tours last about an hour and a half and are quite informative.

Save time to enjoy the Hassayampa Bookstore. It's located in a lovely adobe structure and has books and guides on plants and animals of the Southwest including history, travel guides, and gift items. There's also a reference library the public can use.

There's no picnicking and pets must be left at home. However, this peaceful, serene setting is comfortable even on a warm spring day. Free. But a donation is appreciated. Call for hours. (520) 684-2772.

WHERE TO EAT AND STAY

The Wickenburg Inn Tennis & Guest Ranch. Prescott Highway, 7 miles northwest of Wickenburg on US-89. Not gourmet, but reasonable and pleasant. Come for good American fare—chicken, fish, and steaks. Reservations suggested. $$; (CC). (520) 684-7811.

    Kay El Bar Ranch. Box 2480, Wickenburg 85358. This is a charming historic guest ranch owned and managed by two sisters and their husbands. Listed on the National Register of Historic Places, this small, intimate guest ranch is beautifully maintained and offers visitors an authentic western experience from trail riding to family-style dining. The setting is uniquely territorial-style Arizona. A two-night minimum stay is required, but to get the full flavor of this special get-away guest ranch, visitors will want to spend a week. The Kay El Bar is open from October through April. $$$; (CC). (520) 684-7593.

    Rancho de los Caballeros. Five miles west of Wickenburg and 2 miles south of US-60 on Vulture Mine Road. Located in an especially scenic high desert setting, this "Ranch of the Gentlemen on Horseback" combines a luxurious resort setting with the relaxing ambience that is the hallmark of Southwestern hospitality. A unique combination of golf and riding allows guests to ride through miles of magnificent desert trails and tee off on rolling, challenging fairways in the same day without leaving the grounds. An elegant resort, Rancho de los Cabelleros boasts a superb golf shop on its premises. Fine dining is available along with hearty western favorites. Open late fall to early spring. Reservations suggested. $$$. (520) 684-5484.

    Chaparral Ice Cream & Bakery. 45 North Tegner. This ice cream parlor features homemade ice cream. The best flavor is Hassayampa Mud. You can have breakfast, lunch, or an early dinner here of pastries, soup, and sandwiches. The atmosphere is authentic 1950s with red-and-white-checked tablecloths, roomy wooden booths, and a friendly staff. $-$$. (520) 684-3252.

JOSHUA FOREST PARKWAY

Northwest on US-93, 20 miles beyond Wickenburg, you'll be greeted by one of nature's more unusual welcoming committees: a strange, dense forest of Joshua trees. Located on both sides of the highway, hordes of thick-trunked cacti crowd the landscape and mesmerize passing tourists.

Joshua trees, which are actually tall, bristly yucca plants, were named by Mormon pioneers who thought the upright branches pointed toward the Promised Land. These slow-growing trees provide homes for twenty-five species of birds. In addition, pack rats gnaw off spiny leaf blades, and night lizards find that the rotted-out bark of wind-toppled Joshua trees provides their entire world. Usually found in the Mohave Desert, Joshua trees rarely are found in the Sonoran Desert, which makes this dense stand all the more exciting.

GHOST TOWNS OF CONGRESS, STANTON, AND OCTAVE

You may return to Phoenix from Wickenburg by heading southeast on US-89/A-93. Or, if you are up for adventure and have adequate gas in the tank, follow US-89 north 16 miles on a paved road to Congress for a leisurely journey through some authentic ghost towns. In Arizona, "authentic" means that you won't find snack bars, concession stands, or gift shops. What you *will* find are the ghosts of buildings from Arizona's past—crumbling structures slowly dying in the desert. Consequently, before you turn off onto the back road leading to Congress, Stanton, and Octave, if you see facilities and need to stop, do so.

You may prefer to combine this excursion with your return trip on US-89 south from Yarnell and Peeples Valley (see Day Trip 2, North from Phoenix).

Started as a mining camp, Congress was established in 1887. By 1891, it was estimated that $600,000 in ore was shipped from that mine, although it's possible that more than $1 million actually was taken out. After 1919, mining activity slowed to a trickle and the town faded away. As you drive on this paved road, known only as "the road to Congress," look around at the crumbling foundations and faded memories of a once-glorious past. Only the dump of the mine stands within sight of the present town of Congress Junction.

Continue through Congress Junction about 4 miles and then turn right onto a gravel road. Watch for the sign that says that this is the road to Stanton and follow it. It looks rough, but it is graded and passable for passenger cars. Stanton is about 7 miles from Congress. As you bump along the road to this ghost town, note that it was built by pioneer C. C. Genung in 1871 at a cost of $7,650. Genung paid white men $75 a month, Mexicans received $65 a month, and Indians got 50 cents a day plus beans, flour, sugar, coffee, and venison to build that road. Today Stanton is privately owned.

When you reach Stanton, you'll want to investigate what's left of this mining camp. Originally called Antelope Station, the town was located on an old stage route and renamed for Charles P. Stanton, who was deputy county recorder. Legend has it that Stanton was a defrocked priest. For sure, he was a man of doubtful character as he ran the town, and he and the "Stanton Gang" raked in gold at the expense of the community. It's rumored that his gang cost Arizona settlers "more than all the Apaches put together." Ultimately Charles Stanton met his demise when he was shot by a man who believed that Stanton had insulted his sister.

Travel a few more miles on this same road to reach Octave, which is located 13 miles from Wickenburg. Now a maze of stone foundations, cellar pits, and ruins, it was once a bustling town of 3,000 hardy souls who came here for gold in 1863. Eventually $8 million was taken out of the quartz veins of Octave Mine. The mine continued in operation until World War II. Today it belongs to the wind, sun, and sand and to those adventurous types who love the silent, brooding allure of ghost towns.

As is true of any of Arizona's back roads, don't attempt to navigate the road to Stanton during rainy weather. The slick mountains and the barren desert make flash floods a real hazard. (See the section on Flash Floods at the end of this book.)

LAKE PLEASANT

To complete your day, what better excursion than to get out of the dusty ghost towns and head for Lake Pleasant? To reach this recreation site, go southeast on US–89 and backtrack for about 11 miles. At the junction of US–89 and A–74, follow A–74 east to Lake Pleasant, one of the many man-made lakes dotting the Arizona desert. Arizonans take water seriously—damming rivers for flood control, surface water, and recreation. You may be surprised to know that Arizona has one of the highest boats-per-capita ratios in the country.

Lake Pleasant was formed when the Waddell Dam was constructed on the Agua Fria River. Picnic, rent jet skis, or just enjoy the rocky landscape and cool views before returning to Phoenix. When you're ready to end your day, travel east on A–74 to I–17. Follow I–17 south to Phoenix. Or backtrack west on A–74 and pick up A–93 southeast to Phoenix.

WHERE TO GO

Lake Pleasant Dinner Cruise. Mail Address: 3828 North 28th Avenue, Phoenix, 85017. The newest way to see the lake is to cruise the Lake Pleasant *Desert Princess*. Cruises run year-round with dinner, dancing, and live entertainment nightly and a champagne brunch on Sunday. Unfortunately, the trip is expensive and the food is overpriced and unexciting. The trip takes $2^1/_2$ hours and a paid reservation is required 48 hours in advance. Fee. (602) 230-7600.

Tucson

Welcome to southern Arizona. With Tucson as your base, you can roam back roads, poke around ghost towns, or ascend Kitt Peak to view some of the world's most sophisticated optical instruments. You'll find everything here, from quaint historical settings to a gleaming, growing city. Because southern Arizona encompasses such a vast area, you may wonder how you're going to see it all if you're not familiar with the territory. Relax. As you read through the suggested trips, you'll quickly understand the logical progression described. Several of the day excursions link up easily with each other, creating pleasant opportunities for overnight vacations.

Because of the way this book is organized, some of the best Tucson attractions are listed in the section, Day Trip 3 Southeast from Phoenix. You'll want to check out this Day Trip if you are planning on staying in Tucson!

Historically, agriculture and copper mining served as the basis for the economy in this part of the state. However, tourism quickly is becoming the most important industry. You'll discover, as you travel through this region, that even the smallest towns offer clean, comfortable facilities for visitors.

Before you set off, examine your road map. The land in southern Arizona is owned by a number of different entities. Most of the countryside belongs to Yuma, Pima, Cochise, Pinal, and Graham counties, but the area also includes several national monuments, wildlife preserves, national forests, and Indian reservations, the largest of which is the Tohono O'odham west of Tucson. In Arizona, driving in and out of reservations is like crossing different countries. You won't notice much difference except, possibly, a change in the surface of the road.

You'll also see, if you look closely, that two areas are labeled "Saguaro National Monument." This isn't a mistake. The larger one lies due east of Tucson; the smaller portion of the park is located

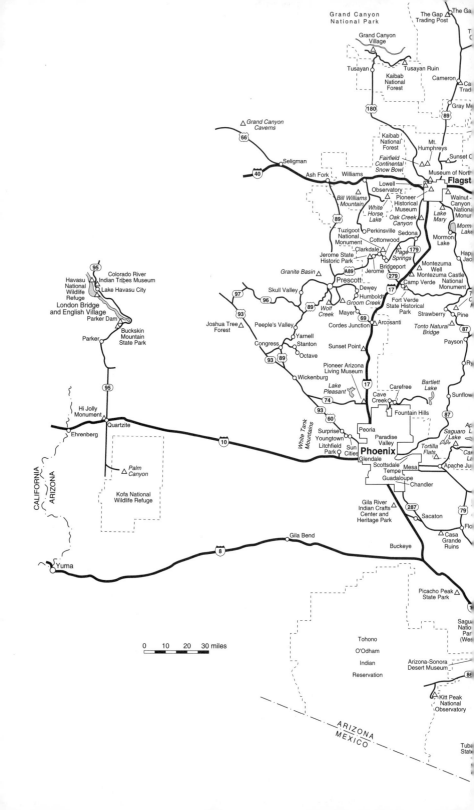

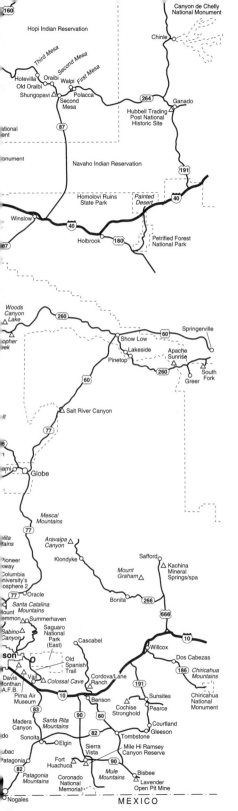

west of the city, and both are referred to as "Saguaro National Monument."

Although southern Arizona is located south of Phoenix, the elevation around Tucson is higher than that of the capital city. You drive "down" to Tucson, but you are actually driving "up." Be prepared for slightly cooler and drier temperatures in the immediate vicinity of the Old Pueblo.

You may want to refer to Day Trip 2, Southeast from Phoenix to brush up on what's available in Tucson before reading this portion of the book.

Sabino Canyon
Mount Lemmon

SABINO CANYON

Prepare for a day in the great outdoors. You'll begin your drive in Tucson, surrounded by the urban scene. But as you head out toward the Santa Catalina Mountains, you'll quickly leave the city behind. One of the beauties of this day trip is that you can enjoy some of the area's most magnificent wilderness so close to a city. To do both areas justice in one day, you'll need to leave early and not linger too long at either. This could be a problem because both Sabino Canyon and Mount Lemmon have endless trails to hike on and acres of serenity to enjoy.

Although this day trip stars Mother Nature at her finest, she is fickle. Take an extra wrap along. Depending upon the season, carry a windbreaker, heavy sweater, or even a ski jacket in the car. As you climb to the summit of Mount Lemmon, you'll experience a major change in climate. You also need comfortable walking shoes. Although primarily an unspoiled area, there are easy trails and nearby amenities.

If you plan to drive to the top of Mount Lemmon during the winter months, it's wise to call ahead to check on the weather. If it's cloudy or rainy in Tucson, it could be snowing at the summit. Although the road to Mount Lemmon is paved, snow can make it impassable. Even the most adventurous types wouldn't get caught without chains or a four-wheel-drive vehicle.

New York City has Central Park, but Tucson has Sabino Canyon, a woodsy respite close to town. Nestled in the foothills of the Santa

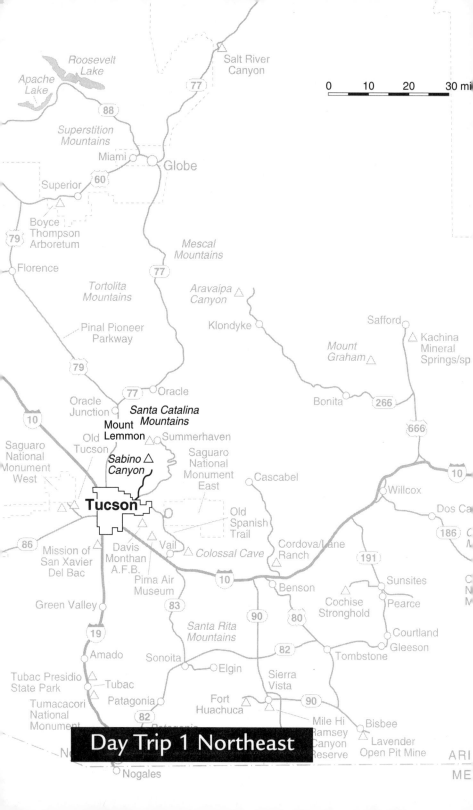

Roosevelt
Lake

Apache
Lake

Superstition
Mountains

Salt River
Canyon

77

88

0   10   20   30 mi

Miami

Globe

Superior

60

Boyce
Thompson
Arboretum

79

Florence

Mescal
Mountains

77

Tortolita
Mountains

Aravaipa
Canyon

Safford

Kachina
Mineral
Springs/sp

Pinal Pioneer
Parkway

Klondyke

Mount
Graham

79

77

Oracle

Oracle
Junction

Santa Catalina
Mountains

Bonita

266

666

10

Saguaro
National
Monument
West

Mount
Lemmon

Old
Tucson

Summerhaven

Sabino
Canyon

Saguaro
National
Monument
East

Cascabel

Willcox

10

Dos Ca

Tucson

Old
Spanish
Trail

Cordova/Lane
Ranch

186

C
M

86

Mission of
San Xavier
Del Bac

Davis
Monthan
A.F.B.

Vail

Colossal Cave

191

Sunsites

C
N
M

Pima Air
Museum

10

Benson

80

Cochise
Stronghold

Pearce

Green Valley

83

90

Courtland

Gleeson

19

Santa Rita
Mountains

82

Tombstone

Amado

Sonoita

Elgin

Sierra
Vista

90

Courtland

Tubac Presidio
State Park

Tubac

Patagonia

Fort
Huachuca

Mile Hi
Ramsey
Canyon
Reserve

Bisbee

Lavender
Open Pit Mine

Tumacacori
National
Monument

82

ARI

ME

Nogales

Day Trip 1 Northeast

Catalina Mountains, Sabino Canyon is a hiker's, picnicker's, and lovers' dream. With its streams and waterfalls, hiking and biking trails, this natural area manages to absorb the hordes of visitors who turn to it every day for a needed dose of calm and quiet.

To get there, follow Wilmot Road north to where it joins with Tanque Verde Road. Head northeast on Tanque Verde and across the Pantano Wash to its intersection with Sabino Canyon Road, which takes you to the visitors center. You must park your car here and proceed either on foot or by tram for the 4-mile trip to the first of several recreation areas. The tram runs frequently and there are regular moonlight rides offered from March through December. Fee. (520) 749-2861.

WHERE TO GO

Pick up a trail map at the visitors center. Then as you walk along, you may observe the different kinds of trees growing here. Pine and fir forest the slopes above the streambed. Deep within the canyon, you'll find other trees, including willow, box elder, and alder. In the lower elevations, Sabino Canyon is host to cactus, paloverde, and even saguaros, while along the streambed, you'll find shady sycamore, cottonwood, ash, and walnut trees.

Why the name Sabino? No one is exactly sure. One school of thought insists that the name comes from a plant called sabino or savino. The more accepted story is that it was named for a Mexican rancher who lived in the area in the 1870s.

Formed about 200 million years ago, the canyon has established itself as an ideal getaway no matter what the season. The tram was installed to help preserve the air quality and environment. Along the way it stops at designated observation sites, and during the summer months, moonlight excursions offer a totally different experience. If you've never taken a guided tour in a national park at night or seen a wild area after sunset, you should do this. Tickets are available next to the visitors center parking area. For more information contact Sabino Canyon Shuttle, Route 15, Box 280, Tucson, 85750, or call (520) 749-2327.

MOUNT LEMMON

To get to Mount Lemmon from Sabino Canyon, follow Sabino Canyon Road south to Tanque Verde Road. Turn east on Tanque Verde to Catalina Highway. Follow Catalina Highway northeast to Mount Lemmon. This is an extremely popular area and is well marked. Watch for signs to Mount Lemmon.

As you drive along Tanque Verde toward Catalina Highway, you will see some elegant residential areas. Tucson is famous for its low-slung, hacienda-style homes and bright blue pools hidden among the saguaros and ocotillos.

Catalina Highway, also called the road to Mount Lemmon, climbs the mountain's southern slope. From this point, the 30-mile drive will take about an hour up the 9,157-foot mountain. Although the road is perfectly safe for automobile traffic, those who can't look down from a tall building may not enjoy this experience. Queasy passengers who still want a view should just look up.

As you head up this queen peak of the Santa Catalinas, you'll pass scenic viewpoints and see areas marked for camping and picnicking. You can even stop and fish; signs will lead you to a lake stocked with trout. Along the way you'll get a graphic lesson in physical geography. Even if you've never taken a course in this subject and know nothing about it, you cannot help but learn something on this trip. Your drive will take you through five distinct life zones — areas that support specific types of vegetation. You'll begin with the Sonoran desert and climb through piñon and juniper. Soon you'll be into elevations supporting fir trees and, eventually, aspen trees. This is the same vegetation change you would observe were you to drive from Arizona to the Canadian border. Not surprisingly, the drive is especially gorgeous in autumn and spring.

Once at the top, hike around. If you've packed a picnic lunch, spread it out and relax. Enjoy the crisp cool air and the views that stretch forever. Remember, while perched in this northern clime, that you are just one hour— and some 7,000 feet — away from the desert floor.

To return to Tucson, retrace your steps down the mountain and follow Tanque Verde Road back into town.

WHERE TO GO

Summerhaven. At the summit of Mount Lemmon. Spend time walking around this friendly mountaintop hamlet. There's an entire community up here, including a lodge offering rustic accommodations, small cabins, campgrounds, and other amenities. You can eat, use the restrooms, and fill the car with gas. Because you're at the top of a 9,100-plus-foot mountain, don't expect too much luxury and you'll be pleasantly surprised by the charm. (520) 576–1400.

Mount Lemmon Ski Lift. In the winter, if the snow is right, Mount Lemmon becomes the southernmost ski area in the United States. In the summer, ride the lift for the breathtaking view. The twenty-five-minute round-trip covers approximately 1 mile. You'll depart near the base area and look over the San Pedro Valley, the Reef of Rocks, and the towns of Oracle and Mammoth. Fee. (520) 576–1400.

WHERE TO EAT

Iron Door Restaurant. In Ski Valley, at the base of the Mount Lemmon ski area. Come for salads, sandwiches, homemade soups, skiers chili, and cornbread. The restaurant is named for a lost mine with an iron door that, legend has it, was operated by Jesuit padres in the Catalinas during the 1700s. According to the story, Apache raiders killed the Indian mine workers and the Jesuits. Lunch only. $$. (520) 576–1321.

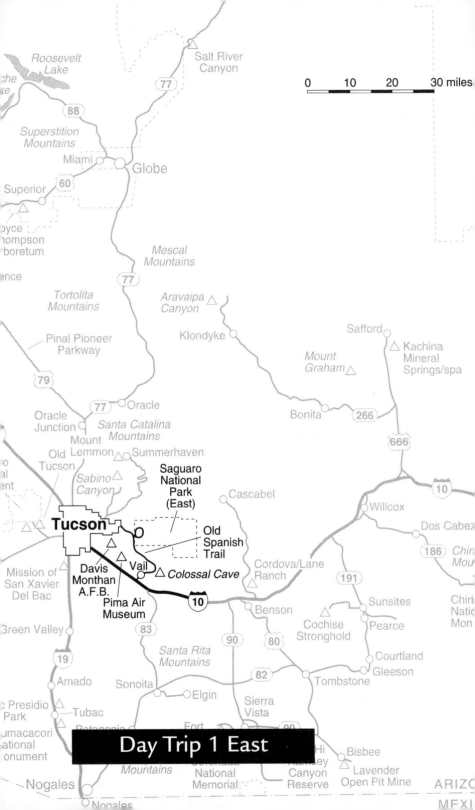

Day Trip 1 East

EAST

DAY TRIP 1

Davis-Monthan Air Force Base
Saguaro National Park (East)
Colossal Cave

DAVIS-MONTHAN AIR FORCE BASE

It's difficult to imagine that this immense base started as a municipal airport established by civic-minded citizens in 1919. Located on Craycroft Road at Golf Links Road in Tucson, Davis-Monthan is named for Lts. Samuel H. Davis and Oscar Monthan, two early Air Corps officers from Tucson.

The Army Air Corps made its first investment in D-M in 1931, and modern paved roads and runways followed in the mid-1930s. Shortly before Pearl Harbor, $3 million was earmarked for expansion, and D-M soon became one of the best heavy bombardment training stations in the nation.

After World War II, the base was nearly deserted until it was designated an Air Technical Service Command storage area. Because of the arid climate, hundreds of aircraft are stored here now.

Currently D-M is a diversified military installation. It is home to the largest outdoor aircraft storage facility in the world, and A-10 combat crew training and OA-37 Forward Air Control operations also are conducted. With all the fighter planes and helicopters constantly in the air, the skies over D-M are rarely quiet.

WHERE TO GO

Base Tours. Craycroft and Golf Links roads. Tours are available every Monday and Wednesday morning. Longer photographic tours are offered the second Saturday of each month. A base bus picks up visitors at the front gate of the base on South Craycroft Road near

145

the intersection of Golf Links. Free. For additional information, write to Headquarters, 836th Air Division, Public Affairs, Attn: Community Relations, Davis-Monthan AFB, AZ 85707, or call (520) 228–4717.

Pima Air Museum. 6000 East Valencia Road, just east of I–10, 4½ miles from the interstate. It houses more than 200 military planes ranging from bombers to drone fighters.

Although not technically part of Davis-Monthan, the facility works closely with the base. The third-largest air museum in the country, it is exceeded in size only by the Smithsonian Institution's National Air and Space Museum in Washington, D.C., and the Wright-Patterson Air Museum in Dayton, Ohio. Ask if a special volunteer is available to take you through the presidential aircraft located on the grounds.

Snacks and soft drinks may be purchased at the museum, which is open every day except Christmas. Fee. (520) 574–0462.

SAGUARO NATIONAL PARK (EAST)

As you look at your map of this area, note that the Saguaro National Park is actually two parks. The larger one, the Rincon Mountain Section unit, is located due east of Tucson, while the smaller park, the Tucson Mountain District unit, lies to the west. Both parks were established March 1, 1933, for the protection of a remarkable stand of saguaro (pronounced sa-wa-ro) cactus found here. Thanks to excellent management, they offer desert travelers a treat for the eyes. Be apprised that there are no accommodations available other than picnic tables at either of these facilities.

Return to I–10 when you leave the Pima Air Museum. Go east on I–10 to exit 275 and continue north on this road to Old Spanish Trail. Turn east on Old Spanish Trail for 2 miles to the entrance of **Saguaro National Park East** or Rincon Mountain Section unit. Take the 9-mile Cactus Forest Drive loop to visitors center. It's open from 7:00 A.M. to sunset.

Driving through a stand of saguaros is unlike driving through any other kind of forest. The profusion of angles will constantly delight you. Some saguaros signal with their arms in crazy directions; others stand almost perfectly symmetrical with arms reaching up in supplication. Although a stately plant, saguaros nevertheless strike some humorous poses.

As you walk or drive through the 62,499 acres of this section of Saguaro National Park, you'll be amazed at the endless variety and sheer numbers of the plants. The visitors center has information on the native vegetation, and you'll get an overview of the biology and geology found in this area of the state. Hopefully you'll come away with a better understanding of how plants and animals adapt to an arid existence. Above all, you'll gain a new appreciation for a wondrous plant, the saguaro.

The saguaro cactus is remarkable. A natural desert condominium, it provides homes for a variety of creatures. Several species of birds eat its seeds, live in its walls, and build nests in its arms. By the time a saguaro grows to 20 feet and has its first branch, the plant has lived through seventy-five years of strenuous desert sun, wind, and rain. With a root structure stretching for miles just barely beneath the surface, the plant is an unparalleled natural balancing act. Superbly adapted to make the most of an unpredictable desert water supply, the plant's accordion-style pleats allow it to shrink during droughts and plump up after rains. Given optimum conditions, secure from bulldozers and development, this queen of the desert can grow to 50 feet and survive to age 200.

Birdwatchers will have a field day at Saguaro National Park. More than fifty species of reptiles also roam around the park. If you've thought of the desert as an empty place, think again. As you wander through this rolling saguaro-studded landscape with its endless shades of sun-bleached green, look for desert tortoises, gophers, coach-whip snakes, ground squirrels, peccaries, coyotes, and mule deer. Listen, too, for the whistle of the curve-bill thrasher, the churring of the cactus wren, and a yipping coyote chorus.

Take a self-guided stroll down one of the more gentle nature trails mentioned in a free pamphlet you can pick up at the visitors center. If you visit between February and May, you may be fortunate enough to witness an outstanding wildflower display. These fragile blooms are dependent upon winter rain, so a superb show is not guaranteed each year. If you're there when these blossoms peak, you're in for a special desert experience.

Outdoor types may prefer hiking in the forest of the Rincon Mountains. A backpacking permit is required in the backcountry. Contact the National Park Service, Saguaro National Park, 3693 South Old Spanish Trail, Tucson, 85730 for more details. Fee. (520) 733–5100.

COLOSSAL CAVE

As you leave Saguaro National Park, continue south on Old Spanish Trail for 10 more miles. You'll see the signs for Colossal Cave, an underground wilderness experience.

Thanks to the work of the Civilian Conservation Corps, touring this cave is easy. Navigable pathways lead through the entire cave. Stairways are lighted. There are no difficult areas to traverse; no narrow spaces to squeeze through. Even the temperature is comfortable. It remains at seventy-two degrees Fahrenheit year round.

Cave buffs who are used to wet caves may be disappointed by the interior. A dry cave means just that. There are no glistening, colorful stalactites and stalagmites to capture your imagination. The formations have dried to a sandy, dusty surface.

The story of the cave, however, is very colorful as it is pure western lore. It seems that three bandits robbed a train in 1887 and made off with $70,000 to $90,000 worth of gold and paper money.

A posse from Tucson hit their trail the next day and went after them. The sheriff was Virgil Earp. Searchers discovered the entrance to the cave and evidence that the robbers were hiding there. The bandits were eventually caught in El Paso without their booty. So, the legend lives on that the gold and money may still be in the cave.

Frequent guided tours ferry visitors through the cavern. (520) 647-7275.

To return to Tucson, continue on Old Spanish Trail from Colossal Cave to Vail. At Vail, pick up I-10 (A-86) northwest and continue into Tucson. Or you can head east on I-10 to Day Trip 2 of this sector.

Benson · Willcox
Ghost Towns of Cochise County

BENSON

Follow I–10 east to Benson about 45 miles from Tucson. This small community, like its neighbor Willcox, was founded along the main line of the Southern Pacific Railroad. During the late 1800s it served as a shipping point for the livestock- and mineral-producing areas to the south. It nestles in an intermountain valley created by the San Pedro River. Although the original streets were designed in a grid on a 160-acre plat, the town grew haphazardly.

Today Benson is emerging as a suburb of Tucson. Surrounded by natural beauty, the immediate area offers a wealth of things to see and do.

WHERE TO GO

Amerind Foundation. Exit 318, south of I–10 in Texas Canyon between Benson and Willcox. Take the Triangle-T-Dragoon exit (318) on I–10 and continue east 1 mile to the Amerind Foundation turnoff. Turn left at the sign FFRANCH-AMERIND.

This museum is a jewel. A privately funded center for archaeological field research, the center also houses a museum and art gallery dedicated to archaeological and ethnographical material on Indians from all the Americas. The gallery contains a superb collection of western, Indian, and American art.

Why a fine museum in the middle of the desert? The answer lies in the passions of one man, William Shirley Fulton, a Connecticut

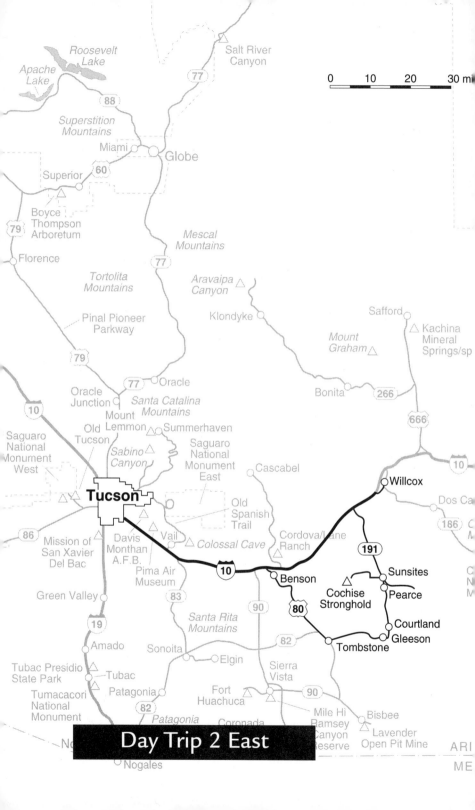

Roosevelt Lake

Apache Lake

Salt River Canyon

(77)

(88)

Superstition Mountains

Miami Globe

(60)

Superior

(79)

Boyce Thompson Arboretum

Mescal Mountains

(77)

Florence

Tortolita Mountains

Aravaipa Canyon

Klondyke

Safford

Kachina Mineral Springs/sp

Pinal Pioneer Parkway

Mount Graham

(79)

(77) Oracle

Bonita (266)

Oracle Junction

Santa Catalina Mountains

(666)

Mount Lemmon Summerhaven

(10)

Old Tucson

Saguaro National Monument West

Sabino Canyon

Saguaro National Monument East

Cascabel

Willcox

(10)

Dos Ca

Tucson

Old Spanish Trail

(186)

(86)

Mission of San Xavier Del Bac

Davis Monthan A.F.B.

Vail Colossal Cave

Cordova/Lane Ranch

(191)

Sunsites

Pima Air Museum

Benson

Cochise Stronghold

Pearce

Green Valley

(83)

(90)

(80)

Courtland

Gleeson

(19)

Santa Rita Mountains

(82)

Tombstone

Amado

Sonoita Elgin

Tubac Presidio State Park

Tubac

Patagonia

Fort Huachuca

Sierra Vista

(90)

Tumacacori National Monument

(82) Patagonia

Coronada

Mile Hi Ramsey Canyon Reserve

Bisbee

Lavender Open Pit Mine

ARI

Nogales

ME

Day Trip 2 East

industrialist. Fulton purchased this property, 65 miles east of Tucson, in the early 1930s and became intensely involved in Native American cultures. As he began to acquire a sizable collection of diverse artifacts, Fulton hired noted architect H. M. Starkweather to design and build a permanent home for his important collection. Starkweather visualized the Spanish Colonial Revival-style structure as an eloquent contrast to the massive natural boulders of this part of Arizona.

Until recently the Amerind Foundation (the name refers to the prehistoric Indians who lived in the Americas) concentrated more on research than outreach. However, the Amerind has redirected its focus to make its impressive collection of artifacts, arts, and crafts more accessible to visitors. Fee. Call for hours of operation. (520) 586-3666.

Cascabel Clayworks. Twenty-four miles north of Benson on Pomerene Road. Expect to travel on a dirt road for many miles to reach this community of artists. Handmade clay works are fashioned in a unique setting with shade trees, the San Pedro River, and a backdrop of gold cliffs. No phone.

Singing Wind Book Shop. Two and one quarter miles north of Benson on Ocotillo Road. Don't be put off by the closed ranch gate. Stop your car, get out, open the gate, and continue driving down the road. (Close the gate behind you!) You'll find a small white ranch house nestled in a scene straight out of a western film. This renowned bookshop contains a complete collection of books about the Southwest and western Americana as well as an amazing assortment of books on nearly any subject. Plan to spend quality time browsing through the many rooms. (520) 586-2425.

San Pedro Valley Arts and Historical Society. 180 South San Pedro. In 1983, the San Pedro Valley Arts and Historical Society purchased a building that had been boarded up for nearly fifty years. After renovating it, the society opened a museum/gallery that features changing exhibits and a permanent display. There's also a gift shop featuring handcrafted items, ceramics, and paintings by local artisans. Free, but donations are appreciated. (520) 586-3070.

San Pedro Southwestern Railroad. 796 East Country Club Drive, Benson. From Benson, take SR-80 one mile south to Country Club Drive. Train afficionados in Arizona rejoiced when the San Pedro & Southwestern RR hit the rails. Passengers can choose from an open air car or climate controlled coaches. The four hour trip departs from Benson and travels south into the pristine San Pedro Riparian National Conservation Area. The scenery is thick with cottonwood and mesquite which are home to an astonishing array of desert wildlife. The route continues past an area that was once busy with silver mills and then passes the ruins of Contention and the historic town of Fairbank. Guests are served a folksy, western BBQ by Ironhorse Ranch. Expect simple fare and fun (but not professional) western entertainment. The journey is narrated and points of interest are well described. In addition to the regular schedule, which runs Thursday through Sunday throughout the year, theme trains are also available. *A word of warning:* If you choose to take an evening summer sunset ride, while it sounds romantic, once the sun goes down it is impossible to see the scenery! Fee. (520) 586-2266.

Texas Canyon. Located 14 miles east of Benson on I-10. This is a lovely natural area with spectacular rock formations. You can picnic here, hike, or simply enjoy the views of nature as the master sculptor.

Zearings Mercantile Store. 305 East Fourth Street. This old-fashioned general store is filled with antiques, guns, and candy from around the world. There's even a mini-museum inside that depicts a general store in the 1800s. The owners are from California and are very knowledgeable about the collection. (520) 586-3196.

WILLCOX

From Benson, follow I-10 east 36 miles to Willcox. This small Arizona community was settled in 1880 as a construction camp for the Southern Pacific Railroad. When the track went down, Willcox sprang to life. It quickly became a focal point in Cochise County for cattle shipping and still holds that position. Some of the largest cattle ranches in the state are located in the broad, grassy valleys in this area.

Often called the "Gateway to the Chiricahua Wonderland," Willcox is rich with Indian lore. Here the United States Cavalry battled the Chiricahua Apaches. Many sites commemorate various skirmishes. This is the country of Cochise, the legendary Apache chief who stalked and struck deep in the valleys and then faded back into the shadowy mountains. This land was holy to all Apaches. The Apache chief Geronimo wrote: "There is no place equal to that of Arizona. I want to spend my last days there and be buried among those mountains."

Today Willcox is known as the home of television, movie, and radio personality Rex Allen. But if ghosts intrigue you more than cowboys, you'll want to see the wonderful old ghost towns and graveyards in this vicinity that lie silently under the Arizona sun. If you pay a visit to the Old Willcox Cemetery, southeast of town, you'll see where Warren Earp, brother of the famous frontier Marshall Wyatt Earp, is buried. For more information about the ghost towns in the area and other points of interest, drop by the Willcox Chamber of Commerce, 1500 North Circle I Road. (520) 384–2272.

WHERE TO GO

Apple Orchards and Pistachio Groves. Follow Fort Grant Road northwest 20 miles from town to arrive at these private orchards and nut groves. Willcox is a major apple-producing area and, in season, hosts popular U-Pick-Em days. Call the Chamber of Commerce at (520) 384–2272 to find out when these days are scheduled.

The Cochise Information Center and Museum of the Southwest. 1500 North Circle I Road, Willcox. Stop for information about this area and tour the museum. When you enter, you'll be greeted with an impressive bust of Cochise. Take the time to read some of his sayings and you'll get an insight into the mind of this unusual man. You may also want to stroll around Heritage Park on the grounds of the center where you'll see a replica of an Indian village, a nature trail, and a mining display. (520) 384–2272.

Cochise Stronghold. Follow I-10 west about 8 miles from Willcox. Take US–666 south about 17 miles. About a mile before you get to the community of Sunsites, there is an unnamed graded road heading west. Look for the sign indicating that this is the road to Cochise Stronghold. Take this road west for 10 miles until it ends at the parking lot and campgrounds.

Cochise Stronghold is the area of the Dragoon Mountains that served as home, headquarters, and safe haven for Apache Chief Cochise. Cochise was a fierce leader, on a par with Geronimo and Mangas Coloradas. As you drive into the mountains, more than one writer has noted a "presence" that seems to linger over the landscape. Somewhere in this tangle of rocks and canyons, towers and domes, and manzanita shrubs lie the bones of Cochise. Even in death, he remains a controversial character.

One legend says that when Cochise died in 1874, his braves buried him in full regalia. They lowered his body into a deep crevice along with his horse, dog, and rifle. According to another story, his men, fearing vandalism by white men, buried their chief on a grassy mesa and then ran their horses back and forth to mask the grave site. In any event, although the exact location of Cochise's body is unknown, his spirit is everywhere.

As you enter the area of the Stronghold, you'll see a Forest Service campground. A good hiking trail into the Dragoon Mountains begins here. If you decide to explore this region, remember that the area is not commercially developed. You won't find any souvenir shops or cafes at the end of your journey, which takes about four hours. If you're prepared for a rugged walk, park at the campground and follow the well-marked 3-mile trail. Some of the climb is steep, but eventually you'll arrive at an open area where you can gaze over a 40-mile vista. This point on the trail is designated as the heart of the Stronghold. As you stand there, surrounded by the cliffs and sculpted spires, it's easy to imagine Apache bands moving in and out of the shadows.

When you start down, you'll need to watch your footing because the path is steep. Around the 2-mile mark, turn to see towering above the walnut and sycamore trees an almost overpowering view of Cochise Stronghold. It's the same scene that greeted General O. O. Howard as he marched into the Stronghold in 1872 carrying a flag of truce. As a result of Howard's trek, Cochise agreed to end the hostilities at last.

No doubt General Howard had other things on his mind than the scenery, but, as you leave the Stronghold, take one last, lingering look at this Apache sanctum. Don't be surprised if you have the distinct feeling that the great Chief Cochise is looking back at you.

A word of caution: This area has no amenities other than picnic tables—not even a telephone.

Stout Cider Mill. Located at I-10, exit 340. This is the only cider mill on Interstate 10 from the East Coast to the West. The apple pies are stuffed to overflowing and are superb. The cider is delicious. Even if you're not hungry, the place is fun for browsing. (520) 384-3696.

Walking Tour. The Willcox Chamber of Commerce has published a historical walking tour of the area that gives you insight into this old western town. If you take the tour, be sure and stop in at the **Commercial Hotel/Brown's Ice Cream Parlor.** The hotel was built in the 1800s and has been restored. It's now operated as an old-fashioned ice cream parlor.

WHERE TO STAY

Mule Shoe Ranch. From Bisbee Avenue (next to the shopping center) go to Airport Road. Turn right and continue for 30 miles on a washboard road. This ranch is owned and operated by the Nature Conservancy and sprawls over 55,000 acres of Sonoran and Chihuahuan deserts. There are seven permanently flowing streams that make this a wonderful riparian habitat. The cabins are comfortable and newly rebuilt. Most have kitchenettes; some have clawfoot tubs, woodstoves, and even corrals. $$. (520) 586-7072.

GHOST TOWNS OF COCHISE COUNTY

To do the ghost towns justice, plan a full day of touring. It's tough to rush ghosts. The entire area—bounded by Sierra Vista, Benson, and Willcox to the north and the Mexican border to the south—is a ghost-town hunter's dream. During the mining boom, this countryside was thick with camps and communities that sprang up with a shout and died out with a whimper when the ore disappeared.

Visitors may stand among the crumbling rubble and easily imagine wild-eyed young men and sassy women who lived here, drunk on the easy money. Even if you don't believe in spirits, ghost towns have a calming effect that infects the most skeptical tourist. As you stand looking at the wisps of streets, pieces of foundation, and crooked walls that defy gravity, you cannot help but hear the whispers of past action.

Each of these communities once burst with activity. They were crowded with saloons and stores and homes, and as long as the gold, silver, and copper came in, so did the men hunting quick fortunes and fast women. Now, although the music has stopped, the energy lingers.

If you visit during the summer months, bring a jug of water and wear a hat so that you don't fade too fast. As you visit the ghost towns, you'll find that at least two communities, Dos Cabezas (Day Trip 3, East of Tuscon) and Pearce, have refused to give up the ghost completely. Real-live people reside in these communities, and you'll even find food and drink at Pearce.

WHERE TO GO

Pearce. From Cochise Stronghold, retrace your route and head east on the graded road to Arizona Sunsites, a new community catering to the family and retirement crowd. One and a half miles south of Sunsites, on your right, is the road to Old Pearce. This is where Ghost Town Trail begins. Follow the signs directing you to the Old General Store.

The Commonwealth Mine put Pearce on the map around 1890 when Johnny Pearce struck gold. More gold came from this mine than from any other mine in the territory. At Pearce you can visit the old cemetery, which is still used today. Abraham Lincoln's bodyguard is buried here as are some Union and Confederate soldiers and a few of Pearce's "tarnished belles" from its more lively era. The Old General Store and museum are full of Old West items that visitors enjoy poking through.

WHERE TO STAY

Grapevine Canyon Ranch, Inc. Call for directions, or write to P.O. Box 302, Pearce, 85625. This is an authentic working guest ranch that backs up to a western view straight out of a John Wayne movie, secluded in the Dragoon Mountains 85 miles southeast of Tucson. This ranch offers guests the opportunity to work on Spring roundups and all aspects of daily life. Horseback instruction is available; food is served family style. And all "hands" are friendly and ready to help "dudes" learn how to cowboy. There are eight casitas and three cabins for thirty-four guests. This working ranch is open year-round. No children under twelve are allowed. The Grapevine is a favorite with international guests because of its remotely splendid setting and real West ambience. There is a two-night minimum. In high seasons, spring and fall, the ranch asks for a four-night minimum stay. $$$ (includes meals); (CC). (520) 826–3185.

WANDERING THE BACKROADS

To visit more ghost towns, continue south on the road past Pearce. It winds through the old mining towns of Courtland and Gleeson, ending up at Tombstone, where you can connect to Day Trip 1, Southeast of Tucson.

Courtland. On Ghost Town Trail to Tombstone. There's one resident in Courtland, and he does not encourage visitors. As you drive by, you may want to take a passing glance at this once-thriving mining camp. If you decide to explore on foot, don't expect to be greeted by any famous Southwestern hospitality.

Gleeson. On Ghost Town Trail 16 miles east of Tombstone. Turquoise put Gleeson on the map. Even before the Spaniards arrived, the Indians in the area mined this stone. Later residents found zinc, copper, and lead. Modern visitors will find picturesque ruins to wander through and a cemetery to explore.

To get a complete listing of Arizona ghost towns, write to the Arizona Office of Tourism, 1100 West Washington, Phoenix, 85001. (602) 542-TOUR. You can spend a day or two exploring the old towns in this region of the state. If you have time, pick up a book on Arizona history. The more you know, the more you'll appreciate what you're seeing.

After Gleeson, you have a choice. Continue to Tombstone (see Day Trip 1, Southeast of Tucson) and stay overnight there or go through Tombstone, heading north on US-80 to I-10, and follow I-10 west to Tucson.

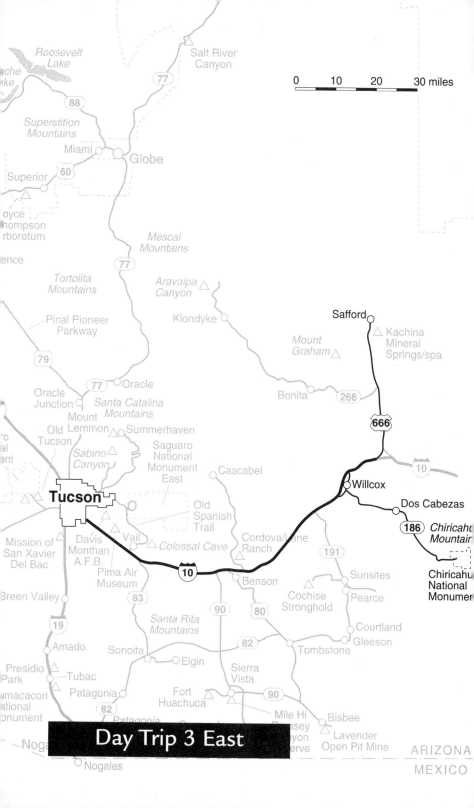

Roosevelt
Lake

ⁿ che
ke

Salt River
Canyon

77

88

*Superstition
Mountains*

0   10   20   30 miles

Miami

Globe

oyce
hompson
rboretum

60

Superior

ence

*Mescal
Mountains*

77

*Tortolita
Mountains*

*Aravaipa
Canyon*

Klondyke

Safford

Kachina
Mineral
Springs/spa

*Mount
Graham*

79

*Pinal Pioneer
Parkway*

77   Oracle

Oracle
Junction

*Santa Catalina
Mountains*

Mount
Lemmon

Bonita

266

666

Old
Tucson

ro
al
ⁿt

Summerhaven

*Sabino
Canyon*

Saguaro
National
Monument
East

Cascabel

Willcox

10

Tucson

Dos Cabezas

Old
Spanish
Trail

186   *Chiricahⁿ
Mountair*

Mission of
San Xavier
Del Bac

Davis
Monthan
A.F.B.

Vail

Colossal Cave

Cordova/Lane
Ranch

191

Chiricahⁿ
National
Monumerⁿ

Pima Air
Museum

10

Benson

Sunsites

*Santa Rita
Mountains*

83

90

80

Cochise
Stronghold

Pearce

reen Valley

19

82

Courtland

Gleeson

Amado

Sonoita

Elgin

Tombstone

Presidio
Park

Tubac

Sierra
Vista

82

maca cori
ational
ⁿument

Patagonia

Fort
Huachuca

90

82   *Patagonia*

Mile Hi
nsey
yon
erve

Bisbee

Lavender
Open Pit Mine

ARIZONA

Nogⁿ

Nogales

MEXICO

Day Trip 3 East

CHIRICAHUA NATIONAL MONUMENT

From Tucson follow I-10 east to Willcox. At the junction of A-186, turn south and follow this road about 20 miles to the Chiricahua National Monument. If you pick up this trip at Safford, take US-666 south to I-10, head west to A-186, and follow it to the park. After paying the entrance fee, proceed to the visitors center. The exhibits here graphically describe both the man-made and natural history of this mountainous area. You may pick up pamphlets or buy guidebooks describing the various trails. If you take the time to go through the visitors center first, you'll appreciate this region of the country much more.

Described as "a wonderland of balanced rocks, volcanic spires, and grotesquely eroded cliffs," Chiricahua National Monument was established in 1924. Endlessly mysterious, this is an ever-changing landscape. One moment shadows caress the spires that rise nearly 200 feet into the air; the next, light plays hide-and-seek with chiseled rocks that stand silently shoulder to shoulder.

Plan this day trip when you have lots of time and energy. If you want advance information, contact the Chiricahua National Monument, Dos Cabezas Star Route, Willcox, 85643. (520) 824-3560.

WHAT TO DO

To see this sprawling park from the comfort of your car, follow Massai Point Drive, a 6¹/₂-mile paved road that leads up Bonita Canyon to Massai Point. From the top you'll get a good view of Sulphur Springs Valley to the west and San Simon Valley to the east. The Massai Point Exhibit Building is a worthwhile stop, for it offers more information on the natural history of the area.

However, you'll experience the sense of the Chiricahuas more if you travel on foot. There are over 17 miles of trails to choose from. If you plan to hike for more than an hour, take water with you. Whether you decide on a twenty-minute stroll or a two-and-a-half-hour hike, you're sure to succumb to the strange beauty of this rocky place. Let your imagination fly—and you may even sense the spirit of Geronimo lurking in the shadows.

From here you can retrace your steps, heading north on A–186 to Willcox and then going west on I–10 back to Tucson, or you can go on to see the ghost towns of Cochise County. If you plan to visit the ghost towns, stay overnight in Benson or Willcox (see Day Trip 2, East from Tucson).

DOS CABEZAS

This is one of several ghost towns in Cochise County. The others can be found in Day Trip 2, East from Tucson. From Chiricahua National Monument, take A–186 north for 9 miles to Dos Cabezas. During its mining heyday, this community was a stage station. Not quite a ghost town, Dos Cabezas supports enough people to maintain a U.S. post office. As you walk around, you'll get a sense of what this place felt like when gold fever raged through the region.

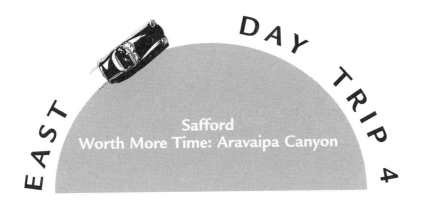

SAFFORD

From Tucson head east on I-10 to its junction with US-666. Go north on US-666 about 34 miles to Safford.

Dwarfed by towering Mount Graham, which rises 10,713 feet above it, Safford has grown as an agricultural and copper mining community. Like many small Arizona towns, this Graham County community offers the casual visitor more outdoor than indoor activities.

Graham County was organized in 1881, but its history dates back to the Anasazi Indians, an ancient people who inhabited the area around the time of Christ. The Anasazi were followed by the Hohokams, farmers who disappeared in the thirteenth century, and finally by the Apaches, who were nomadic fierce fighters. Although Coronado visited this area in 1540, it wasn't until tiny Camp Goodwin was established in 1864 that white men made their presence known in this area. Not surprisingly, the Apaches were not about to give up this land easily, and they battled to keep their territory. The last of the Apache chieftains, Geronimo, finally surrendered in 1888.

As you drive through the sculpted countryside with its broad valleys and secluded canyons, you will be enthralled by the strange, twisted beauty and may understand why the Apaches believed this landscape was worth fighting for.

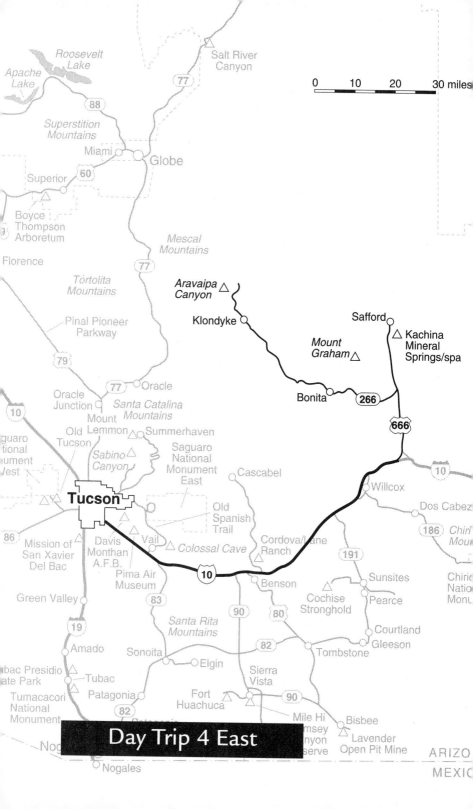

WHERE TO GO

Mount Graham. About 9 miles south of Safford, off US-666, you will see A-366, or Swift Trail. Turn right and follow this road for a spectacular journey to the summit of Mount Graham. Like the drive to Mount Lemmon, this takes you through five of the seven ecological zones of western North America. You'll begin in desert cactus and end in mountainous aspen.

When you see a sharp right-hand turn leading to Marijilda Canyon, *don't* take it. This road is not recommended for passenger cars. (As you travel around Arizona, *always obey a sign that says:* NOT RECOMMENDED FOR PASSENGER CAR OR SEDAN TRAVEL. These roads can go from rough to impassable fast!) Instead, continue on Swift Trail. The first 22 miles are paved, but then the road becomes well-maintained gravel. With its many switchbacks, you'll need about two hours to make it to the top. As you traverse the 36 miles to the summit, you'll pass campgrounds—complete with showers—and picnic grounds. Pull off at the scenic turnouts to drink in the views.

Although the drive is worth the trip, Mount Graham has nine major trails to hike on, once you ascend. Dutch Henry Trail originates at Ladybug Saddle; Ash Creek Trail begins at the summer-home area of Columbine at 9,500 feet. You can pick up Grant Goudy Ridge Trail at Soldier Creek Campground. Try the Round-the-Mountain Trail, covering 14 miles and touching on some of the most popular features of the area, or High Peak Trail, originating a short distance southeast of Columbine at 9,600 feet. In addition, you can hike on Clark Peak Trail in the Taylor Pass and West Peak area, Bear Canyon Trail, Snake Trail, and Arcadia Trail. Pick up information and trail guides at the Safford-Graham County Chamber of Commerce, 1111 Thatcher Boulevard, Safford, 85546. (520) 428-2511.

Kachina Mineral Springs Spa. Six miles south of Safford, just off US-666. For a relaxing interlude, soak up the natural hot mineral springs that come out of the ground at 108 degrees Fahrenheit. Bathe in tiled Roman-style tubs. Enthusiasts believe that the stimulating combination of bathing, sweating, and massage cleanses both the body and the mind. Fee. (520) 428-7212.

WORTH MORE TIME: ARAVAIPA CANYON

You *must* contact the Bureau of Land Management (BLM) before making a trek into this jewel of a wilderness area, and there is a fee. Write to the Bureau of Land Management, 711 14th Avenue, Safford, 85546, or call (520) 428-4040.

To get to Aravaipa Canyon from Safford, take US-666 south to A-266. Follow A-266 west to Bonita and then pick up the secondary road to the village of Klondyke. Follow this road to the canyon entrance. Park your vehicle and proceed on foot.

Aravaipa is located in the Galiuro Mountains and the creek supports an abundance of wildlife. More than 230 species of birds have been recorded here including some rare black-and-zone tailed hawks and yellow warblers. To protect the wildlife only 50 people per day are permitted to hike on the trail and permits should be obtained in advance. It is always important to ask about the condition of the canyon in terms of weather.

This canyon is *not* for the casual hiker. Aravaipa is designated as a wilderness area; it is not a picnic ground. The area covers 4,044 acres and offers hikers and backpackers a relaxing-to-challenging experience. Bring water and a trail map (which you receive when you contact the BLM), even if you plan to spend only a few hours in this desert splendor.

Today Aravaipa is such a tranquil place that it's difficult to remember its violent history. The confluence of Aravaipa Creek and the San Pedro River, however, was the original site of Camp Grant (now Fort Grant). Although the U.S. Army swore that the Aravaipa Indians had not been responsible for raiding the white settlements, both the white men and the Papago (now Tohono O'odham) Indians were unconvinced. In 1872, a group of Tucson citizens and Papagos approached the Aravaipa Reservation and, before the sun rose, massacred eighty-five men, women, and children.

As you hike in the canyon, you'll be flanked by cliffs rising 700 feet or more on either side of you. In some areas you must squeeze through narrow stone hallways. If you choose to follow Aravaipa Creek, plan on having wet shoes at times. You'll be wise to move quietly and carry a good camera to catch much of the endangered wildlife. Bighorn sheep take refuge here, and the largest number of native fish in any stream in the state populate the water. Aravaipa is also a birdwatcher's paradise.

While hikers wax eloquent about an autumn backpacking trip into Aravaipa Canyon, enthusiasts insist it's ideal any time of year.

To return to Tucson after such a full day, follow US–666 south to I-10 and head west back to the "Old Pueblo." Or you can go on to Chiricahua National Monument (Day Trip 3, East from Tucson).

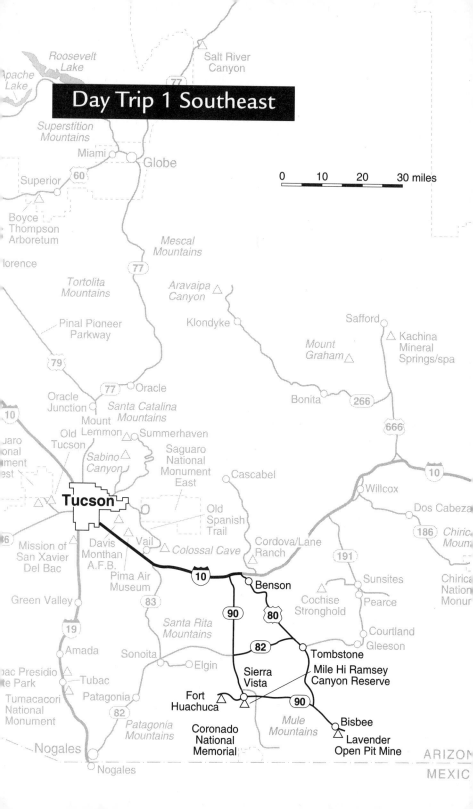

Although this day trip can be done in one day, you may prefer this as a more leisurely two-day excursion. Plan to arrive in Tombstone by midmorning and reach Bisbee by suppertime. Stay overnight in Bisbee and then drive on to Sierra Vista, Fort Huachuca, and back to Tucson the following day.

Should you decide to cover this portion of southern Arizona in one day, know at the outset that you can't see everything described below. Choose carefully among the attractions. There is so much to see that if you aren't careful, you'll arrive home in the wee hours of the morning, overtired and oversatiated.

TOMBSTONE

Begin in familiar territory by taking I-10 east to Benson. At US–80, head south to Tombstone. Here's where all your western fantasies will come true. This is "The Town Too Tough to Die." It's where Ed Schieffelin went prospecting in 1878 for silver, warned that all he would find in this Apache-infested land was his tombstone. Instead, he found one of the richest silver strikes in the country.

Tombstone is no false-front, made-up western town. This is the *real* thing. Once it boasted a population of about 10,000 wild and respectable souls. Today the community caters to tourists, but all the legends are alive and well here. As you walk along the dusty streets, you'll see the O.K. Corral, the Bird Cage Theater, the Crystal Palace, and other historic sites. Tombstone is the Wild West preserved at its raunchiest and best. It personifies the frontier experience in those wild days before the century turned.

What was it like to live here? George Parsons, an early settler, noted in his diary in 1880 that "a man will go to the devil pretty fast in Tombstone. Faro, whiskey and bad women will beat anyone." And Wyatt Earp once commented, "We had no YMCA's."

As you come into town on US–80, you'll hit Fremont Street. Park anywhere. Since the entire town is a living museum, you'll want to see this national historic site on foot.

Begin with a liberal dose of history. Stop at the **Tombstone Epitaph,** 5 South Fifth Avenue, and pick up a map describing the points of interest.

Take a moment to familiarize yourself with the town. Most of what you'll want to tour lies within a few main streets. The sites are concentrated in a square framed by Fremont and Toughnut streets to the north and south, and Third and Fifth avenues on the west and east.

Since most of the attractions have an entrance fee, you may prefer to stop in at the O.K. Corral or Tombstone Historama and buy a combination ticket rather than pay separately for each. The combination ticket saves you a little money and a lot more time waiting to buy other tickets.

For more information before you go, write the Tombstone Tourism Association, 5 South Fifth Avenue, Tombstone, 85638, for a map and a brochure.

WHERE TO GO

Tombstone Courthouse. Toughnut Street between Third and Fourth avenues. This elegant structure was built in 1882 for the then amazing sum of $43,000. It served as the Cochise County Courthouse until 1929 when the county seat was moved to Bisbee. Two floors of exhibits await visitors. There's a ghoulish side trip out the side door to see the hangman's platform, a room devoted to cattlemen, another to lawyers, and rooms full of costumes, jewelry, and china. This is a good first stop to get you in the mood for the 1880s.

Tombstone Historama. Allen Street between Third and Fourth avenues, next to the O.K. Corral. Enter this bright, airy building and slide back into time thanks to this unique, informative electronic presentation of Tombstone's history. You'll be seated in a small theater to watch an excellent mini-sound-and-light production, and will gain an understanding of the forces that shaped this tough little town. Fee. (520) 457-3456.

O.K. Corral. Allen Street between Third and Fourth avenues. This is where it all happened, where history was made that bloody, dusty October day in 1881 when the Earp brothers and Doc Holliday faced off against the Clanton and McLaury brothers. You'll see the lifelike figures positioned as they stood in the dust that fateful day, and you'll marvel that a major gunfight was staged in such a small space. Even non-western history buffs will be strongly affected by this site. Fee. (520) 457-3456.

Bird Cage Theatre. On Allen Street just east of Fifth Avenue. Here tired miners bragged of strikes yet to come. Gamblers and gunmen cavorted. The law kept order and pretty young girls charmed them all. Preserved as it was in the 1880s, this theater was the gathering place for Tombstone citizens looking for fun. There's less glamour than you might expect, but remember that in the 1880s, this place was "it." Fee. (520) 457-3421.

Rose Tree Inn Museum. Toughnut Street between Fourth and Fifth avenues. The world's largest rose bush, which grew from one slip sent to a Scottish bride living in Tombstone, spreads over 7,000 square feet. Inside the museum antique furnishings give visitors a glimpse of how people lived in Tombstone a century ago. Fee. (520) 457-3326.

Crystal Palace Saloon. Allen Street and Fifth Avenue. While the Bird Cage Theatre was bawdy, the Crystal Palace was more refined. Here the elite and not-so-elite gathered for food and drink. You can belly up to the bar and eat and drink (both soft drinks and alcohol) in the carefully preserved interior. Come for good food, atmosphere, and loud, vintage 1890s saloon music. $ at the bar. (520) 457-3611.

Tombstone Epitaph. Fifth Avenue near Fremont Street. Visit the original newspaper building where people continue to publish the famous *Tombstone Epitaph.* Purchase a subscription for $7.00 and keep up on Tombstone once you are home.

Boot Hill. You pass the sign to Boot Hill as you come into town on US–80. You can stop either on the way in or on your way out of town to discover the many infamous gunslingers who are buried at Boot Hill. Read the epitaphs as they are wonderfully cryptic and humorous. Open daily. Donations suggested.

Tombstone has many other museums and points of interest. Depending upon your time and enthusiasm, spend a full day or just a few hours to get the flavor of this bawdy, rugged place.

WHERE TO EAT

Longhorn Restaurant. 501 Allen Street. Come for breakfast, lunch, or dinner and feast on Italian, Mexican, and American food. Ask about the lunch special; it's always good. $$; (CC) Visa and Mastercard only. (520) 457-3405.

Lucky Cuss. 414 Allen Street. Sample food cooked the original 1880s way on wood-burning stoves in this historically charming saloon. Slow-cooked ribs are the specialty. $$; (CC). (520) 457-3561.

WHERE TO STAY

Best Western Lookout Lodge. On US-80 about 1 mile northwest of town. This is the largest motel in the area, featuring forty units and a swimming pool. Although there is no restaurant, a continental breakfast is served. US-80 West, P.O. Box 787, Tombstone, 85638. $$; (CC). (520) 457-2223.

BISBEE

Continue south about 25 miles on US-80 to Bisbee. Just 6 miles north of the Mexican border, this charming community is famous for its mountainous setting, steep, winding streets, and crazy patchwork of architectural building styles. You'll enter town on US-80 through Mule Pass Tunnel. A third of a mile long, it is Arizona's longest tunnel. As you get near town, watch for the Bisbee business loop, which will be on your right. Follow it to Old Bisbee, and you'll wind up on Main Street.

Bisbee has been described by Arizona writer Joseph Stocker as a "larger and newer version of Jerome." (See Day Trip 2, North from Phoenix.) Like Jerome, Bisbee began as a mining town. During its heyday, this was *the* place to stop between New Orleans and San Francisco. Millions of tons of copper, gold, and silver were pulled from the Mule Mountains surrounding the town, until by the late 1880s, Bisbee offered every cultural, culinary, and sporting diversion found in any major American city.

The Phelps Dodge Corporation closed its copper operations in Bisbee in the mid-1970s, but instead of dying, the community determined to survive as a tourism center of southeastern Arizona. During the late 1960s and 1970s, hippies heard about the community and flocked here in droves, attracted by the temperate climate and inexpensive housing. Today most of the hippie culture has vanished, but some artists, poets, and artisans remain in residence. Thanks to a strong dose of community spirit, Bisbee is succeeding as a tourist center, and visitors appreciate the blend of historical charm and modern-day convenience the town offers.

Bisbee is quite small, a population of less than 10,000, but it supports a lively cultural scene. Classical concerts are presented at the Bisbee Women's Club. There are gallery openings by local artists, poetry readings, dinner theater, even melodramas. Most weekends the town hums with activities.

The unique blend of Victorian and 1930s Art Deco images have inspired many creative people who have come to work here. The late world-renowned Arizona artist, Ted De Grazia, once lived in Bisbee and managed the now restored Lyric Theatre.

During the final weekend in April, Bisbee is the scene of La Vuelta de Bisbee four-day cycling competition. If you like cycling and bike-related fun, don't miss this weekend.

You'll want to wander around "Old Bisbee," as it's called. Don't be deceived by the sleepy facade. This isn't a living museum like Tombstone. Rather, this is a very much alive community populated with Bisbee boosters. You'll enjoy touring the old residential sections where turn-of-the-century homes are squeezed onto narrow steep streets wedged into equally narrow, scenic canyons. The result is an intriguing web of tangled mountain roads and architecturally interesting structures.

If possible, do take a complete walking tour of downtown. Stop in at the Chamber of Commerce, 78 Main Street, and pick up a brochure. Even if your time is limited, plan to walk around some of Bisbee's historical district to savor its past. If you aren't up to a strenuous stroll, take a bus tour of Old Bisbee and the hilly residential neighborhood known as the Warren area. Each tour lasts approximately one and one-half hours and allows you plenty of time to take pictures. Fee. For information regarding hours of departure, call (520) 432-2071.

WHERE TO GO

Queen Mine and Lavender Open Pit Tours. Number 1, Dart Road. To get to the Queen Mine building, drive or walk immediately south of Old Bisbee's business district off the US–80 interchange. Underground mine tours leave daily at scheduled hours. As you explore the mine with your guide, you'll hear about George Warren, who, having celebrated with a few too many on the Fourth of July, bragged that he could outrun a horse and rider. In a burst of inebriated pluck, he bet his mining claim, the Copper Queen Mine, on the race. He ran and lost. Eventually his claim panned out, ultimately worth more than $40 million. Today George Warren's biggest claim to fame is that he was the model for the man who stands with his shovel in the center of the Arizona State Seal.

During this educational tour, you'll learn how Bisbee miners coaxed minerals from the mountains. Much of the original mining equipment stands in place. Although you walk into the Copper Queen, you'll ride out on small train cars. Bring a sweater. The mine remains a chilly forty-seven degrees Fahrenheit. Fee. For information about the time of tours, call (520) 432–2071.

Lavender Open Pit. Drive to a viewpoint on US–80 three-quarters of a mile beyond the Queen Mine building to see the open pit, or take a guided tour that leaves from the Queen Mine building every day at noon. As you gaze into this huge bowl scooped out of the landscape, you'll marvel at how man ever carved such an immense niche in the earth. Although the Lavender Open Pit shimmers with color, the name comes from a mine manager, Harry Lavender. Fee. (520) 432–2071.

Brewery Gulch. 13–17 Brewery Avenue. Also known as the Muhlheim Block, this street shoots dramatically uphill or downhill (depending upon your vantage point) from Howell Avenue. Completed in 1905, Brewery Gulch was once home to the Bisbee Stock Exchange, brothels, restaurants, lodging facilities, and saloons. Now under restoration, it emits old echoes of wilder days when gamblers and miners traipsed up Brewery for excitement. Today visitors can poke through new shops and art galleries along this narrow street.

Bisbee Mining and Historical Museum. In front of the Copper Queen Hotel. The permanent exhibition opened in September 1991 and combines mural-size photography, artifacts, minerals, and hands-on displays. The mineral collection is small but select and features a variety of copper-related materials, such as azurite, that can be found in the area. A one-hour visit will explain the political, economic, and labor history of this mining camp turned cosmopolitan town. The Mexican Revolution lives in photographs and commentary; the World War I labor section describes how Arizona cleaned up prostitution and gambling so it could join the Union. A rare faro table illustrates gambling; prostitution is left largely to the imagination.

A poignant exhibit tackles discrimination. Through a mirror device, visitors' faces are superimposed on heads of an Oriental man and a black woman. The question asked is: Does it make a difference?

The museum is located in a historic structure built in 1897. Fee. For information, call (520) 432-7071.

Old Phelps Dodge General Office Building. 5 Copper Queen Plaza. This structure was completed in 1895 and was designed as the general offices of the copper company. On the National Register of Historic Landmarks, the Old Phelps Dodge building is located in Bisbee's "Grassy Park." It is now the town's Mining and Historical Museum. Here you can see early mining equipment and a diorama describing a mining operation. In another setting, such a display may not excite you, but it springs to life in Bisbee. Fee. (520) 432-7071.

Covenant Presbyterian Church. 19 Howell Avenue. Next to the Copper Queen Hotel, this imposing European-style church was built in 1903. At the time it was built, a 579-pipe organ was installed. Over the years the organ has been enlarged and it remains in excellent condition. Free. (520) 432-4327.

WHERE TO STAY

Bisbee has experienced an explosion of good to terrific Bed & Breakfast inns making this a great place to spend the night in southern Arizona. Here are some suggestions.

The Bisbee Inn. 45 OK Street. This old hotel has been renovated to bring back a feeling of Bisbee at its heyday. Not as luxurious as the Copper Queen, it is nevertheless a good choice for travelers who want to experience life in the Old West. Originally built in 1916 as a miner's hotel, the Bisbee Inn offers 20 guest rooms. *A special note:* The original name of the hotel was "La More" which leaves little of its history to the imagination. $$. (520) 432-5131.

Copper Queen Hotel. 11 Howell Avenue. This famous hotel was built by the Copper Queen Mining Company (later Phelps Dodge Corporation) shortly after the turn of the century when Bisbee was the largest mining town in the world. It is Arizona's oldest hotel — having been run continuously as a hotel since that time. The present owners have restored most of the rooms to their former glory making this a good choice for travelers. The rooms are large and each one is different. Some bathtubs come with feet attached; wallpapers are period restoration. Although the lobby still feels dark and old, the renovated rooms are bright and cheery. The Copper Queen may not be quite as quaint as you may hope it to be, but it is authentic. When you sleep here you are in good company. Theodore Roosevelt stayed at the Copper Queen as did General John J. Pershing when he was on his way to Mexico to catch up with Pancho Villa. Ask, too, about the special Murder Mystery Weekends.

The dining room at the Copper Queen is recommended. The fare is sophisticated and well prepared. Have breakfast, lunch, or dinner here. Dine outdoors at the patio cafe or sit inside in the historic, restored dining room. The varied menu features old-fashioned American food spiced with a liberal dash of Mexican dishes. The Copper Queen, P.O. Box CQ, Bisbee, 85603. $$; (CC). (520) 432-2216.

Clawson House Bed & Breakfast. 116 Clawson Avenue. This B&B was built in 1895 for the manager of the Copper Queen Mine. It sits on four acres high atop Castle Rock which is Bisbee's most distinctive geographic feature. Completely restored, the home has a formal parlor, dining room and spacious guest rooms. Small children and pets are not accommodated. $$; (CC). (520) 432-5237 or (800) 467-5237.

High Desert Inn. 8 Naco Road. The best luxury inn to open in Bisbee, the High Desert Inn bills itself as "A Modern Hotel in a Timeless Town." It is an apt description. The inn features five rooms — each designed with a unique historic yet contemporary feeling. With queen-sized, wrought iron beds from France, craftsman tables and other fine appointments, the rooms are exceptionally inviting. The High Desert Inn offers full hotel services. A small intimate bar and unique dining room are open Thursday, Friday, and Saturday evenings and certain holidays. The Cordon Bleu-trained chef offers seasonally changing menus that emphasize fresh ingredients that are locally grown. A small but excellent wine list is available. $$; (CC). (520) 432-1442 or (800) 281-0510.

The Inn at Castle Rock. 112 Tombstone Canyon Road. This B&B was once a miner's boardinghouse and located on Main Street in Old Bisbee. The three-story, red Victorian structure, trimmed with cream-colored balconies — is on the National Register of Historic Buildings. Castle Rock features fifteen rooms and suites, each with private bathrooms. In addition there are gardens and parlors guests are invited to enjoy. The Inn at Castle Rock offers guests and Bisbee visitors the opportunity to dine at Eccentricity's Restaurant which features French-Flemish cuisine. Fine wines and cocktails are available. $$; (CC). (520) 432-4449 or (800) 566-4449.

The Greenway House. 401 Cole Avenue. The rooms are filled with antiques, kitchens are provided in the rooms, and each guest has a private bath. No smoking is allowed. Continental breakfast is served. $$; (CC). (520) 432-7170 or (800) 253-3325.

The Oliver House. 26 Soule. The B&B has fourteen units. The house, in the heart of town, was supposedly haunted. A full breakfast is served; king-sized beds and suites are available. $$; (CC). (520) 432-4286.

School House Inn. 818 Tombstone Canyon. Nine units (non-smoking) are available in a 1918 schoolhouse. A full breakfast is served and private baths are provided. $-$$; (CC). (520) 432-2996 or (800) 537-4333.

The White House. 800 Congdon Avenue. This is a lovely B&B with two units. Guests enjoy patios and private baths. No smoking is allowed, but rooms have electric fireplaces and sitting rooms. $$. (520) 432-7215.

SIERRA VISTA

From Bisbee, backtrack 9 miles north on US-80 and follow A-90 west 20 miles to Sierra Vista. Perched at an elevation of 4,623 feet, this fast-growing city is nestled on the slopes of the Huachuca Mountains. Surrounded on all sides by mountain ranges and never-ending views of the San Pedro Valley, the climate is as awesome as the scenery. Sierra Vista ranks as one of the three most temperate regions in the nation, and its cool summers and moderate winters make this city increasingly popular with newcomers and tourists.

With an abundance of outdoor pleasures nearby (everything from hiking trails to ghost towns and a mountain lake), Sierra Vista has become an important southern Arizona town. In the past, its biggest claim to fame was nearby Fort Huachuca. While the economy remains closely tied to the military installation, Sierra Vista is establishing itself as a manufacturing, wholesale, and retail center.

WHERE TO GO

The Mile Hi/Ramsey Canyon Preserve. Six miles south of Sierra Vista on A-92. Turn right onto Ramsey Canyon Road and drive 4 miles to The Mile Hi. This small and limited facility, owned by the Nature Conservancy, is sheltered in a deep gorge within 280 acres of the Huachuca Mountains. It's a favorite place for birdwatchers and others who are interested in learning more about this unique, fragile environment. Should you decide to spend time here, try to arrive on a weekday. It's much less crowded, and you'll have more opportunity to walk along the two nature trails and enjoy the serenity of this preserve.

Both nature trails open windows to a world populated by a great variety of birds, reptiles, and other animals. Guided hikes can be arranged by contacting the Ramsey Canyon Preserve manager in advance. A bookstore, gift shop, and nature reference library are on the grounds.

When you plan a trip here, remember that not every type of bird can be seen at the canyon during all times of the year. Ramsey Canyon is known as a hummingbird sanctuary, but these delicate creatures are in residence only from April through August. During the winter, they migrate farther south.

Because of the comparatively small size and ecological fragility of the area, certain rules are strictly enforced. No picnicking is allowed within the confines of the preserve, and parking is extremely limited. *All parking reservations must be made in advance!* RVs and campers cannot be accommodated. Whenever possible, car pooling is encouraged. In addition, pets are not allowed on the property. Visitor hours are strictly enforced. For more information, contact The Mile Hi, 27 Ramsey Canyon Road, Hereford, 85615. Fee. (520) 378-2785.

San Pedro National Conservation Area. The visitors center, San Pedro House, is 8 miles east of Sierra Vista on A-90. This 46,000-acre area stretches 33 miles from the Mexican border near Palominos to about 3 miles south of St. David. It includes one of the most significant broadleaf riparian ecosystems in Arizona and perhaps the entire Southwest. More than 350 species of birds, eighty-two of mammals, and forty-seven of reptiles and amphibians may be seen here. This is a wonderland for hikers, birdwatchers, and nature lovers. For more information, contact the Bureau of Land Management, R.R. 1, Box 9853, Huachuca City, 85616. (520) 457–2265.

WHERE TO STAY

Casa de San Pedro. 8933 South Yell Lane, Hereford. From Sierra Vista take A–90 Business Loop to the intersection of A–90 and A–92 in Sierra Vista. Travel south on A–92 for 18.5 miles to Palominos Road. Turn north on Palominos Road for 2 miles to Waters Road. Turn east on Waters Road for 1 mile. This charming, new bed and breakfast is backed by the San Pedro riparian area and is situated on 10 acres bordering the San Pedro River. Cottonwood and willow along the river provide a verdant habitat for a variety of wildlife — more than 330 species of birds, eighty-two species of mammals and forty-seven species of reptiles and amphibians. A birders' paradise, this special B&B is an ideal get-away for any traveler seeking peace and relaxation. Built in Territorial style around a courtyard and fountain, this property has ten guest rooms. All are well appointed and have private patios. A comfortable Great Room invites lounging and reading and superb breakfasts are served in the sunny dining room. The hosts are personable; the facility is superb. A list of special events from lectures to hikes is available. $$; (CC). (520) 366–1300.

GHOST TOWNS

Want more ghost towns?! Cochise County is your place. From Sierra Vista, go north on A–90 and A–92 approximately 9 miles to the junction with A–82. Go east on A–82 for 10 miles to Fairbank. From Fairbank, take an unnumbered dirt road that goes south for approximately 6 or 7 miles to Charleston. To return to Sierra Vista, either continue 8 more miles on that road, which will take you to the junction of A–90 and A–92, or retrace your steps.

There are more than thirty ghost towns in Cochise County, all that remain of once-vital mining towns. Charleston, for instance, was once described as tougher and livelier than Tombstone but was abandoned in 1886 after the Tombstone mines closed. Fairbank was named for Nathaniel Kellogg Fairbank, who helped finance the building of the railroad and organize the Grand Central Mining Company in Tombstone in 1879.

While you're in the area, see the Brunckow cabin, which has one of the bloodiest histories in Arizona. It's considered by some to be haunted and is located on Charleston Road before the Charleston bridge on the way to Sierra Vista from Tombstone. Watch on the left side of the road for an adobe building. Just behind that building is Brunckow cabin, the site of at least twenty murders. The first victim to have been murdered there was Frederick Brunckow himself, who in 1860 met his demise along with two coworkers. His mine was sold to Major Milton B. Duffield, Arizona's first U.S. Marshal, who was appointed by Abraham Lincoln. Major Duffield was shot at the former Brunckow mine in 1874. A newspaper account of the shooting stated, "It is claimed by some good men that he [Major Duffield] had redeeming qualities. Such may be the case, but we could never find them."

These roads are rutted but passable for cars. Be careful if you travel after a rain or during rainy weather for the roads can become impassable. For more information on the area, call the Bureau of Land Management (520) 457-2265.

WHERE TO STAY

The Mile Hi. Ramsey Canyon Preserve. This is one of the few Nature Conservancy properties in the country with overnight accommodations on the grounds. The name, The Mile Hi, comes from a private ranch the conservancy bought in 1975. As a result of this purchase, six cabins are available for rental. Each comes equipped with outdoor barbecue grill, picnic table, fully equipped kitchens, and linens. You'll need to bring your own food. Although you may rent the cabins by the day or week, during the spring and summer months you must reserve cabins for a minimum of three nights. Call in advance, or write to The Mile Hi, 27 Ramsey Canyon Road, Hereford, 85615, $$. (520) 378-2785.

Ramsey Canyon Inn. Next to Ramsey Canyon Preserve. Also

known as the Bed and Breakfast, this delightful B&B is owned and operated by Shirleen Desantis and is a great alternative for couples or nature lovers who crave ambience. There are six rooms and a cabin all lovingly decorated with antiques. Guests enjoy herb teas, fresh brewed coffee, and a variety of gourmet breakfasts. Order a fluffy omelette, German apple pancake, or the specialty, Dutch babies. Or sample fresh-fruit cobblers before heading out to hike. The B&B has a beautiful living area with large fireplace. All rooms have private baths. $$. (520) 378–3010.

CORONADO NATIONAL MEMORIAL

Located 20 miles south of Sierra Vista off A-92, Coronado National Memorial salutes the Spanish explorer Francisco Vasquez de Coronado, who searched for the Seven Cities of Cibola looking for gold.

From Sierra Vista head south on A-92. Turn west onto Montezuma Canyon Road and continue for 5 miles until you come to the visitors center and museum. The road is paved for just about a mile west of the visitors center, and then it becomes a mountainous gravel path that leads to Montezuma Pass, a narrow passageway over the Huachuca Mountains. Park and pick up the hiking trail of your choice. From the pass, you can gaze west over the San Rafael Valley and Patagonia Mountains toward Nogales (see Day Trip 3, South of Tucson).

The Coronado National Memorial is the name given to this entire area and includes both natural and man-made historical features. There is no plaque or statue commemorating Coronado's adventures. Instead, hiking trails lace the 4,976 acres that are home to a variety of birds, animals, and plants.

Told that cities existed where streets were paved with gold, Coronado arrived in Mexico in 1535. On February 23, 1540, he headed north with 336 Spanish soldiers and four priests to search for treasure. Instead of finding golden cities, Coronado found mud houses—adobe pueblo—inhabited by Indians. Pushing on, he ultimately came upon Hopi Indian villages in northeastern Arizona. Driven by the promise of gold, he continued to search past Acoma and onward to the upper Pecos River. Finally, discredited and disheartened, Coronado admitted defeat and died in relative obscurity. Although he never found gold, Coronado did change the course of

Southwestern history. The Spaniards left behind horses that helped the Indians dominate the plains and mountains, and they introduced the white man's religion to the region. Historians agree that the Coronado expedition formed the basis for contemporary Hispanic-American culture.

If you have a car that can go over miles of dirt road — and you have the time — the trip over Montezuma Pass is well worth the effort. It is perhaps the most outstanding physical feature in this Memorial. The pass is located at an elevation of 6,575 feet and once at the top, visitors are treated to sweeping views of the San Rafael Valley to the west and the San Pedro River Valley to the east. The road has steep grades and tight switchbacks and the top of the pass serves as a parking area for hikers who are exploring the Memorial's trails. Standing at the top of Montezuma Pass is a living lesson in the geography and history of this area. You can easily imagine how it must have been when Coronado discovered this place and determined to conquer it. A picnic area near the visitor center is open from dawn to dusk but there are no facilities at the top of the pass other than an excellent National Park plaque that describes the sweeping vista. The road continues to Sonoita. The scenery is spectacular but the going will be slow. Or you can turn around and return to the visitor center.

The Coronado National Memorial is well known for the variety of birds that live in the area. The Park Service reports that more than 140 species have been recorded including 50 resident birds. Free. (520) 366-5515.

FORT HUACHUCA

From the Coronado National Memorial, return to Sierra Vista on A-92, then drive west for 4 miles to Fort Huachuca. To get to the main gate, follow A-90 south to where it intersects with Squier Avenue. The main gate is on the corner of Squier Avenue and A-90.

This 73,000-acre installation lies within the boundaries of Cochise and Santa Cruz counties and is closely tied to the history of Arizona. Now the largest employer in southern Arizona, Fort Huachuca was established in 1877 as a base for American soldiers during the Indian wars of the 1870s and 1880s. Fresh running water, high ground, and shade trees convinced the Army that this was a wise location for a fort. When Geronimo surrendered and the Indian hostilities ended,

Fort Huachuca was kept active to guard against problems around the Mexican border.

Many well-known units were stationed here, but the most famous is the "Buffalo Soldiers," the Tenth Cavalry Division of black fighters who accompanied General Pershing when he chased Pancho Villa into Mexico in 1916.

Closed down after World War II, Fort Huachuca was later reactivated and in 1953 became the home of the U.S. Army Electronic Proving Ground. Again, its physical setting saved the fort because the mild, dry climate and open spaces made it a natural for the electronics field. Today the base buzzes as a center for intelligence and worldwide communications. For information regarding the base, write: Headquarters, Fort Huachuca, ATTN: ATZS-CDR, Fort Huachuca, AZ 85613. (520) 533-3638.

Fort Huachuca Historical Museum. Corner of Boyd and Grierson streets, overlooking the Brown Parade Field. The museum is housed on the historic Old Post where almost all of the original buildings are still in use. Opened in 1960, the museum tells the story of Fort Huachuca and of southwestern Arizona. It showcases military memorabilia from the 1800s to the present. Because Arizona history is closely tied to the military, the exhibits will help you understand events leading up to this young territory becoming the forty-eighth state. There's ample parking, and a gift shop features items and books related to the Southwest. Free. (520) 533-5736.

To return to Tucson from Fort Huachuca, drive north on A-90 to I-10, then west on I-10 to Tucson.

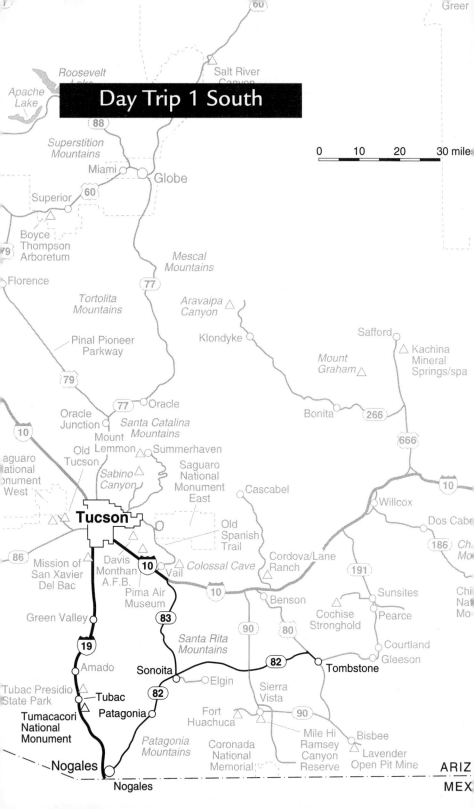

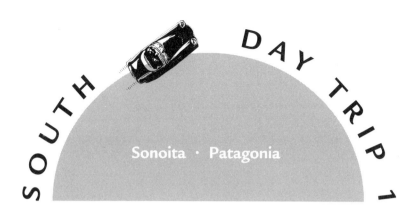

SOUTH DAY TRIP 1

Sonoita · Patagonia

This day trip can also be done from Phoenix if you don't mind adding an extra two hours driving time each way. If you do it from Tucson, it's an easy hour or less to Sonoita and Patagonia.

From Tucson take the scenic drive southeast on I-10 toward Nogales. Go south on A-83 for 27 miles to Sonoita. The route takes you through magnificent country studded with cactus, beveled with foothills, and ringed with wide, open valleys. As the road climbs toward Sonoita, the landscape grows more lush. Not only are you climbing in elevation, the area is also nurtured by Sonoita Creek. Even during the summer, when the rest of the Arizona desert is bleached to a coarse yellow, the high grasses here retain their green tint.

If you decide to stay overnight in Tombstone (see Day Trip 1, Southeast of Tucson), you can start this day trip by heading south the next morning. Follow US-80 north of Tombstone to A-82 and continue west on A-82 to Sonoita and then south on A-82 to Patagonia and Nogales. You can return to Tucson by driving north on I-19, stopping at Tumacacori and Tubac on your way back. This makes a pleasantly packed two- or three-day mini-vacation. Spend the first night in Bisbee, the second in Tombstone, and arrive in Tucson the third evening.

If you make this trip in a single day from Tucson, plan on a long, full day to travel to the Mexican border and return to the Old Pueblo. Everybody likes to visit Mexico at least once while in Arizona. What makes this trip easier than most Mexican vacations is that you don't drive across the border. You'll park in Nogales, Arizona, and walk across the international line into Nogales, Mexico. Once you leave Arizona and enter the state of Sonora, Mexico, you'll feel worlds away from the United States. Border towns are usually safe as long as you stay on the main streets. If you're a naturalized citizen or not an American citizen, be sure to bring your *proof of citizenship* or *passport* so that you can re-enter the United States.

SONOITA

Sonoita is a very old community that dates to around 1699. Originally it was the site of a Vista, a mission that only occasionally received personal visits by Spanish padres.

According to Arizona historian Marshall Trimble, the modern-day town of Sonoita owes its existence to the Benson-to-Nogales railroad line, which was built in 1882. Today this community is still on the transportation "line" for visitors who take what locals call "the back way"—the scenic and more interesting non-interstate route—to Nogales.

More than a place along the way, Sonoita is coming into its own as the site of Arizona's flourishing wine industry.

WHERE TO GO

Sonoita Vineyards. On Canelo Road, 12 miles southeast of town and 2 miles south of Elgin. Take the delightful tour through the winery, and sample some excellent wines being made in southern Arizona. In the past ten years, Arizona has experienced a growth of wineries, as its climate and soil are similar to that found in the Napa Valley area around San Francisco and the great wine country of France.

Sonoita Vineyards was selected for the 1989 Inaugural Food and Wine Gala for President George Bush. The winery is situated in rolling hills and is surrounded by grape arbors with the Huachuca Mountains clearly visible in the not-far-off distance.

Sonoita Vineyards makes Private Reserve Cabernet Sauvignon, Pinot Noir, Fume Blanc, Cuvee Sonoita, Sonora Blanca, Sonora Rossa, Arizona Sunset, and Cochise County Colombard. Wines are available for purchase and sampling. Tour requires a fee, but includes wine tasting. (520) 455–5893.

R. W. Webb Winery. Near Vail. This is just off I-10, right before the A-83 turnoff. Robert Webb is a third-generation Arizonan from Douglas who turned his wine hobby into a growing wine industry. The winery is Spanish Mission-style and was constructed in 1986. It can produce 25,000 cases of wine per year. Patio parties featuring Webb wines and hors d'oeuvres are held the third Saturday of each month. (520) 885-7782.

Kokopelli Winery. Off I-10 exit 336. This winery produces the state's only organically certified wines. The name of the wine is the grape that is grown there. The tasting room is open only noon to 5:00 P.M. on Saturday and Sundays; however, the owners also run a wine festival in January. (520) 384-3800.

The Chapel of Santa Maria. Located in the village of Elgin. The chapel is overseen by the Monks of the Vine, a Wine Brotherhood of vintners. The Santa Fe-style chapel is a nondenominational shrine. Local legend is that vines planted around the shrine are thought to come from cuttings from the earliest Conquistador cultivars. In April the "Blessing of the Vine Festival" is held with music, processions, and food and wine tastings.

Village of Elgin Winery. Within walking distance from the Chapel of Santa Maria in Elgin. The winery is located in an old brown hay barn. It is open daily from 10:00 A.M. to 4:00 P.M. (520) 455-9309.

Naveh Vineyard. This is a kosher winery that makes great white wine. Call for appointment. (520) 455-5375.

Callaghan Vineyards. Elgin. Call for directions and appointment. (520) 455-5532.

PATAGONIA

Patagonia is a picturesque town that lies in a narrow valley bounded by the Santa Rita Mountains to the north and the Patagonias to the south. The mountains and the town were named after the now closed Patagonia Silver Mine, which operated there in 1858. Also known as the Mowry Mine after Sylvester Mowry purchased it in the 1850s, it produced more than $1.5 million worth of ore during its heyday. By the early 1900s the veins were too diminished to merit any more activity.

Today Patagonia has some of the finest quarter horse and cattle ranches in the Southwest. It is known throughout the state for its inviting location and, thanks to the higher elevation, slightly cooler temperatures.

In recent years Patagonia has begun to become its own tourism destination. There's an excellent arts-and-crafts gallery to peruse and two excellent restaurants in the vicinity. In addition the Patagonia-Sonoita Creek Sanctuary has become a birdwatcher's paradise.

The town is also attracting film industry people from Los Angeles who appreciate the serenity and majesty of the hillsides. Beautiful ranch homes are sprouting in the hills, most of which are hidden from passing motorists' eyes.

There are only two main streets in town, McKeown and A-82. You can't get lost in "downtown" Patagonia.

WHERE TO GO

Mesquite Grove Gallery. 371 McKeown Avenue. Owner Nancy Merwin and Manager Regina Medley have assembled a special array of art, most locally done. You'll find sculpture, needlework, jewelry and wood, and dozens of other kinds of artwork all crafted with high style and talent. The prices are excellent, and the work is uniformly fine. (520) 394-2358.

The Patagonia-Sonoita Creek Preserve. South of Patagonia on A-82 between Patagonia and Nogales. As you enter Patagonia on A-82, watch for the Stage Stop Inn and the Patagonia Market. Turn right onto Third Avenue. You may want to stop at the filling station in town to use the restrooms since there are no facilities at the sanctuary. Continue south on Third Avenue to Pennsylvania Avenue and turn east onto Pennsylvania. Follow the road across a small creek and watch for signs that say nature conservancy. (The conservancy operates the sanctuary.) Look for Gate 2, which will be on your left. Turn in and drive to the Information Center. All visitors must register at an entrance gate.

Birdwatchers and naturalists flock to this 312-acre preserve. Located in a narrow floodplain, the sanctuary features a majestic stand of cottonwood trees interspersed with Arizona walnut and velvet ash. Avid birdwatchers from all over the world know that this is the place to see more than 200 species.

To protect the fragile character of the sanctuary, rules are strictly enforced. Pets are not allowed on the grounds. There is no picnicking, camping and fires are prohibited, and motorized vehicles are not allowed on trails within the conservancy. This is especially lovely to visit in the spring and fall. Free. For information, contact the Nature Conservancy, P.O. Box 815, Patagonia, AZ 85624. (520) 394-2400.

WHERE TO EAT

Karen's. 3266 A-82, Sonoita. Take the Sonoita exit from A-82. Turn left at the stop sign, and you will see the restaurant just down the road. Watch for signs! Karen's made its name in Elgin when it was in a charming, renovated home. It has now gone upscale in Sonoita. Salad dressings are still homemade and the food is still good. $$-$$$; (CC). (520) 455-5282 .

Ovens of Patagonia. 292 Naugle Street. Owners Monika and Tom Aylward specialize in gourmet food. Monika is German, Tom is Irish, and their food is excellent—not at all what you'd expect to find in a tiny town. $-$$; (CC). (520) 394-2483.

WHERE TO STAY

The Duquesne House. 371 Duquesne Street. This B&B is almost directly across the street from Cady Hall and was once miners' apartments. The charming adobe building has been renovated with love and attention to detail by Regina Medley, who has furnished it with antiques. Medley is an artist and manages the Mesquite Grove Gallery. $$. Call for reservations. (520) 394-2732.

The Little House. Call for directions. The house is the fifth house on the left, on Sonoita Street. Owners Don and Doris Wenig provide private, serene quarters for their guests. This B&B offers two rooms, each with private bath and private patio, and a host of special amenities. Breakfast is sumptuous and conversation is delightful. Doris, a former librarian, stocks her B&B with wonderful books that guests are free to check out and send back. There is also a collection of CDs to make bedtime even more pleasurable. Reservations are a must. $$. (520) 394-2493.

Circle Z Ranch. Write or call for directions. P.O. Box 194, Patagonia, 85624. A working ranch, Circle Z is open November 1 through May 15. Requires a week stay in season. There are rooms, suites, and cottages for forty guests. The ranch is located in the rolling grasslands just north of the Mexican border. $$-$$$. (520) 394-2525.

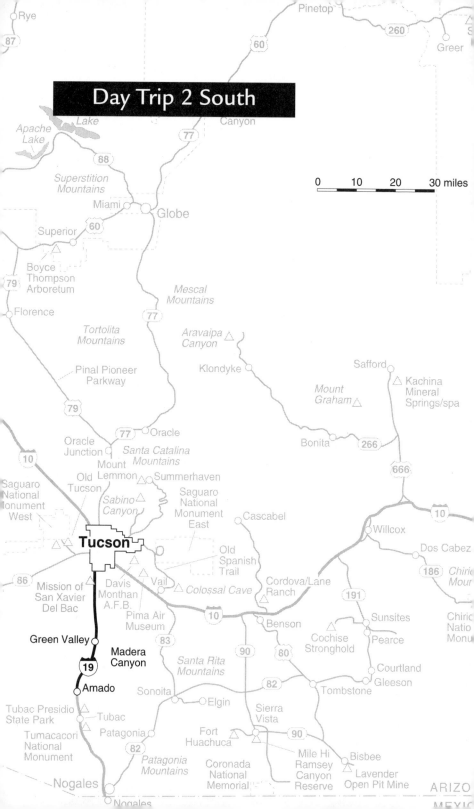

Day Trip 2 South

SOUTH DAY TRIP 2

Amado
Green Valley · Madera Canyon

From Tucson follow I-19 south toward Nogales, Arizona, and Nogales, Sonora, Mexico. This day trip is devoted to man-made wonders of the high-tech world. Because of the time involved for the tours, if you want to cover both sights, I recommend going first to Amado and Whipple Observatory and then seeing the Titan Missile Museum on the way back to Tucson. This is not recommended for young children, but older children and teenagers will enjoy it.

AMADO

Follow I–56 to exit 56 (Canoa). Then follow directions to the observatory.

Fred Lawrence Whipple Observatory. From exit 56, turn left and drive under the freeway to the frontage road on the east. Turn right and drive south 3 miles to Elephant Head Road. Turn left and drive east. Follow the signs to Mount Hopkins Road for about 7 miles to reach the observatory office.

Operated by the Smithsonian Institution and the University of Arizona, Whipple Observatory sits atop Mount Hopkins, the second-highest peak in Arizona. It commands a heavenly panorama north beyond Tucson and south into Sonora, Mexico, over hundreds of miles of saguaro-studded Coronado National Forest, desert floor, and rolling mountain ranges.

Visitors take a daylong tour that describes a brief history of astronomical time and includes visits to the computer laboratories, massive telescopes, optical arrays, and celestial mirrors.

From the visitor center everyone boards a bus for the forty-five minute climb to the top of the mountain and the observatories. The bus travels through various Arizona life zones, from desert to high chaparral to pine forest. The first stop is at 7,600 feet for a tour of 48-inch and 60-inch telescopes and a gamma ray collector. After lunch (you bring it; it's not provided), there's a short, steep ride to the 8,550-foot summit where the Multiple Mirror Telescope (MMT) stands. You learn that the building rotates slowly so the "eyes" stay focused. Computers synchronize the entire operation. With its new 276-inch mirror, Whipple claims the world's largest telescope.

Whipple Observatory is open March through Thanksgiving. Fee. The tour departs at 9:00 A.M. and returns by 3:00 P.M. (520) 670-5707.

From Whipple Observatory, head back to Tucson via I-19 to Green Valley. This is less than a twenty-minute drive, and you can still make the last (4:00 P.M.) tour at the missile museum.

GREEN VALLEY

Pima Air Museum's Titan Missile Museum. From I-19 south, take exit 69. Go west ¹/₁₀ mile past La Cañada. Turn right. This is the only intercontinental ballistic missile complex in the world that is open to the public. This museum is dedicated as a memorial to all loyal Americans who served their country so valiantly in peace and in war. Guided tours are available through the complex and the silo Wednesday through Sunday, May 1 through October 31. The museum is open daily November 1 through April 30. Closed Christmas. The last tour starts at 4:00 P.M. *Note:* High heels cannot be worn at this museum! Fee. (520) 625-4759.

MADERA CANYON

From I-19 south, follow the signs to Madera Canyon. This wooded riparian island in the sky offers an excellent choice of well-marked hiking trails. Trails range from moderate to difficult and the Nature Trail and Amphitheater Trail are both good choices for beginners. Madera Canyon, with its abundance of trees and a running creek, is especially gorgeous in fall and spring. For information about trails and the park, call San Rita Lodge (520) 625-8746. Free, but donation suggested.

WHERE TO STAY

Rex Ranch. Call or write for directions. P.O. Box 636, Amado, 85645. Located thirty minutes south of Tucson, the Rex Ranch is also only thirty minutes from Mexico. The property offers sixteen adobe casitas, each furnished with unusual antiques and collectibles from around the world. Food service is only available for groups and must be arranged in advance. There are good, homey restaurants nearby. $$-$$$; (CC). (520) 398-2914.

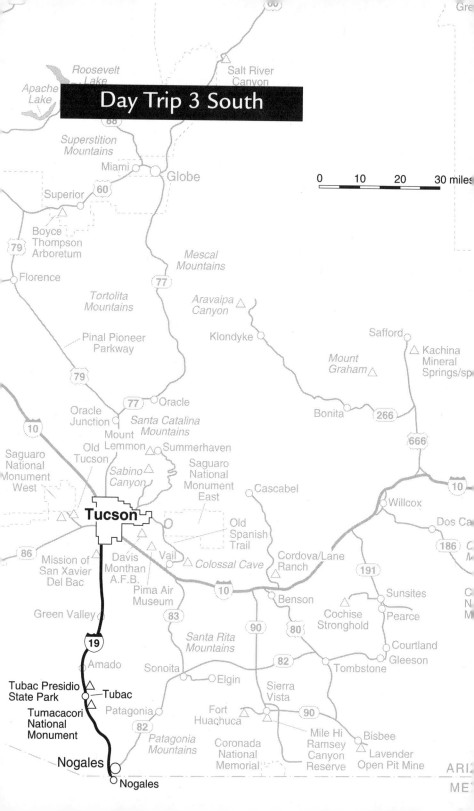

This day is filled with arts and crafts and great shopping. It's not recommended for non-shoppers, but anyone with even a passing interest in local art and native culture will find it very enjoyable. This trip can be combined with seeing the Titan Missile Museum (Day Trip 2, South from Tucson).

Don't be concerned about driving to Mexico. The drive to Nogales is an easy one, with divided highway much of the way. Americans can conveniently park on the United States side and walk across the border.

TUBAC

From Tucson follow I-19 south for 45 miles to Tubac. According to archaeologists and anthropologists, the Santa Cruz River area has been home to many different people for perhaps 10,000 years. It is likely that the prehistoric Hohokam tribe lived here between A.D. 300 and A.D. 1400 to 1500. The Ootam (Pima and Tohono O'odham) arrived here in the 1500s.

The Spaniards came in the 1600s, led by Father Kino, who explored Arizona beginning in 1691. In 1821 the area belonged to Mexico, which won it along with its independence. Since 1853, when the Gadsden Purchase was signed, Tubac has been part of the United States.

Tubac claims to be the first European settlement in Arizona and housed the state's first newspaper and state park. It also had the first schoolhouse. In 1751 the Pima Indians swept through Tubac,

burning and murdering. They were defeated, and the Spanish established a garrison, the Tubac Presidio, to defend the missions and the
Spanish settlers. The Presidio was moved to Tucson in 1776, leaving
the town open to Apache attacks. The area quieted, and R. Toribio de
Otero applied for and got a land grant in 1789.

When the United Sates took possession with the Gadsden Purchase of 1853, Tubac was a ghost town. But when ancient mines were
discovered and minerals unearthed, it became a favorite spot for
prospectors, miners, and journalists.

The Tubac Presidio State Historic Park, Arizona's first, was established in 1959 and the museum opened in 1964.

Today Tubac is a center of arts and crafts for southern Arizona,
touted as the place where "art and history meet." For once, hype is
not far from the truth, for Tubac is a unique artistic community.

In 1948 Dale Nichols opened an art school, and over the years,
potters, painters, and designers of batik, gold, silver, and wood have
all "discovered" Tubac. Today more than fifty galleries and studios
are located here. Tubac sponsors many festivals. Check with the
Chamber of Commerce, (520) 398-2704, for dates. Two festivals are
scheduled in December: the Fiesta—Annual Intercultural Fiesta—
and Fiesta Navidad, when the village is lit by luminarias. The Tubac
Art Festival is held in February, and the Artwalk is scheduled for
early March.

WHERE TO GO

The Presidio Museum and Ruins. Tubac Presidio State Park. As
you continue on Tubac Road past the business area, it becomes
Wilson Road after it crosses Burruel Street. Then, as it curves toward
the Presidio, it is called Presidio Drive.

The Presidio Museum offers a glimpse into life in a Spanish fort
around 1750. An underground exhibit includes some of the original
wall and floor. Open daily. Fee. (520) 398-2252.

WHERE TO EAT AND STAY

The Tubac Country Club. P.O. Box 1297, Tubac, 85646. When you
take the Tubac exit off I-19, continue north on Frontage Road for
1½ miles. The public is welcome at the club restaurant, which offers

the most relaxing place to eat between Tucson and Nogales. The menu is mostly American, although some south-of-the-border dishes are included.

This picturesque resort sports a golf course and hotel accommodations surrounded by patio homes. Book a room by the day, week, or for the entire season. Reservations are suggested in the summer and necessary during the rest of the year. $$-$$$; (CC). (520) 398-2211.

WHERE TO SHOP

Gift shops, arts and crafts galleries, and boutiques are clustered within an area bounded by Tubac Road and Camino Otero, Calle Baca, and Presidio Drive. Here you find many one-of-A-kind items created by local residents. Most shops are open Monday through Saturday, and many have Sunday hours as well. Ask for a free illustrated map of the area at any store.

Tubac Center of the Arts. Plaza Road (there are no street addresses in Tubac). As you head toward Tubac on Frontage Road, Plaza Road intersects with Frontage. You're welcome to browse during the season, October through May. This is the home of the Santa Cruz Valley Art Association, which showcases a variety of styles and types of art by local painters, sculptors, and craftspersons. The center is open Tuesday through Sunday from October through May. Donations are suggested. (520) 398-2371.

TUMACACORI NATIONAL MONUMENT

From Tubac continue south on I-19 for 3 miles to Tumacacori National Monument.

The Tumacacori mission is a national monument that rises from the desert floor like a half-finished cathedral. Built by the Franciscans around 1800, for five years this church was a functioning religious center. Then the Franciscans were expelled and the church was abandoned. Unattended, the mission was gutted repeatedly by Apaches and fortune hunters.

In 1929 the National Park Service restored it to its former, if unfinished, glory. Visitors can take a self-guided tour and see a scale model of how Tumacacori might have looked around 1820. If you call ahead, arrange a guided tour. For information, write Tumacacori National Monument, P.O. Box 67, Tumacacori, 85640. Fee. (520) 398-2341.

NOGALES, ARIZONA, U.S., AND NOGALES, SONORA, MEXICO

Back on I-19 continue to Nogales, Arizona, and Nogales, Sonora, Mexico. Notice the colors of the houses on the Mexican side and how different the two cities look even from a distance. As you continue into town, you'll be in the heart of Nogales, Arizona, where A-89 and A-82 join I-19.

The community on this side is a bustling place complete with a good manufacturing and retail base. Nogales, Sonora, is an equally active area. The Mexican city projects a south-of-the-border feeling. Even though you're only a few feet into Mexico, the mañana atmosphere prevails, and the more you compare the two cities, the more you'll realize how far away Arizona seems once you step across the international line. This is Old Mexico with bullfights, fiestas, and streets lined with small shops.

The border is always teeming with cars and trucks that are jammed with people and packages. Some of the guards will check every package thoroughly, so allow enough time to get across the border on the return trip.

It's recommended that you park your car on the Arizona side and do not attempt to drive into Mexico. Obey signs and don't park illegally. Parking is usually available by the railroad tracks on the Arizona side, and you can proceed across the border on foot. Should you decide to drive into Mexico, take out Mexican automobile insurance first, since United States insurance doesn't cover you in foreign countries. You can buy Mexican car insurance by the day in Tucson or in Nogales, Arizona, at several agencies.

WHERE TO GO

In Mexico walk up any of the main streets in Nogales and browse. You'll find good shops on Elias Calles, Lopez Mateos, and Obregon Avenues and on Hidalgo Street. Think of the shopping area as a long rectangle bounded by Elias Calles Avenue and Hidalgo Street, stretching from the border to Andonegui Street. Look for good buys on pottery, baskets, leather, wrought iron, and Mexican silver. You can also find lovely embroidered clothing as well as linens and crystal. Remember, this is Mexico and you are expected to bargain! Take your time and look around. You'll find the shop owners friendly and happy to make your trip worthwhile.

When you buy in Nogales, you'll deal in U.S. dollars. When you return to the United States, you must verbally declare your U.S. citizenship and purchases. You are allowed to bring back up to $400 of merchandise duty free, including one quart of liquor and one carton of cigarettes per adult.

La Roca. 91 Elias Street, Nogales, Sonora. After you cross the border, turn left and cross over the railroad tracks. Continue two blocks, turn right onto Elias Street, and walk two more blocks to La Roca, an elegant, enclosed shopping center resembling a large pinkish-red, adobe-style hotel. Inside you'll find more expensive items than on the main shopping streets. Most shopkeepers here accept credit cards. You'll encounter some rough sidewalks and high curbs en route to La Roca, so be careful where you walk.

Arizona Vineyards. 2301 Patagonia Highway. Two miles east of Nogales. Visit a rural, nineteenth-century European-style winery. The owner has decorated the interior with oil paintings he has done, pottery, wooden gargoyles, folk art, sculpture, a hat collection and winged horses. Everything is done by hand and visitors can watch the entire process and taste the production. This winery is open daily from 10:00 A.M. to 5:00 P.M.. (520) 287-7972.

WHERE TO EAT

La Roca. 91 Elias Street. Mexican food is an obvious specialty here. The upstairs dining room offers margaritas and nachos as well as complete lunches and dinners. $-$$; (CC). 2-0760 (Mexico).

WORTH MORE TIME

Sasabe. Rancho de la Osa. P.O. Box 1, Sasabe, AZ, 85633. Attention: Veronica. From Tucson follow I-19 south to A-86 or Ajo Way. Turn west (right) for 24 miles to Robles Junction which is A-286. Turn south (left) for 44 miles. At the sign for Sasabe, turn right for $1^1/2$ miles to the ranch. *Note:* If you reach the Mexican border, you have gone 1 mile too far.

The only and best reason to go to Sasabe is to visit the historic Rancho de la Osa. The ranch dates back to 1730. The 16-room guest ranch has just been refurbished with Mexican antiques and handmade linens. The old adobe ranch has been reborn into a gourmet Southwest experience. Rooms have private entrances and wood-burning fireplaces.

This intimate ranch is set amid magnificent desert wilderness and offers lots of birdwatching opportunities. The ranch has always been a favorite with Tucsonians who wanted a true get-away destination. The new owners have replaced the old ultra-rustic experience with one which is much more guest-oriented.

Guests can reserve a place at lunch or stay daily or weekly depending upon the season. While the horses are gentle, the riding is challenging because of the mountain landscape. However, the staff at the ranch provide enough instruction for guests to feel comfortable after a few days. $$; (CC). (520) 823-4257.

KITT PEAK AND KITT PEAK NATIONAL OBSERVATORY

From Tucson pick up A–86 (Ajo Highway) and follow it southwest for 37 miles. At the junction of A–386, turn left (the only way you can) and begin the 12.2-mile climb to Kitt Peak. Although this is an excellent road, it twists and winds around the mountain, giving passengers sometimes breathtaking views of sheer drop-offs and broad valleys.

The Kitt Peak National Observatory is located on top of Kitt Peak in the Quinlan Mountains. At an elevation of 6,882 feet, this giant eye-in-the-sky houses the largest concentration of facilities for stellar and solar research in the world. The primary mission of Kitt Peak National Observatory is optical astronomical research. Solar astronomers work from sunrise to sunset; stellar and planetary astronomers work during the hours of darkness but also, thanks to special scientific equipment, during daylight.

Scientists from all over the world regularly visit Kitt Peak. Although the astronomy center employs more than fifty people, only the necessary support staff live on the mountaintop. The rest make the daily round-trip to the summit. There is plenty for the public to see here. You can spend an hour or a full day, depending upon your interest in astronomy.

Stop first at the visitors center. You can pick up an illustrated brochure for a self-guided walk, or you can join one of the regularly

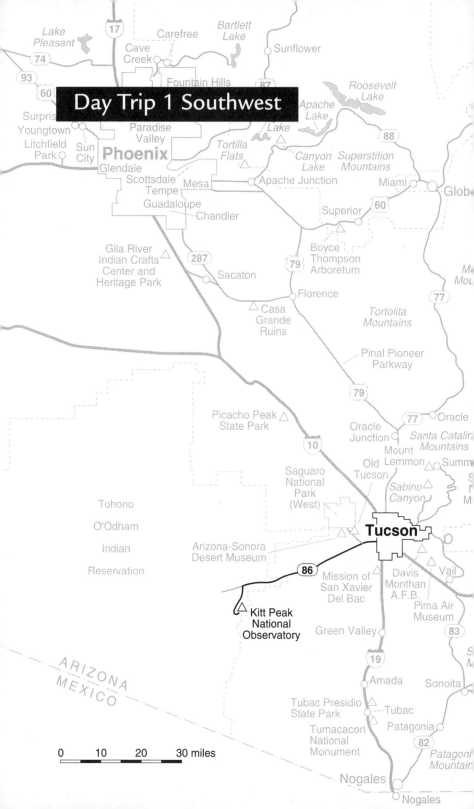

Day Trip 1 Southwest

Lake Pleasant

17

Carefree

Bartlett Lake

Sunflower

74

Cave Creek

93

60

Fountain Hills

87

Roosevelt Lake

Surpris
Youngtown

Paradise Valley

Apache Lake

88

Litchfield Park

Sun City

Phoenix

Tortilla Flats

Canyon Lake

Superstition Mountains

Miami

Glob

Glendale

Scottsdale

Mesa

Apache Junction

Tempe

Guadaloupe

Chandler

Superior

60

M
Mou

Gila River Indian Crafts Center and Heritage Park

287

Sacaton

79

Boyce Thompson Arboretum

Florence

Tortolita Mountains

77

Casa Grande Ruins

Pinal Pioneer Parkway

79

Picacho Peak State Park

10

Oracle Junction

77

Oracle

Santa Catalin Mountains

Mount Lemmon

Summ

Old Tucson

Saguaro National Park (West)

Sabino Canyon

M

Tohono

O'Odham

Indian

Reservation

Arizona-Sonora Desert Museum

Tucson

86

Mission of San Xavier Del Bac

Davis Monthan A.F.B.

Vail

Kitt Peak National Observatory

Green Valley

Pima Air Museum

83

ARIZONA

MEXICO

19

Amada

Sonoita

Tubac Presidio State Park

Tubac

Patagonia

Tumacacori National Monument

82

Patagoni Mountain

0   10   20   30 miles

Nogales

Nogales

scheduled tours conducted twice daily, including weekends, that begin at the visitors center. You also will find exhibits and models to study, films to watch, and even a model of the large telescope that you can operate.

As you walk out of the visitors center, look out over Altar Valley. Some 18 miles to the southwest, you will see Sells, headquarters of the Tohono O'odham tribe. Due south, there is a dome-shaped mountain peak called Baboquivari, the traditional home of the Tohono O'odham Indian god I-I'toy.

While at the Kitt Peak National Observatory, you'll want to see the McMath Solar Telescope, which is the largest solar telescope in the world. It is always aligned with the celestial North Pole at Tucson's latitude, and the entire structure housing it is encased in copper. Coolants are piped through the scope's outer casing, or "skin" as it is called, to ensure that this sensitive instrument is maintained in a uniform temperature.

Another fascinating device to see is the Nicholas U. Mayall Four-Meter Telescope, the nation's second-largest optical instrument. It allows astronomers to study objects six million times fainter than the dimmest star visible with the naked eye.

Only candy and soft drinks are sold on Kitt Peak, so if you decide to make a day of it, pack a picnic lunch. Follow the signs to the picnic area, complete with tables and fire pits.

Since it's usually about fifteen degrees cooler at the top of the mountain than in Tucson, take a jacket or sweater. Free, but donations are suggested. For more information including arrangements for group tours, write to National Optical Astronomy Observatories (Kitt Peak National Observatory), 950 North Cherry, Tucson, 85726-6732, or call (520) 318-8600.

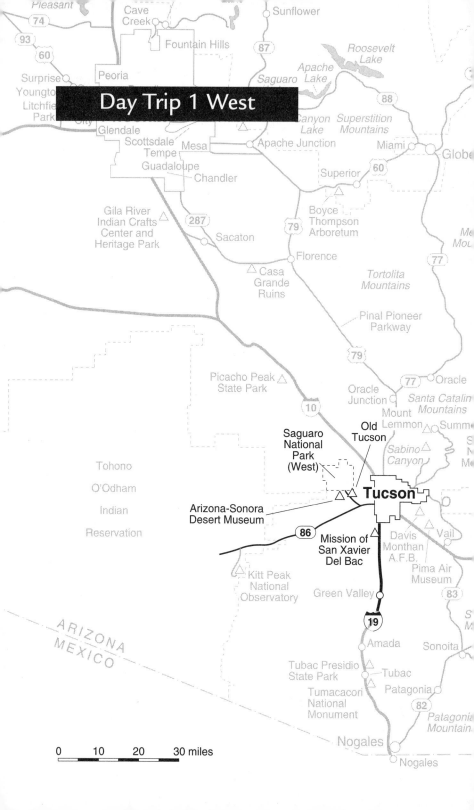

Day Trip 1 West

WEST

DAY TRIP 1

Mission of San Xavier del Bac
Old Tucson
Arizona-Sonora Desert Museum
Saguaro National Park (West)

Just 14 miles from Tucson is a cluster of worthwhile attractions. This day trip takes you through one of the most majestic forests of saguaro cacti you'll ever see. You can spend a full day of glitz and glamour combined with a liberal dose of science and education and unparalleled natural beauty. Visit each of these attractions in separate half-day trips and spend a few hours, or spend an entire day, seeing each one of them. If you decide to take in all four at once, be ready for a long, full day—not because the distances are great, but because there's so much to see at each destination.

MISSION OF SAN XAVIER DEL BAC

Pick up I–19 and head south for this 9-mile trip through Tucson and South Tucson to San Xavier del Bac (Ha-veer). At Valencia Road, turn west and enter the San Xavier Indian Reservation. Small houses and broad, tilled fields stretch in all directions.

In the distance, you will see the White Dove (as it's called) rise dramatically from the desert floor. Dazzling white, San Xavier shimmers like a bird caught between the brown-beige land and indigo sky. With its imposing dome and lofty parapets and towers, the Mission contrasts brilliantly against the violet of the nearby mountains. You'll quickly see why it has been called the finest example of mission architecture in the United States.

Turn south at Mission Road and follow it to the church. Constructed over a period of fourteen years, from 1783 to 1797, San Xavier is a graceful blend of Moorish, Byzantine, and late Mexican

Renaissance styles. Mass is celebrated daily every morning and in three services on Sunday. A vital, living mission, this church is used regularly by the nearby Tohono O'odham and San Xavier Indians. (The vast Tohono O'odham reservation is just west of the San Xavier land.)

Stand outside and contemplate the structure. The entire building is a series of domes and arches, and every surface is intricately adorned. Notice that wood was used only in the door and window frames. Look carefully to see a cat and a mouse carved into the facade of the building, one in each tower. Legend has it that if the cat ever catches the mouse, the world will end.

Walk inside. As your eyes become accustomed to the interior of the church, you'll see that, thanks to a cleaning project undertaken by Italian restorers and local residents, the mission is alive with vibrant color once again. A profusion of statues and paintings give this mission a warm lived-in feeling.

Father Kino, a Jesuit padre widely revered in this area, visited this site in 1692. The padre laid the foundations for the first church, which was 2 miles north of the present mission, and named it San Xavier in honor of his chosen patron, St. Francis Xavier, who was the illustrious Jesuit "Apostle of the Indies." The reclining statue to your left, as you face the main altar, is St. Francis Xavier.

To many people in the Southwest, this image of St. Francis Xavier has become a place of pilgrimage. If possible, plan to sit a while inside the church and experience the special ambience. A taped narrative provides an educational commentary about the mission.

Outside once again, visit the mortuary chapel and then climb the hill east of the mission to see the replica of the grotto in Lourdes, France. Be sure to pick up a brochure as you enter the church for a more detailed explanation of the history of San Xavier del Bac. Free, although donations are accepted. (520) 294–2624.

OLD TUCSON

Old Tucson. 201 South Kinney Road. From San Xavier, travel north on Mission Road to Ajo Road (A–86). Take Ajo Road west to Kinney Road. Follow Kinney north to Old Tucson.

If you are coming from Tucson, rather than from San Xavier, drive west on Speedway Boulevard to where it joins Anklam Road and becomes Gates Pass Road. As you continue west, you'll climb quickly into the foothills of the Tucson Mountains. Soon you'll be engulfed by the desert. As you get near Gates Pass, the road will twist and dip and climb until even the sky seems filled with mountains and saguaros. Once you are over the mountaintop, you'll gently descend into the valley. Watch for Kinney Road to your left. You'll turn south on Kinney and follow that a few miles to Old Tucson. If you are driving a large motor home or towing a trailer, take the Ajo Road-Kinney Road route and avoid Gates Pass.

Old Tucson is great fun for the entire family. This complete frontier town is peopled with characters who perform stunts, do trick riding and have shootouts. Visitors like to get a part in a saloon musical or appear in a Western film shoot. Youngsters and oldsters will get a kick out of the almost-real gunfights. There are movie sets to ogle and a narrow-gauge railroad that takes you around the grounds. Enjoy amusement park rides, climb aboard a stagecoach, or take a tour behind a sound stage. Naturally, it's a little bit fake, but after all, Old Tucson never pretended to be authentic.

Old Tucson serves up plenty of good western grub — mesquite broiled steaks and barbecue and authentic Mexican dishes. There are lots of places to shop here with stores filled with western wear, movie memorabilia and gifts.

Built originally in 1939 as a set for an epic movie, *Arizona,* this location continues to attract crowds. Cinematographers and tourists love the place. Since *Arizona,* more than one hundred other movies, television shows, and national commercials have used Old Tucson as a setting. Fee. (520) 883–0100.

ARIZONA-SONORA DESERT MUSEUM

The museum is on Kinney Road. From Old Tucson head north on Kinney Road. Continue on Kinney as it bends northwest and follow the signs to the entrance of the Arizona-Sonora Desert Museum.

If you think of museums as stodgy places you visit when it rains, think again. This one has a well-defined mission: to tell the story of life in the Sonoran Desert and of all the creatures who call this region home. An exciting combination of a zoo, an aquarium, and a botanical garden, this one-of-A-kind place defies a simple definition.

Look carefully. You'll see samples of nearly everything that crawls, runs, climbs, flies, or slithers in the desert as well as a wondrous display of plants indigenous to this special environment. Some are gorgeous; others almost grotesque. If you've ever wondered what a Boojum tree looks like, this is the place to see one.

Stroll along manicured garden paths to see well-designed, educational exhibits. With the addition of the Earth Sciences Center, the Desert Museum has created an exhibit that mimics the underworld. Through an ingenious display, it opens this little-seen place to visitors. There's even an imitation limestone cave where stalactites and stalagmites "grow."

Another section of the Earth Sciences Center transports you back billions of years to the time when the desert began. Thanks to films, photographs, and maps, this exhibit enables you to understand how this part of the world was formed.

In the earth-science cave, you can follow a loop trail for 75 feet. There is also a mineral exhibit that covers almost every known mineral on earth, from large crystals to ones so tiny they can only be seen through the microscopes provided.

Before you leave the museum grounds, be sure to browse through the gift shop, which is filled with various arts, crafts, and scientific displays.

If you have time to see only one museum in southern Arizona, this is the place to visit. To make your day more enjoyable, try to arrive during the morning so you can observe the creatures when they are most active. (Like all smart residents of the desert, they siesta in the afternoon.) Please leave your pets at home. Temperatures in unventilated vehicles, especially during the summer, can be fatal to animals. Fee. (520) 883-1380. 2021 North Kinney Road, Tucson, 85743-9989.

SAGUARO NATIONAL PARK (WEST)

This is the western (Tucson Mountain) park of Saguaro National Park (see Day Trip 1, East from Tucson for information on the eastern Rincon unit). There are two areas that make up Saguaro National Park: one lies to the east of Tucson, and the other to the west. Both are worth your time.

As you leave the Arizona-Sonora Desert Museum, continue northwest on Kinney Road to the Red Hills Information Center in the Tucson Mountain section of the Saguaro National Park. Pick up a map at the information center, or sightsee from your car by taking the Bajado Loop drive. To do this, continue on Kinney Road until it becomes Golden Gate Road. Follow this road until you see Hohokam Road to your right. Take Hohokam Road south back to where it meets Kinney.

In a recent poll of Arizona's most visited sites, Saguaro National Park (East and West) ranked just behind the Grand Canyon in popularity. While traffic can be slow over Gates Pass, the area is so vast that visitors who choose to get out of the car and hike can always be assured of plenty of "get away" space.

If you aren't walked out from Old Tucson and the Desert Museum, there are several good hiking trails, some of which lead to the 1,429-foot-high **Wasson Peak.**

This section of Saguaro National Park is slightly smaller than the Rincon Mountain area. However, the 21,078 acres contain an unusually dense and vigorous saguaro forest. The cacti, coupled with dramatic foothills and mountain views, make this a favorite photographic and relaxation stop. Although firewood and water are not available in the park, you will find picnic areas, scenic overlooks, and restrooms. At the end of a long day, you may be happy to just drive through and save the hiking for another time. Free. (520) 733-5100.

From Saguaro National Park, it's an easy trip south on Kinney to either Gates Pass Road or Ajo Road to Tucson.

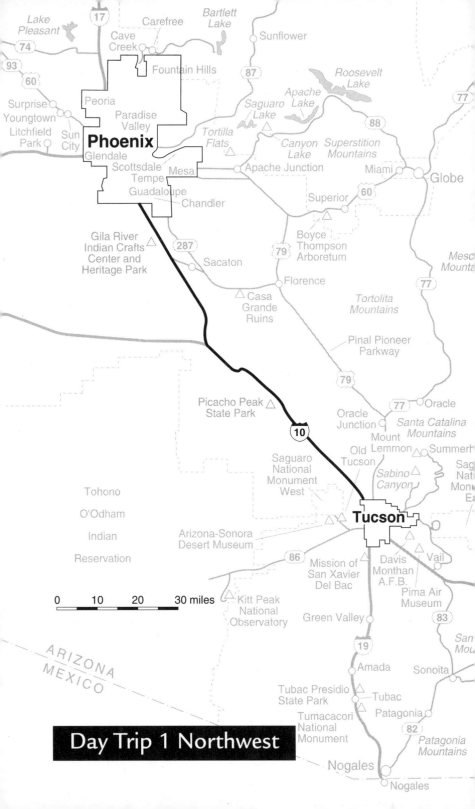

Day Trip 1 Northwest

PHOENIX

From Tucson, follow I-10 northwest to Phoenix. This is an easy freeway drive that takes two or two and a half hours.

Contemporary Phoenix, which is the sixth-largest city in the nation, cherishes its desert, water supply, sunshine, and famous leisure lifestyle. A fine climate translates into the good life. With 3,177,016 acres of city, state, and county parks, federal lands, and freshwater lakes within one hour's drive, play's the thing in Phoenix. Outdoor sports are de rigueur here. People jog, climb, swim, and bike all year long. Everyone who stays comes to appreciate the natural setting. Men who didn't know a maple from an oak tree when they lived "back East" move to Phoenix and become connoisseurs of cactus.

In the old legend, the Phoenix bird spread her wings and rose from the ashes. Today's version stars its own legendary "bird"—the construction crane. The city is growing fast. Some look at the spread-out shape of Phoenix and call it "urban sprawl." Others smile and say that's what they moved west for—space.

Even with all the development, there's plenty of room here. The 13,000-acre South Mountain Park is the largest municipally owned facility in the world. Squaw Peak, the Phoenix Mountain Preserve, and North Mountain Parks each provide many more thousands of recreational acres.

Yet with all its emphasis on the big and the new, Phoenix is equally proud of its beginnings. A former mayor spearheaded the move to restore and dedicate a special section of downtown as Heritage Square. A stretch of freeway leading to Sky Harbor Airport, called the Hohokam, is painted with designs derived from ancient Indian symbols.

As you approach Phoenix, don't be put off by its size. It's an easy town to get around. Washington Street runs east and west and is the zero ("0"), or starting point for all north and south addresses. Central Avenue runs north and south and is the starting point ("0") for east and west addresses. East of Central, the roads are labeled as streets, while west of Central they are called avenues. Keep this in mind and you won't find yourself at Thirty-fifth Avenue looking for a number that is on Thirty-fifth Street.

Stop first at the Phoenix & Valley of the Sun Convention & Visitors Bureau, 1 Arizona Center, 400 East Van Buren, Suite 600, Phoenix, 85004, or call (602) 254-6500. Here you can inquire about accommodations, attractions, special events, and dining and pick up brochures describing these in more detail.

WHERE TO GO

Following is a sample of what Phoenix has in store for visitors. For a more complete listing, read the brochures from the Phoenix & Valley of the Sun Convention & Visitors Bureau.

The Old State Capitol. 1700 West Washington Street. Pick up Washington in downtown Phoenix and follow it directly west to the Capitol Building. There is ample free parking in two large lots on the east side of Seventeenth Avenue. When you park and turn toward the west, you'll be facing the Old Capitol building with its copper dome. Inside is a museum that features an exhibit of territorial and Arizona history and government. You can take either a self-guided or guided tour. This is a recommended trip for people who have a strong interest in the state. Free. Call for tour hours. (602) 542-4675.

Arizona Gem & Mineral Museum. 1502 West Washington. With the restoration of the old El Zaribah Shrine near the Arizona capitol at Fifteenth Avenue and Washington, the Arizona Mineral and Mining Museum acquired a shining new gem in a lustrous old/new setting. Outside, the blue and white structure has been restored to vintage 1922 elegance. Inside, more than 3,000 minerals collected from Arizona and the world are on display. (The collection includes more than 8,000 pieces.) Rockhounds of all ages will find much to marvel at here, and friendly lapidary club volunteers are on site to answer questions. Be sure to visit the separate Governor Rose Mofford room at the museum. The former governor has donated the collection of artifacts and gifts she acquired from her more than four decades of public service. Free. (602) 255-3791.

Heritage and Science Square. Sixth Street and Monroe Street. In this area, you'll find the best of the old, and, with hotels and the convention center looming nearby, the most dazzling of the new that symbolize contemporary Phoenix. The centerpiece of Heritage Square is the **Rosson House,** a restored home built in 1894. With its spires and turrets, it casts a benevolent shadow on downtown. Surrounded by other houses, including the **Silva House, Stevens House,** and **Stevens-Haugsten House,** and topped off with the airy **Lath House,** Heritage Square has become a favorite gathering place for residents and tourists.

As you walk through this charming block of homes, you'll be transported to a gracious time when people slept on open sleeping porches to survive the desert summer and ladies fanned themselves and sipped cool lemonade. A fee is charged to tour the Rosson House, but the others are free of charge. (602) 262-5071.

Arizona Doll and Toy Museum, 602 East Adams. Children and adults will enjoy this constantly changing scenario of dolls and toys from the past and present. An authentic 1912 schoolroom features antique dolls as the "students." Free. Closed August. (602) 253-9337.

Arizona Science Center. 600 East Washington Street. Located in Science and Heritage Square. The museum is the work of famous Albuquerque architect Antoine Predock and is one of the city's newest points of civic pride. Inside find an array of hands-on exhibits geared for preschool to junior high students to explain the natural and man-made world—from health to astronomy, technology to weather. The museum is organized around thoughtful topics such as "Communication" or "All About Me" and contains colorful exhibits on all floors. In addition there are classrooms in the adjoining building as well as a lunch cafe. This is a favorite destination for families, but it is also appealing to adults with or without kids. Another plus is the museum gift shop, Amazing Atom. Visit the Dorrance Planetarium, the first public planetarium in Phoenix, and enjoy the full-size theater that shows IWERKS films. Visitors to the Arizona Science Center can select which programs they want to see and pay for those separately (e.g. museum exhibits, the planetarium or IWERKS). Fee. (602) 716-2000.

The Civic Plaza. 225 East Adams Street. From the Rosson House, you can walk west to the Civic Plaza, which contains the **Phoenix Civic Plaza Convention Center and Symphony Hall.** Both are focal points for business and entertainment for the entire valley. The convention center can host the world's largest conventions, and top-name talent is booked into Symphony Hall throughout the year. Don't miss the elegant life-sized sculptures of dancers on the plaza. These are the work of Arizona artist John Waddell, a nationally acclaimed sculptor. Parking is available under the Civic Plaza complex. For more information on the convention center, call (602) 252-6823. To inquire about events at Symphony Hall, call (602) 262-7272.

Phoenix History Museum. 105 North Fifth Street, located in Heritage and Science Square, at Sixth Street and Monroe. Visit this impressive contemporary-design museum, located in Science and Heritage Square, to learn about the history not only of Phoenix but of the entire Salt River Valley. Well-designed exhibits bring history to life, enabling visitors of all ages to enjoy the collection and understand how the valley grew from its Hohokam beginnings into the modern metropolis it is today. Don't miss seeing the Calendar Stick carved by the last known Pima Carver, Owl Ears. The Pimas carved these sticks to record their history. Fee. (602) 253-2734.

The Phoenix Art Museum. 1625 North Central Avenue, on the corner of Central Avenue and McDowell Road. Long known for its fine collections of both Oriental and Mexican art, the newly remodeled and expanded museum also is home to an impressive collection of western American art. Each October the Cowboy Artists of America ride into Phoenix to hold their annual show and sale at this facility. The museum's permanent collection concentrates on eighteenth- and nineteenth-century American and European art and sculpture. There is a distinguished collection of exquisitely detailed Thorne Miniature Rooms, and the museum is home to the Arizona Costume Institute, which affords the facility an elegant display of period clothing.

This museum underwent extensive renovation in 1995. In addition to the museum's own collection, visitors can view fine traveling exhibitions scheduled throughout the year. Tours led by museum docents are available by special arrangement. The museum shop is a good place to find unusual gift items and art books. Open daily except Monday. Free. (602) 257-1222.

The Heard Museum. 22 East Monte Vista Road. Considered one of the finest anthropological museums in the world, the Heard has an impressive permanent collection, an inspiring audiovisual exhibit, and important traveling shows. All of this excitement is encased in a lovely hacienda-style building that shows off old Phoenix at its best.

Your first stop should be the audiovisual production shown in the Main gallery. Sit on a bench and lose yourself in this thirty-minute experience, "Our Voices, Our Land." As you watch and listen, you'll begin to understand something of the deep relationship that exists between the Indian people and their lands.

After the show, continue through the gallery. There's a time-line on the wall that graphically traces the development of the Southwest from the Paleo-Indian era (c. 1500 B.C.) through the present day. This is the Heard's major exhibit, "Native People of the Southwest, " and it lets you into a special world illustrated by life-sized Hopi, Navajo, and Apache dwellings. The exhibit presents a scholarly and beautiful explanation of the relationship between the environment and Indian culture. For instance, rather than demonstrate how corn is ground, it explains why the Hopis believe that corn is life. This is done through a sensitive blending of art, natural history, and anthropological information.

Next visit the **Kachina Gallery,** which holds a dazzling display of nearly 1,000 Kachina dolls. These hand-carved, hand-painted wooden figurines represent various Hopi religious spirits. You can trace the progression of this important art form from old, crudely carved figures to today's slick, sophisticated statues collectors vie for. Be sure to spend time in the museum's art galleries, as well, where different artists are showcased. On your way out, browse through the spacious gift shop. Here you can find fine works by both established and undiscovered Native American artists. After visiting the Heard Museum, you'll know why this facility is the pride of the entire Southwest. Call for hours. Fee. (602) 252-8848.

Squaw Peak Mountain Park. 2701 East Squaw Peak Drive. Head east on Lincoln Drive to Squaw Peak Drive. Turn left at the light. For a quick desert experience in the heart of the urban scene, drive into Squaw Peak, park, and hike. If you have the inclination, join the crowds who religiously trek up and down the well-marked trail to the summit. The park has many *ramadas,* shelters that offer shady areas for picnicking. Water and restrooms are available. You can call ahead to reserve one of these roofed areas for a large gathering. Since mountain parks are very popular with local residents during the fall, winter, and spring, reserved space is often at a premium.

The trail to the summit is 1.2 miles and is an excellent aerobic exercise as well as a fine social activity. It's a crowded trail. Know that parking spaces can be scarce. The hike up starts at 1,400 feet and climbs to 2,600 feet. There are also excellent trails that circle around Squaw Peak. While these don't offer the strenuous climb, they have the advantage of being more peaceful ways to experience Squaw Peak. Free. (602) 262–4889.

South Mountain Park. 10919 South Central Avenue. Take Central Avenue south to the far end of town, a fifteen- to twenty-minute drive beyond downtown Phoenix. Eventually Central Avenue will curve to the west and you'll approach the park. This more than 13,000-acre mountain range was a gift to the city of Phoenix in the 1920s by a group of farsighted Phoenix boosters including Clare Boothe Luce and Elizabeth Arden. As you enter the park, the ranger at the stone gatehouse will ask you not to bring any glass containers or alcoholic beverages.

Take a scenic drive up to a mountaintop for a thrilling look down at Phoenix, or park your car and walk along the trails. There are many opportunities here for serious biking, walking, or hiking. Picnic facilities and restrooms are plentiful. Free. (602) 495–0222.

The Papago Trail. This route takes you through the heart and soul of the Phoenix metropolitan area. Encompassing miles of picturesque natural desert and studded with outstanding man-made attractions, the Papago Trail links the 1,496-acre Papago Park with the Rio Salado project, which is being developed across the Salt River in Tempe. When that project is complete, it will add 5 miles of linear park paralleling the Salt River.

Within the Papago Trail:

Arizona Historical Society Museum. 1300 North College Avenue. This museum is located at the crossroads of Sixty-eighth Street and Curry. Sixty-eighth Street is called College after it crosses McKellips. A new museum housed in an impressive structure, this contemporary history museum features exhibits on agriculture, tourism, mining, World War II, and other aspects of Arizona's diverse history. A large, outdoor replica of Roosevelt Dam describes how this structure was made and the importance it plays in Arizona life.

The permanent exhibits are exceptional. Start with the "people" who represent those groups who settled the state. Inside are historic rooms, films and outstanding photographs. Be sure to go upstairs to enjoy the "Fair." The main agricultural exhibit is designed to attract and teach children about the important contribution of agriculture. Kids can have a lot of fun answering the questions posed. But so can grownups! This museum will continue adding exhibits as fundraising is complete, so it will always be worth repeat visits. Free. (602) 929-0292 .

Arizona Military Museum. 5636 East McDowell Road in the National Guard Complex. Enter through the main gate of Papago Park Military Reservation. This museum houses the weapons, uniforms, photographs, maps, etc., of Arizona's military history dating from the sixteenth through twentieth centuries. The building served as a prisoner of war camp during World War II. Free. (602) 267-2676.

Desert Botanical Garden. 1201 North Galvin Parkway (next to the Phoenix Zoo in Papago Park). The Desert Botanical Garden presents a living museum of desert plant life and is one of the nation's only informal science centers dedicated to the desert, desert plants, ecology, and conservation. Here are more than 10,000 plants and 3,500 different species of cacti, succulents, trees and flowers, and attendant wildlife. Adults and children should experience the exhibit entitled "Plants and People of the Sonoran Desert." Gardeners will enjoy the Demonstration Garden and the new Desert House, which demonstrates how technology that is available in the 1990s can produce an environmentally pleasing home. There is also a book and gift shop on the grounds.

Be sure to visit the Desert Discovery Trail, the brick-paved path that leads to all trailheads and facilities. This will take you to the Cactus House and Succulent House. The Plants & People of the

Sonoran Desert Trail is a one-third mile, hands-on trail that illustrates how Sonoran Desert plants have been used by people for centuries to provide food, fiber, and shelter. The Sonoran Desert Nature Trail is a one-quarter mile trail which is somewhat steep. It affords panoramas of the distant mountains as well as close-up views of the desert butte which is the backdrop for this special garden. The fourth trail, the Center for Desert Living, showcases desert landscaping displays, vegetable gardens, herb gardens and the Desert House exhibits. Fee. (602) 941-1217.

Hall of Flame. 6101 East Van Buren. Turn south on Project Drive from Van Buren to see the world's largest display of firefighting equipment. More than one hundred pieces are in this private collection including hand-to-hand, horse-drawn, and mechanized firefighting equipment dating from 1725 to 1955. Fee. (602) 275-3473.

Papago Park. This 1,200-acre desert island gets its red color from iron oxide-hematite. Formed six to fifteen million years ago, this is a sedimentary formation and among the oldest exposed rock found anywhere in the state. You can wander 13 miles of hiking and biking trails, fish the Urban Fishing Waters, climb to Hole-in-the-Rock, or play golf at the public course within the park. Full picnic facilities are available. Free. (602) 262-6111.

Papago Park, Tempe. Curry Road and College Avenue. This 296-acre park is contiguous with the Phoenix Papago Park. In addition to natural desert and picnic facilities, there are a softball field, Frisbee, golf course, lake/lagoon, playground, and nature trail. Free. (602) 350-5200.

The Phoenix Zoo. 455 North Galvin Parkway. Rated as one of the ten top zoos in the country, this 125-acre zoo presents more than 1,400 animals including 200 endangered species. Special exhibits not to be missed are the African Savanna, Arizona Trail, Sumatran tigers, and Tropical Flights. Even grown-ups will be wowed by the Phoenix Zoo, where giraffes gambol freely in a natural grassy setting framed by the Papago Buttes.

The Children's Zoo is self-contained. There are complete food and beverage facilities, gift shop, and shaded picnic areas available. Strollers and wheelchairs may be rented, and the Zoo Train offers a convenient way to cover the vast grounds. Fee. Open daily. Summer hours, May 1 through Labor Day, 7:00 A.M. to 4:00 P.M. (602) 273-1341.

Pueblo Grande Museum and Cultural Park. 4619 East Washington. Art and architecture have ancient histories as **Pueblo Grande Museum and Cultural Park** in East Phoenix reminds. This in-town Indian ruin is replete with platform mound and remnants of an ancient canal as well as a small but charming museum of artifacts and art. The discovery of the ruin and subsequent park development prompted Phoenix to hire an archaeologist on city staff, the first city in the country to do so.

Occupied from A.D. 500 through A.D. 1450, Pueblo Grande was an important village that sported a ball court, homes, ceremonial mound, and canals. The canals and platform mound can be visited on the grounds. Permanent and rotating exhibits inside the museum describe the art and culture of the Hohokam and other prehistoric Indians. Fee. (602) 495-0901.

Red River Opry. 730 North Mill Avenue. Take Curry Road west to Mill Avenue and turn left. It's on the corner. The Opry stages live variety shows featuring country music, comedy, and nostalgia. Fee. Call for show times. (602) 829-OPRY.

Salt River Project History Center. 1521 Project Drive. Off the main lobby of the Salt River Project Administration Building. A small but well-designed museum describes the history of irrigation and water in the Phoenix Valley. Artifacts are displayed, and video presentations run to explain the Hohokam Civilization and Roosevelt Dam.

Tempe Arts Center. First Street and Mill Avenue. Here are 12,000 square feet of sculpture gardens and a large public gallery. Free public exhibitions are featured and musical performances are staged. Free. (602) 968-0888.

WHERE TO EAT

Phoenix offers every type of cuisine—from Mongolian and Mexican to Thai and elegant continental. Ask anyone in Phoenix to name a favorite dining spot and you'll get a different answer. All of the major resorts also offer fine dining. Here are a few local favorites:

Eddie's Grill. 4747 North Seventh Street. Eddie is one of the Valley's most inventive chefs who blends Southwest cooking with his own creative style. Eddie's Grill is a local favorite and the decor of the restaurant adds to the fun. $$-$$$; (CC). (602) 241-1188.

Windows on the Green. The Phoenician Resort, 6000 East Camelback Road, Scottsdale. One of the finest restaurants in the city, the menu features unique dishes such as ostrich with blueberry sauce. The creative menu is superbly prepared and always outstanding and the ambience, overlooking the green fairways of the Phoenician Resort, is one of the best in the Valley. $$$; (CC). (602) 423-2530.

Eddie's Grill at the Phoenix Art Museum. 1625 North Central Avenue. A terrific cafe featuring some of Chef Eddie's best cuisine in the elegance of the Phoenix Art Museum but with the convenience of fast food service. A great place for lunch when you are doing the Phoenix downtown museums. $$$; (CC). (602) 257-2191.

Los dos Molinos. 8646 South Central Avenue. Authentic Mexican fare—pronounce that VERY HOT—served in a unique hacienda setting in South Phoenix. Very much worth the trip for those who love true Mexican food. Since there is usually a wait for seating, plan to visit the gallery on the grounds. See their other location in Mesa. $-$$; (CC). (602) 243-9113.

Roxsand. 24th Street and Camelback in Biltmore Fashion Park. Southwest gourmet cuisine served in great style is Roxsand's trademark. She also does outstanding vegetarian fare. $$-$$$; (CC). (602) 381-0444.

Rustler's Rooste. 7777 South Pointe Parkway at South Mountain. (That silent "e" on "Rooste" tells you that this is one of The Pointe's resort centers.) There's a slide for those who choose to use it that deposits you into the restaurant. The specialty here is hearty western fare, especially barbecued items. It's all a mite corny, but it's a good place to see city lights twinkling over the desert. $$-$$$; (CC). (602) 431-6474.

Vincent Guerithault on Camelback. 3930 East Camelback Road. Vincent has joined the rare list of fine American chefs whose specialties feature native ingredients with superior and artistic presentation. One of Arizona's most outstanding restaurants, Vincent is open for lunch and dinner. Reservations are suggested. The atmosphere is elegant yet relaxing; the food is outstanding. $$$; (CC). (602) 224-0025.

WORTH MORE TIME: MARANA

Rocky Mountain Cattle Moo-vers. 8100 Tangerine Road, Marana, 85653. This Colorado-based company offers "City Slicker" cattle drives October through May in Arizona. (The same service is available in Phoenix, near the Sun City West area, beginning mid-October 1997.)

The Cattle Moo-vers experience is available to all levels of riders, novice to experienced. Would-be cowboys can choose from a combination of all day or half-day cattle drive or jeep tours. Although the company caters to tours, individuals can reserve space by calling at least 24 hours ahead to join the drive rounding up Mexican Corriente steers.

Experienced riders have an opportunity to ride off the trail and help work the cattle. In addition to the ride, the company offers New England clambakes in the desert, jeep tours, rodeos and cowboy entertainment. Visitors also have a choice of riding a haywagon instead of four-legged critters. $$-$$$; (CC). (520) 628-2088 or (800) 826-9666.

Flagstaff

With Flagstaff as your base (see Day Trip 4, North from Phoenix), the entire northern third of Arizona is open to you. You'll see wonders of the ancient world such as the Grand Canyon, the quiet beauty of lakes and forests, and remote Indian villages whose inhabitants live very much as their ancestors did hundreds of years ago.

As you plan your trips, remember that northern Arizona is different from the southern and central sections of the state. During the winter, snowstorms can rush in quickly, covering the highways and turning an easy drive into a snowy challenge. If you're planning a visit during the fall, winter, or early spring, phone ahead to check the weather.

In summer, temperatures around Flagstaff remain moderate, with warm days and cool evenings. But as you travel into the high desert areas of the northeastern section of the state or to the far western border near California, you're back in the sizzling heat. In these areas, don't forget to carry water in your car and be prepared for high temperatures.

The following trips are planned to include a maximum amount of sightseeing in a minimum of time. For northern Arizona, stretch your time limit for a day trip from two to four or even five driving hours one way. Many of these trips are better done in tandem—doing one trip one day and picking up the following trip the next day without heading back to Flagstaff. Combining trips cuts the driving distance and lets you maximize out-of-the-car time.

However, if you don't have a weekend or can't string a couple of days together, relax. You can make each of these a separate overnight experience as long as you're prepared to go the distance to get back to Flagstaff.

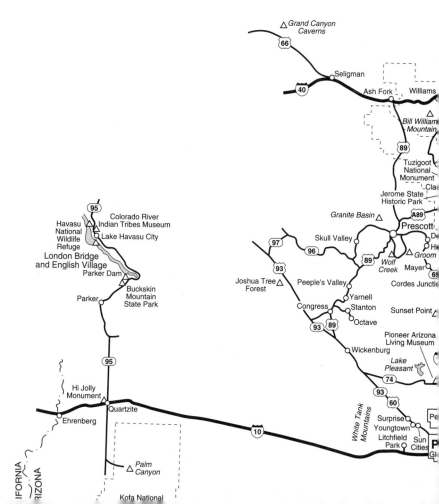

Grand Ca
National

G

Tusay

Grand Canyon
Caverns

66

Seligman

40   Ash Fork   Williams

Bill William
Mountain

89

Tuzigoot
National
Monument

Cla

Jerome State
Historic Park

95   Granite Basin △   A89

Havasu   Colorado River   Prescott
National   Indian Tribes Museum
Wildlife   Lake Havasu City   De
Refuge   97   Skull Valley   H
London Bridge   96   Groom
and English Village   89   Mayer
Parker Dam   Wolf   69
93   Creek
Buckskin   Cordes Junctio
Mountain   Joshua Tree △   Peeple's Valley
Parker   State Park   Forest
Yarnell
Congress   Stanton   Sunset Point
93   89   Octave
Pioneer Arizona
Living Museum
95   Wickenburg
Lake
Pleasant
Hi Jolly   74
Monument
93
Ehrenberg   Quartzite   60
Surprise   Pe
10   Youngtown
Litchfield   Sun
IFORNIA   Park   Cities
RIZONA   Gl
△ Palm   P
Canyon
Kofa National

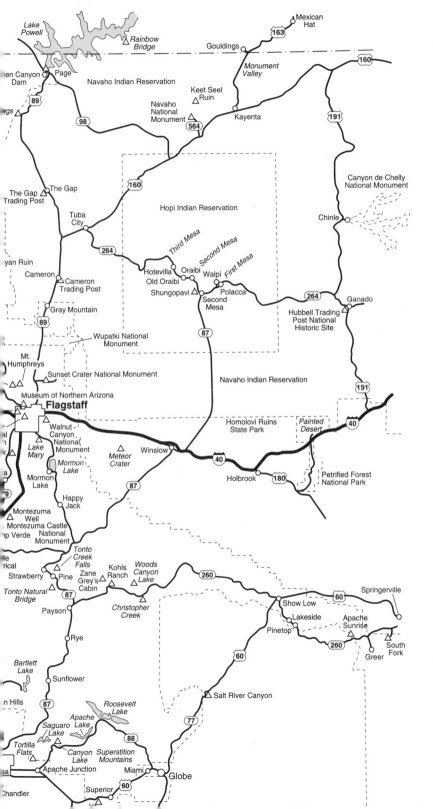

One last piece of advice: This vast area is sparsely inhabited. You are wise to carry some food in the car, as well as water, soft drinks, or juice. Clean, well-equipped rest stops are often few and far between, so when you see a decent-looking gas station, you should stop if your tank is below two-thirds full or somebody needs to use a restroom. Often you won't see another gas station for miles. Forewarned, you shouldn't get caught in the wilds.

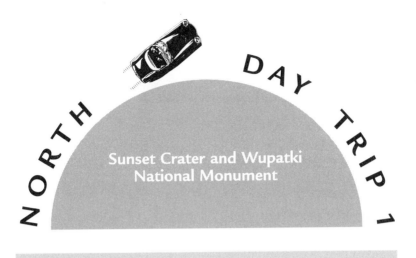

SUNSET CRATER AND WUPATKI NATIONAL MONUMENT

From Flagstaff, head north on this scenic drive to enjoy past treasures.

Scenic Drive

Volcanoes and Ruins Loop. The complete tour will take two to three hours and cover 70 miles. Drive 12 miles northeast on US–89 to the Sunset Crater-Wupatki turnoff. Turn east (right). It's about 36 miles around this road back to US–89 and then 22 miles back to Flagstaff. The road passes through the most recently active portion of the San Francisco volcano fields that surround the city. The last eruption occurred around A.D. 1250, but wounds heal slowly in an arid land, so much of the area looks as if it had been fuming and spurting just yesterday.

During this excursion, plan to stop at the visitor centers at both Sunset Crater and Wupatki.

Sunset Crater National Monument is a 1,000-foot-high historic cone. Here you will find strange rivers of lava that erupted 900 years ago that look as though they happened yesterday. There are many trails to hike along and explore; visitors, however, are asked to stay on the trails and not forge their own. The lava flow is brittle and can

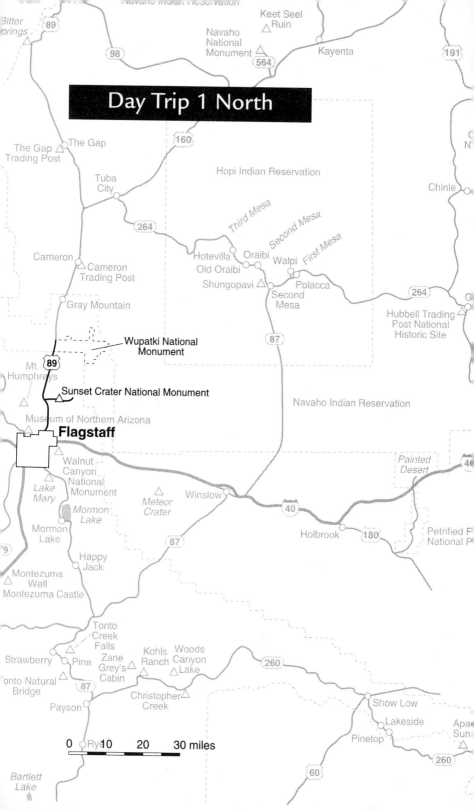

Day Trip 1 North

be damaged easily. John Wesley Powell, who was the first man to successfully run the Colorado River, named Sunset Crater for the red-orange hue that is found near its peak. This is a strange and eerie landscape, but one that is well worth a visit. Fee. (520) 556-7042.

Wupatki National Monument. These well-preserved Indian ruins are the remains of structures built by the Sinagua Indians. The Sinagua were prosperous traders and farmers who left behind 35,000 acres of prehistoric ruins containing apartment houses, ball courts, and artifacts. The ball court is considered very rare by archaeological standards.

There is a Park Service Station and Interpretive Center that explains the history and geology of the area. Self-guided trails make it easy to stroll among these structures and understand the significance of the sites. Fee. (520) 556-7040. From Wupatki, return to Flagstaff on US-89.

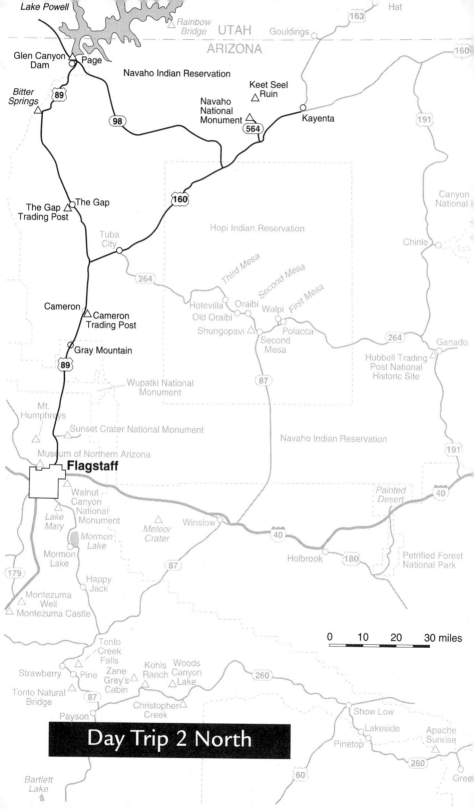

Day Trip 2 North

PAGE AND GLEN CANYON DAM

From Flagstaff go north on US-89 to Page and Lake Powell. You may want to plan to spend the night at Lake Powell before going on to the Navajo National Monument. You can also pick up the Northeast day trip at Kayenta or stay overnight in Page, then go on to Navajo National Monument the next morning and pick up the Northeast day trip at Kayenta. Taking two days to see Lake Powell and Navajo National Monument allows ample time to explore, visit Page and Lake Powell and tour Navajo National Monument. If you have only one day to cover this, you'll drive through Page, see Lake Powell from the shore, and take a fast trip to the Navajo National Monument. But cramming all this into one day will leave you hungry for more.

As you proceed north on US-89 from Flagstaff, you'll pass the tiny hamlet of **Gray Mountain.** Here you enter the vast expanse of the Navajo Indian Reservation. Summer travelers need to move their watches ahead one hour: while Arizona doesn't observe daylight saving time, the Navajo Nation does. This time change can be confusing and even frustrating if you aren't forewarned. You don't want to plan to arrive somewhere by 5:00 P.M. only to find that it's 6:00 P.M. and you've missed what you want to see.

Eight miles north of Gray Mountain on US-89, you'll see the **Cameron Trading Post,** the first of a number of Indian trading posts in this region. Cameron is actually a complex of buildings made of lovely native stone and wood. Discover a treasure trove of

229

items—some exquisite, others tourist trinkets. There's also food service in a lovely, spacious dining room as well as some very nice overnight accommodations. Don't miss the display of Navajo weavings inside the trading post.

After leaving Cameron, the highway crosses the Little Colorado River, one of the major tributaries of the Colorado River. Another 31 miles up the road you'll come to a second famous trading post, **The Gap.** Both Cameron and The Gap played important roles in opening the Arizona Territory. Trading posts helped to establish an economy that benefited both the white and Indian societies. To today's casual observer these places appear to be scenic tourist stops, but they aren't. Years ago trading posts were lifelines for the Indians and traders who depended upon them. The Indians traded rugs, jewelry, and other handcrafted items for groceries and needed supplies. Occasionally, a Navajo man or woman would pawn a prized piece of jewelry for money, and the trader would keep the item until the owner could redeem it. Some owners never were able to get their heirlooms back, and "pawn jewelry," cherished by collectors, eventually was sold.

With a full day facing you, unless you need to stop, push on and explore these posts another day. Page and the wonders of Lake Powell await.

At Bitter Springs US–89 bends east. Continue on US–89 to Page. Like all towns built to support generating plants, this community owes its life to power and glory—the power of Glen Canyon Dam and the glory of the Grand Canyon. The dam was built in the 1950s; the canyon has been under construction for millions and millions of years.

Glen Canyon Dam was constructed at a cost of $260 million, a hefty sum, especially when you consider that to replace that plant today would cost $800 million. It was October 15, 1956, when President Dwight D. Eisenhower pushed a button on his desk in the White House 2,100 miles away to set off the first blast. Four years later, June 17, 1960, the last of 4,901,000 cubic yards of concrete was poured. The resulting dam, a 583-foot-high wall, holds back the second-largest man-made lake in North America. (Lake Mead, also formed by the Colorado River, is the largest.) Glen Canyon conserves water from a 246,000-square-mile watershed, provides electricity for the Pacific Southwest and the Rocky Mountain areas, and gives Page a reason for being.

A small, friendly community dedicated to tourism and electricity,

Page was first staked out as a temporary government construction camp in 1957. It was named for the first commissioner of the Reclamation Service established under President Theodore Roosevelt. Since then, the town has thrived. There are a busy airport, visitor center, museum, library, and eleven churches side by side on just one street. (Two other churches are located elsewhere in town.)

Near Page, US-89 climbs, and you'll get your first view of Glen Canyon Dam below. Behind it, the magical blue world of Lake Powell spreads out, improbably set into a rocky abyss of this far-eastern section of the Grand Canyon. Lake Powell is renowned throughout the world for its astonishing beauty, and no tourist yet has been disappointed by the views.

Just outside of Page visitors will often find Navajo artists selling their wares. It's fun to stop and browse and even shop. Often you can meet the artists who are happy to describe the work to you. While it's fine to bargain with them, if you want to take a picture of the artists, always ask permission first. If you do take their photograph, and don't purchase anything, it's good form to leave a "thank you" in the form of a tip.

WHERE TO GO

Glen Canyon Dam and Carl Hayden Visitor Center. On US-89. This is a highly recommended stop. In the visitor center, an illustrated history depicts the construction and use of the dam. If you have time, watch the audiovisual program. If not, at least browse through the easy-to-follow displays, which reveal fascinating details about the dam. You can easily spend thirty minutes in the Carl Hayden Visitor Center. If you have time, take the guided tour of the generating plant given almost every hour. Visitors can also tour the dam on their own. They are taken from the crest of the dam down one of three elevators into the power plant where they can see the inner workings of the turbines and understand how this dam delivers power to much of the western United States. Nearly an hour in length, the tour is not strenuous; you'll walk about a third of a mile. It's a cool fifty degrees Fahrenheit down under, so bring a wrap. Free. (520) 645-2511.

The Page Visitor Center/Museum. 6 Lake Powell Boulevard. Continue north on US-89 until you see a sign for the business district of Page. Follow the signs. Drive over the bridge and take Lake Shore Boulevard to the Chamber of Commerce and Visitor Center and Museum, all located in one building. Check with the visitor center for additional information on the area, and then take a quick trip through the museum, which is filled with artifacts and memorabilia commemorating John Wesley Powell and his expeditions.

Major Powell is acknowledged as the first explorer of the Colorado River and the Grand Canyon. A Civil War veteran, he lost his right arm at Shiloh before setting out on this expedition. The thirty-five-year-old adventurer first conquered the Colorado in 1869, settling in at Green River, Wyoming. He went back in 1871 and did the trip again. Thanks to his meticulous personal journal, generations of "river rats" (people who run the rapids in the Grand Canyon) and canyon and river enthusiasts relive his experiences and can identify with his thought-provoking impressions. Free. (520) 645-4095.

Wahweap Lodge and Marina. Four and a half miles from Glen Canyon Dam on US-89 northwest of Page. Turn right at the sign for the marina (the only way you can turn) onto a paved road that leads to Wahweap. One of four marinas on Lake Powell, Wahweap (pronounce Waa-weep) is the most accessible for tourists. Here you'll find overnight accommodations, fine dining, a gift shop, and a host of tours and adventures. Even if you don't plan to spend the night or eat at Wahweap, you'll want to stroll through the lodge to lose yourself in the views of the lake. Lake Powell is a complete recreational wonderland—the fishing is great, the views better, and the deep, cool, blue water and the out-of-the-way beaches are the best. Other lakes in Arizona may be closer to major cities or have more sandy beaches, but only Lake Powell, with its fjords and inlets, scallops and gulleys, wrapped in a golden desert sun, comes so close to perfection.

WHAT TO DO

There's so much to do in this area that you can spend a week or an entire season at Lake Powell. In addition to the trips listed below you can rent a personal watercraft with a top speed of 35 mph. The Tigershark is easy to ride with a jet drive. While it is not inexpensive to rent, the thrills are worth it. All of the trips listed below depart from Wahweap. Even if you can only squeeze in a two-hour excursion, do so. You'll see the lake from the shore, but you can only *experience* its mystic setting when you're on it and surrounded by its sandy, sculpted mountains. To make reservations for boat tours or accommodations, or to inquire about adventures in the area, contact Del E. Webb Recreational Properties, Box 29040, Phoenix, 85038, or call (800) 528-6154 toll free or (602) 278-8888 if calling from Phoenix.

Here is a sampling of the cruises you can take on the lake:

The Canyon King. Make arrangements at Wahweap Lodge and Marina, where the boats depart. Treat yourself to a ride on the only genuine paddle wheeler operating west of the Rockies, or enhance this experience with a sunset/moonlight dinner cruise. *The Canyon King* ferries 150 guests at a time and is closed December–March for maintenance. You can also make special arrangements for large groups or parties through Del E. Webb Recreational Properties, Box 29040, Phoenix, 85038. Fee. (520) 645-2433.

All-Day and Half-Day Rainbow Bridge Tour. Both tours leave from Wahweap Marina. The half-day involves a five-hour trip; the all-day allows for more side channel cruising. You'll depart from Wahweap in the early morning and follow the main channel of Lake Powell to Rainbow Bridge. This natural wonder literally fills the sky as you approach the docking area. You can read the dimensions, but the size of the stone arch will still astound you. The dome of the United States Capitol building could fit underneath it. After your boat docks, there's a short hike to get to the base of the bridge. Be sure to read the inspiring commemorative plaque.

Glen Canyon Dam was built over strong environmental objections. People grieved over the flooding of Glen Canyon, which John Wesley Powell considered one of the most beautiful areas in the Grand Canyon. They feared what traffic would do to fragile places like Rainbow Bridge. The dam did doom the canyon to a watery death, but the trade-off was Lake Powell, a shimmering body of water that dances between the intricate, spidery spires and rolling sandstone mountaintops. Neither the water nor the exposed desert canyon seem aware of the other's presence. You'll see the two worlds of lake and land meeting but not merging.

Since the dam was built and Lake Powell formed, more people see Rainbow Bridge each month than had ever seen it before the dam was built. But so far, visitors are considerate, and the area surrounding the bridge appears to be surviving well. Fee. For more information contact Del E. Webb Recreational Properties, Box 29040, Phoenix, 85038. (520) 645-2433.

The Navajo Tapestry Cruise. This short excursion on Lake Powell (two and one-half hours) gives travelers a fast but true flavor of this wonderland. You leave from Wahweap Lodge and the boat glides between the walls of Antelope Canyon, cruises through Navajo Canyon (from which the cruise takes its name), and then returns via Antelope Island, Warm Creek, and Castle Rock Strait. This is a brief, but intensely satisfying way to see Lake Powell. Fee. Contact ARA Leisure Services, Box 56909, Phoenix, 85079. (800) 528-6154 or (602) 278-8888.

Houseboating. Enjoy the water for a couple of days and nights or stay a week on a well-equipped, luxurious floating house. The best speeds for a houseboat are "slow" and "stopped," so wise houseboaters dock their boats at secluded coves early on and use a speedboat to water ski and explore the thousands of skinny little canyons that lead from the main body of the lake. With 1,900 miles of shoreline to choose from, you can houseboat on Lake Powell repeatedly and never explore the same spot twice. Be prepared to get lost on Lake Powell. Most first-timers do, but keep reading your maps and you'll come out fine. During the height of the summer season, you'll need to reserve a houseboat far in advance. This is an ideal family experience. For price information and availability, contact ARA Leisure Services, Box 56909, Phoenix, 85079. Fee. (800) 528-6154 or (520) 278-8888.

Colorado River Float. Departs from the Page Museum, 6 Lake Powell Boulevard. For would-be river runners who don't like white-water craziness, a float trip provides the ideal alternative. You'll float for a day through the polished splendor of Marble Canyon, stop for lunch on the bank, and see ancient petroglyphs from the canyon floor. After the 15-mile float trip, you'll feel as if you've "done" the Colorado. This is great fun for families with young children and anyone who wants the see the Grand Canyon the most scenic way—from the bottom up. Fee. Inquire about float trips by calling (800) 528-6154, (520) 278-8888, or (520) 645-3279 at Wahweap.

Page Loop Trail. Mountain bikers can have a blast on this 10-mile loop that is partly single track and rough four-wheel drive road.

Beginning riders can complete the loop in about two hours with an occasional dismount for the more difficult sections. Experienced riders can do it in about one hour. There's also a three hour ride that incorporates a detour to enjoy the slickrock. This is recommended for experienced riders only. The trail begins at the Nature Trail at the north end of Page near Lake View School. Free.

Gunsmoke Theater. At The Dam Bar & Grille. 644 North Navajo. Definitely corny—but fun, this attraction is billed as an all-American music show. The Gunsmoke features country western performers and celebrity impersonators. The "greats" are all here — from Elvis to Willie and Dolly. The ticket price includes a prime rib or chicken dinner and the show. All seats are reserved so call in advance; this is a popular destination for tour buses. Performances take place June through September. $$. (520) 645-1888.

WHERE TO EAT

The Dam Bar & Grille. 644 North Navajo. Trendy and fun by any standards, this restaurant is Page's most upscale spot. Find casual dining, a great bar and wonderful historic photographs of when Glen Canyon Dam was constructed. Notice the etched glass "mural" that is dedicated to the water and power theme. This is a popular gathering spot for locals and visitors. $-$$. (520) 645-2161.

Wahweap Lodge. Wahweap Marina, Lake Powell. The main dining room has a dazzling view of the lake. At night the room shimmers with elegance, and by day you can gaze out on the blue expanse. The specialty is prime rib, but the menu is varied and well prepared. Ask about the daily specials. $$; (CC). (520) 645-2433.

WHERE TO STAY

Wahweap Lodge. Wahweap Marina, Lake Powell. The rooms are large and spacious, but if you aren't on the ground floor, be prepared to tote your own luggage up the stairs. You can reserve rooms at the Lake Powell Motel, get a housekeeping unit, or rent space for a camper or RV through the central reservation service. While the views and locations are excellent, the rooms, while spacious, are basic "motel"—not exciting but clean and comfortable. Contact ARA

Leisure Services, Box 56909, Phoenix, 85079, or call (800) 528-6154
or (520) 278-8888.

The Holiday Inn. 287 North Lake Powell Boulevard in Page. This
is right up the street from the Page Chamber of Commerce/visitors
center/museum building. Although not on the lake, the motel units
are quite nice. Call (520) 645-8851.

Note: In the past few years a number of excellent new hotels have
been built that serve all price ranges.

NAVAJO NATIONAL MONUMENT

When you're ready to push on another 88 miles, leave Lake Powell
and drive southeast on A-98 for 66 miles to US-160. At the junction,
head northeast on US-160 toward Kayenta. Twelve miles farther,
you'll see a sign for A-564. Turn left and follow it north for 9 miles.

This drive will take about two hours, during which time you'll
cross the Navajo Indian Reservation, an often desolate landscape.
Watch for the Navajo hogans, low, round houses that many Navajo
families still use as homes. The hogan doorway will always face east,
where the sun rises. When you reach A-564, you'll be on a paved road
leading to Navajo National Monument. This is a collection of three
wonderfully preserved Indian ruins: all that is left of pre-Columbian
communities known as Keet Seel, Betatakin (pronounced
Be-tah-tah-kin), and Inscription House. Remote enough to be off
the beaten tourist track, and romantic, these ruins provide an unusually personal look into the past for travelers who have the stamina and time to go the distance.

As is recommended for all national parks and monuments, your
first stop should be the visitors center. Here you'll get your bearings.
Although this is called the Navajo National Monument, the name
refers to its location on the Navajo Reservation. The remnants of
dwellings are from the Anasazi civilization, a pre-Columbian people
who inhabited this area around 1200 B.C. The exhibits and the slide
program at the center describe the life and items of the Anasazi.
You'll learn about their homes and crops and also get a quick lesson
in the geology of this area. For more information on Navajo National Monument, write HC 71, Box 3, Tonalea, AZ 86044-9704.
Free. (520) 672-2366.

WHERE TO GO

Betatakin. Guided tours are available to this Anasazi cliff dwelling throughout the year. Take an easy walk along Sandal Trail, which leads to an overlook of Betatakin. As you peer into this ruin, you'll sense that these people have left only momentarily and are due to return soon. During the season, June 1 to mid-September, there are three daily tours. After September, there is just one tour a day scheduled.

Betatakin means "house on a ledge," and this cluster of dwellings is literally set into a massive cavern in the canyon wall. The most accessible of the ruins here, Betatakin was constructed and abandoned in two generations between 1250 B.C. and 1300 B.C. The 135 rooms constituted a total community. There's a kiva, or ceremonial chamber, granaries, and living quarters.

Discovered in 1909 by Byron Cummings, a pioneer archaeologist of the Southwest, and John Wetherill, a rancher and trader, Betatakin was made safe for exploration in 1917 by Neil M. Judd of the Smithsonian Institution. The 1-mile round-trip walk from the visitors center takes about an hour. Bring binoculars to see these dwellings from the vantage of the rim. Ranger-guided tours, which descend into the ruin, are limited to twenty people at a time because of the fragility of the area. These excursions take about three hours and involve some strenuous climbing. The canyon is 700 feet deep, equal to a seventy-story building, and the altitude is 7,200 feet, which can be tiring for anyone, even those who are physically fit. Anyone with a heart condition should not attempt this climb. Free.

Inscription House. As of this printing, tours are no longer available. The site is closed for stabilization to make it safe and to prevent erosion under the stress of future exploration and tours.

Keet Seel. Tucked away in a remote canyon 8 miles from the visitors center, Keet Seel is the largest cliff dwelling in the state and can only be reached on foot or on horseback. Either way, it's a strenuous trip, but the journey is well worth the trouble for people who have adventurous hearts, strong legs, and iron seats.

You must make arrangements for this trip with a ranger ahead of time, because visits to Keet Seel are limited to twenty tourists a day. A Navajo family leads tours on horseback to Keet Seel, and if you are up for this rugged trip, be ready for some rough riding. The horses have two speeds: walk and wild gallop. Sure, you'll take a ride on the wild side, but when you reach Keet Seel, you'll forget your soreness and marvel at this extraordinarily well-preserved Anasazi ruin. Make arrangements for this experience at the visitors center. Fee for renting the horse.

From Navajo National Monument you can head south on A-564 to US-160, then south on US-160 to US-89, and US-89 south back to Flagstaff. Or, you can return to Page for the night.

NORTHEAST DAY TRIP 1

Kayenta
Monument Valley, Utah

KAYENTA

Kayenta is located 150 miles northeast of Flagstaff and the trip takes about three hours. Go north on US–89 to its junction with US–160 and continue northeast on US–160 to Kayenta. This is a tiny town by American standards, but it is a major community on the Navajo Reservation.

Be sure to visit the Navajo Nation Cultural Center that is part museum, part gift shop. This is one of the new enterprises of the Navajo Nation Department of Tourism. The arts and crafts and other objects displayed here for sale are authentic and prices are reasonable. The purpose of these centers is to help the Nation support its own craftspeople and artists and they are a visual statement of an aggressive program to help the Navajo Nation expand its economy through tourism.

The center is located at the crossroads of US–160 and US–163 on the northwest corner. Kayenta is the jumping-off point for Monument Valley, your next destination. From Kayenta, turn north on US–163 to Monument Valley and Mexican Hat.

WHERE TO EAT

The Golden Sands Cafe. On US–163 1 mile north of the Kayenta Holiday Inn. Feast on the Golden Sands Navajo taco, a delectable combination of chili and Navajo fry bread. You can choose from two sizes of tacos. The place is a favorite of locals and tourists, and there

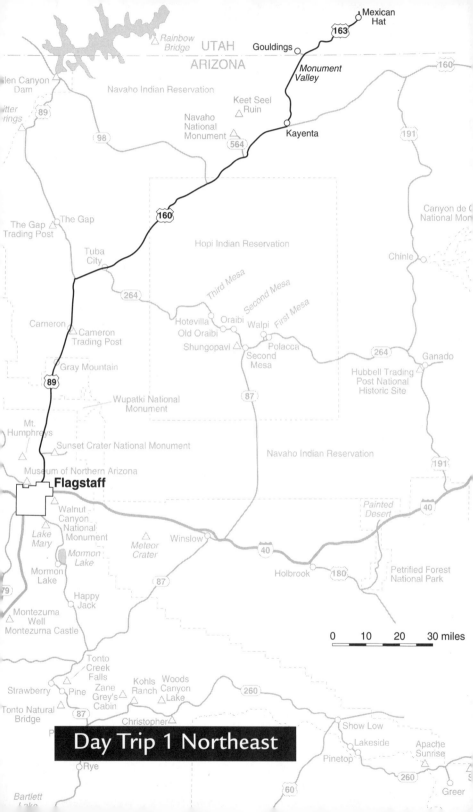

Day Trip 1 Northeast

is usually a collection of pickup trucks in the parking lot. The portions are huge, the prices reasonable, and the atmosphere is authentic Navajo Indian Reservation. $-$$. (520) 697-3684.

WHERE TO STAY

The Holiday Inn, Kayenta. At the junction of US-160 and US-163. You'll find clean, adequate accommodations. Nothing fancy, but considering the remote location, this Holiday Inn offers a surprisingly nice option for travelers. There's even a swimming pool. $$; (CC). (520) 697-3221.

MONUMENT VALLEY, UTAH

From Kayenta, take US-163 north approximately 20 miles. At a crossroads just over the Utah state line, bear right to the Monument Valley Visitors Center. If Salvador Dali had sculpted a landscape, this would be it. Stark spires rise abruptly from the sandy floor, and the rock formations appear to have been dropped onto the flat earth, as if some ancient people flew in from the stars, deposited their rocky cargo, and disappeared.

Monument Valley is not a national park but, rather, a Navajo Tribal park consisting of 29,816 acres owned and managed by the Navajo Tribal Council. The valley was made famous by John Wayne, who starred in many classic westerns that were filmed here.

At the visitors center, you'll see a sign pointing to a 17-mile unpaved scenic loop through the park. You can pick up a brochure inside, which describes a self-guided tour. Along the way there are eleven numbered scenic stops. Although the signs say you can drive your car on this road, think twice before you do so. The road is narrow, rutted, and banked by deep sands. In short, it isn't terrific. Most people prefer to take a guided jeep tour, especially since many of the more spectacular rock formations can be seen only from off the road.

During the summer season, expect high daytime temperatures and long lines to get into the visitors center or the park, but know that it's well worth any inconvenience. In the winter, Monument Valley is often closed because of snow. Fee. (801) 727-3287 or (801) 727-3353.

WHERE TO EAT AND STAY

Gouldings. Six miles west of the visitors center just over the Utah state line off US-163. As you approach Monument Valley, you'll see a cluster of reddish-colored buildings built into the cliff to your left. Gouldings Trading Post complex is a wonderful blend of nostalgia and convenience.

Meals are no longer served family style here, because a new, modern restaurant has been built. While it is efficient, it is less charming than the old, small dining room. The food is adequate and the atmosphere is modern and clean, and the native help is unfailingly pleasant and helpful.

Accommodations are clean and pleasant, and the views are spectacular. There is even a swimming pool—perfect for a dip after a trip out into the sands of Monument Valley.

Be sure to visit the small theater on the property. It shows a breathtakingly beautiful film. The museum is charming and informative and traces the history of Gouldings, which has long been a favorite place for western movie makers. The gift shop offers a nice collection of native-made artifacts.

Even if you are not an early morning person, make a point of getting up to watch a sunrise in Monument Valley. Both day's beginning and end are spectacular sights in this ethereal land of vast spaces and otherworldly rock formations.

And do take a Gouldings open vehicle tour of Monument Valley. Open vehicles are the most pleasant way to tour this impressive place. Guests can take either all day or half day trips. Goulding's guides are well versed in history and lore. If you're up for adventure, you can take a horseback day trip or overnight into Monument Valley with Indian guides. There are two stables in the park to choose from. These trips are not recommended for novice riders. $$; (CC). For reservations or information, P.O. Box 1, Monument Valley, UT 84536. (801) 727-3231.

From here you can retrace your steps to Flagstaff or pick up Day Trip 2, Northeast from Flagstaff. If you have the time, combining these trips can make a marvelous four- to seven-day vacation. *One word of caution:* Outside of Monument Valley enterprising Indians have set up a "village" to display and sell crafts. Buy with caution. Not all of these items are authentic. This is a problem that the Navajo Nation is well aware of and is trying to fix. Examine items carefully, and if you are not certain that a piece is authentic, don't purchase it! Save your money for reputable outlets such as those sponsored by the Navajo Nation or galleries.

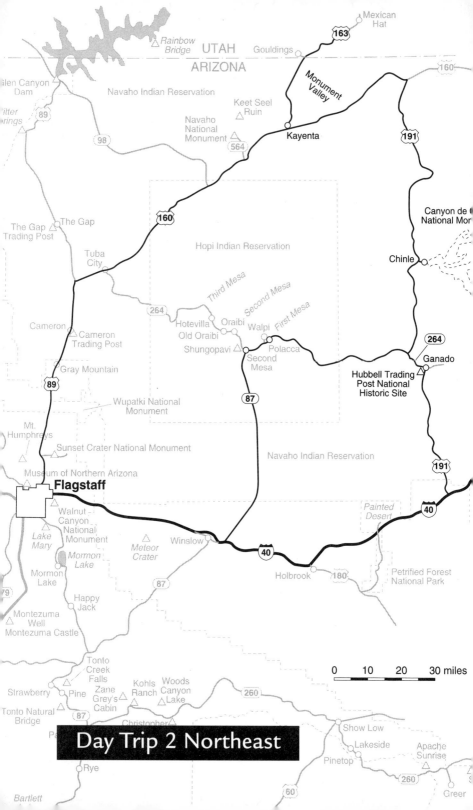
Day Trip 2 Northeast

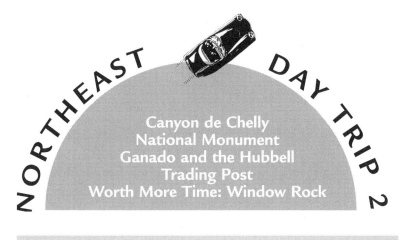

NORTHEAST DAY TRIP 2

Canyon de Chelly
National Monument
Ganado and the Hubbell
Trading Post
Worth More Time: Window Rock

CANYON DE CHELLY NATIONAL MONUMENT

Canyon de Chelly Monument is approximately 135 miles southeast of Monument Valley on Indian Route 64. From Monument Valley, drive south on US-163 to Kayenta. At the junction of US-160 and 163, drive east on US-160 about 40 miles to where US-160 meets US-191. Go south on US-191 for 75 miles to Chinle and the entrance to Canyon de Chelly (pronounced de Shay). To see Canyon de Chelly properly requires at least one overnight if you are coming from Monument Valley and two if Flagstaff is your base.

Canyon de Chelly is quite unlike Monument Valley. Where Monument Valley is stark and golden desert, Canyon de Chelly is pink and warm. It is one of the most appealing of Arizona's canyons. As you enter the canyon on Indian Route 64, you will see the visitors center directly ahead of you.

This park boasts towering sculpted rock formations, sheer and colorful cliffs, and picture-postcard scenery. It is inhabited both by modern-day Indians and memories of ancient ones. The Pueblo Indians, who vanished from this area around A.D. 1350, abandoned their dwellings forever. Their spirit infuses the ruins within the canyon walls. Hundreds of ancient communities, many of them poised on sandstone ledges within colorful caverns, give witness to the earlier vitality of this place.

The Navajos arrived in the area sometime before the eighteenth century. Even today a small enclave of Navajo families lives in modern dwellings on the canyon floor, tends sheep, and grows crops.

WHERE TO GO

Self-guided tours. Pick up brochures describing these tours at the Canyon de Chelly Visitor Center. When walking or driving on the rim, be sure to obey all signs. In places, it's a dizzying 400-foot drop onto the canyon floor.

The walk to White House Ruins is a pleasant hike along a well-marked path. The walk down takes less than an hour. But remember to add extra time to hike back up again! Wear tennis shoes and carry some water.

At the bottom you will cross the sandy wash that, in the winter and spring, can be running. So be prepared to get wet. Once across you can gaze at this well-preserved ruin and imagine what it was like for these prehistoric people to live and farm in this incredible canyon.

Usually a native jeweler is seen here, his blanket laden with rings and bracelets and necklaces that he's made. The prices are good, so if you see something that catches your eye for a reasonable price, don't hesitate to buy it. It could be handmade.

As you drive around this canyon, remember that the best way to see Canyon de Chelly is outside of your car. Many trails beckon. Take advantage of them and enjoy the views. Pay attention to signs and respect the natural site.

Canyon de Chelly is a favorite spot for Native American entrepreneurs, who also sell their wares on the canyon rim. Again, buy with care as not everything you'll see is authentic.

Guided jeep tours. To fully appreciate the geology, history, and anthropology of this exquisite canyon, take a guided half-day or full-day jeep tour. Make arrangements at the Thunderbird Lodge, P.O. Box 548, Chinle, AZ 86503. Unless you have an extensive interest in ancient Indian civilization, the half-day trip is your best bet; a full day could leave you exhausted. In summer, as you bounce along the canyon floor in an open jeep, you may need the protection of sunscreen and a hat. You may even want to take a canteen or thermos with water. Open daily. Fee. (CC). (520) 674-5841 or (520) 674-5842.

WHERE TO EAT

Thunderbird Lodge Motel. On US-191. The food tends to be heavy and starchy, but it's prepared and served by a Navajo staff in a charming building, circa 1896, which was the original trading post. The only dining establishment in the immediate area of the canyon, this is your only choice. Open daily during breakfast, lunch, and dinner hours. $-$$; (CC). (520) 674-5842 or (520) 674-5841.

WHERE TO STAY

Thunderbird Lodge Motel. On US-191. This historic lodge offers the most complete facilities in Navajoland. The rooms are clean and moderately priced, and the location, at the mouth of the canyon, is magnificent. You'll find a gift shop to browse through, and you can make arrangements for tours right at the lodge. Make sure you bring a light jacket or sweater for summer evenings if you visit from April to November. In the winter, you'll need to bundle up. For information, write to Thunderbird Lodge Motel, P.O. Box 548, Chinle, 86503. $$; (CC). (520) 674-5842 or (520) 674-5841.

Canyon de Chelly Motel. As you enter Chinle, south on US-191, turn left at the intersection—the only one in town. Don't depend upon the road signs in this area. Often, if the road is under repair, the signs come down. (Take solace in the fact that Chinle is tiny and you really cannot get lost.) $$$; (CC). (520) 674-5288.

GANADO AND THE HUBBELL TRADING POST

Hubbell Trading Post National Historic Site. One mile west of Ganado. Before returning to Flagstaff from Canyon de Chelly, you can continue south 30 miles on US-191 to the intersection of A-264, then 5 miles east to Ganado and the Hubbell Trading Post National Historic Site. A national treasure, the trading post is worth the visit.

The rug room at the Hubbell Trading Post rivals any museum collection in the world. If you're in the market for a Navajo rug, this is an ideal place to shop. The knowledgeable salespeople will be happy to tell you about the patterns and weavers. The only modern-day touch is that, along with the name of the weaver, you'll also occasionally find a Polaroid photograph of the weaver attached to the ticket. You also can browse through exquisite jewelry, sandpainting, books, and trinkets or even pick up food supplies if you plan to camp in the area. Groceries are sold in the front room.

John Lorenzo Hubbell was the dean of traders for the Navajos, and his trading post continues to act as a bridge between the Indian and Anglo worlds. In its heyday, the post offered a place for Navajos to socialize as well as to conduct business. VIPs of every culture who passed through northeastern Arizona during the late 1800s and early 1900s stopped here. The guest list includes presidents, generals, writers, scientists, and artists.

Today business continues as usual in this elegant pocket of the state. The atmosphere hasn't changed; Navajos and tourists still come by to trade and talk.

Hubbell's career spanned critical years for the Navajos. When he came to the territory to open his trading post, the Indians were adjusting to life on a reservation and were attempting to cope with the restrictions placed upon them by the United States government. Hubbell offered his friendship when great numbers of Navajo were struggling to free themselves from the confines of Fort Sumner in New Mexico. He sympathized with the Navajo and often spoke out on their behalf. When he died in 1930, one of Hubbell's native friends eulogized him at the memorial service saying:

> You wear out your shoes, you buy another pair;
> When the food is gone, you buy more;
> You gather melons, and more will grow on the vine;
> You grind your corn and make bread which you eat;
> And next year you have plenty more corn.
> But my friend Don Lorenzo is gone,
>   and none to take his place.

After browsing through the trading post, walk around the grounds to see the Hubbell home. Limited tours are available and restricted to four tours per day. Free. (520) 755-3254.

From Ganado, there are several ways to return to Flagstaff. The fastest route is US-191 south to I-40. Then head west on I-40 to Flagstaff. Another alternative is to take A-264 west to A-87, turn south on A-87, and then west on I-40 to Flagstaff. Get some sleep at Canyon de Chelly if you plan to head west on A-264 to Polacca for Day Trip 3, Northeast from Flagstaff, after visiting Ganado.

WORTH MORE TIME: WINDOW ROCK

Window Rock. The capitol of the Navajo Nation, Window Rock is worth a visit. The trip to Window Rock will take about two hours from Ganado. The capitol of the Navajo Nation is located about 30 minutes from Gallup, New Mexico. From Hubbell, take US-191 south to A-264 and continue east to Window Rock. In Window Rock visit the Navajo Nation Cultural Center which includes a museum and indoor and outdoor Theatre, and of course, see Window Rock—the rock that gives this town its name.

WHERE TO STAY

Navajo Nation Inn. A-264 and A-12. This very well-equipped modern inn has excellent amenities including a good dining room that features some traditional Navajo dishes. The rooms are bright and immaculate; the ambience is distinctly Navajo and very comfortable. The Inn also offers individual and family tours of the area. The only drawback is the gift shop. It is surprisingly inadequate for an inn that draws so much traffic. However, the Navajo Nation Cultural Center is well within walking distance and here you'll find a superb display of all Navajo arts and crafts. Prices are fair (don't expect bargains!), but both the quantity and quality are good. $$; (CC). (800) 662-6189 or (520) 871-4108.

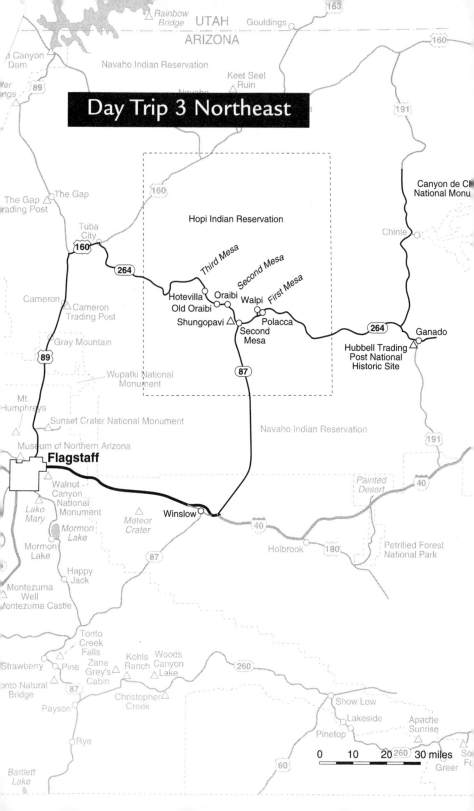

Day Trip 3 Northeast

UTAH
ARIZONA

Rainbow Bridge

Gouldings

163

160

Navaho Indian Reservation

Keet Seel Ruin

191

n Canyon Dam

89

Canyon de C National Monu

The Gap Trading Post

The Gap

160

Hopi Indian Reservation

Chinle

Tuba City

160

264

Third Mesa

Second Mesa

First Mesa

Hotevilla
Old Oraibi

Oraibi

Walpi

Cameron

Cameron Trading Post

Shungopavi

Polacca

Second Mesa

264

Ganado

Gray Mountain

89

Wupatki National Monument

87

Hubbell Trading Post National Historic Site

Mt. Humphreys

Navaho Indian Reservation

191

Sunset Crater National Monument

Museum of Northern Arizona

Flagstaff

Walnut Canyon National Monument

Painted Desert

40

Lake Mary

Meteor Crater

Winslow

40

Petrified Forest National Park

Mormon Lake

Mormon Lake

Happy Jack

Holbrook

180

Montezuma Well
Montezuma Castle

Tonto Creek Falls

87

Kohls Ranch

Woods Canyon Lake

Strawberry

Pine

Zane Grey's Cabin

260

nto Natural Bridge

87

Christopher Creek

Show Low

Payson

Lakeside

Apache Sunrise

Rye

Pinetop

Bartlett Lake

0   10   20 260 30 miles

60

So Fr

Greer

INDIAN COUNTRY

This is a wonderful trip that shouldn't be rushed. Because of the great distances in this part of the state, visiting more remote areas means stretching your usual day trip time limit.

As you plan, consider that the Hopi Reservation roads found in this sector are often narrow, two-lane byways. You won't make fast time, so add another hour to your excursion limit.

You can begin the trip in Flagstaff, heading east on I-40 to Winslow and picking up the turn-off for A-87 north 3 miles east of there. Follow A-87 north for 65 miles to Second Mesa on the Hopi Indian Reservation, then turn right (east) for 7 miles and actually start at Polacca on First Mesa.

A better option might be to combine this trip with Day Trip 2, previously described. Time permitting, you will enjoy this journey more if you can begin it refreshed after a good night's sleep at Canyon de Chelly. After driving 30 miles south to Ganado and stopping at the Hubbell Trading Post (see Day Trip 2, Northeast from Flagstaff), head west on A-264 to Polacca.

If you look at a map, you'll see that the Hopi (pronounced Ho-pee) nation is plunked down in the middle of the vast Navajo Reservation. Although they live in close proximity, the Hopi and the Navajo couldn't be more different. Historically the Hopi, whose ancestors are the Anasazi, have been pueblo dwellers—homebodies content to build permanent villages and cement family ties. The Navajo, in contrast, are nomadic farmers and sheepherders. In fact, the word "hopi" means "the peaceful ones," and traditionally these people have led a peaceful agrarian life.

The windswept mesas of the Hopi Reservation have long been a source of inspiration to the Hopi and non-Indians alike. As you drive through this reservation on A-264, you'll feel a subtle pull, the magic that makes life in the fast track seem ridiculous. At first, the landscape seems barren, but look again. Everywhere you will see corn growing, even in the most improbable corners of backyards and in the rockiest soil. To the Hopi, corn represents life, and they cherish this food for its nutritional and spiritual values.

If this is your first trip to the Hopi Reservation, or Hopi, as it is more commonly called, you may wonder where the ancient villages are. Etched against the horizon, high on flattened mountaintops, the tiny pueblos jut against the sky like jack-o-lantern teeth. Although the Hopi have lived here for hundreds of years, they do not intrude upon Mother Earth. They live gently and inconspicuously, coaxing life from this rocky soil they call their land.

All but one of the villages you may visit are located on or near the areas called First, Second, and Third mesas. The names refer to the chronological shift of the Hopi population from A.D. 1500 to A.D. 1900. First the Hopi settled in Walpi (the area now known as First Mesa), and they gradually moved westward to Oraibi and Hotevilla.

Life goes on here, in many instances as it always has, with families living in ancient pueblo dwellings high on treeless cliffs. Some villagers have moved down from the mesa, spending most of the year in modern, government-built housing at the foot of the mountains. These Hopi go back to the old village only for festivals and holidays.

During the year, Hopi dances are frequently held on the mesas. These ceremonies are often open to the public. To inquire when public dances are scheduled, call the Hopi Cultural Center at (520) 734-2401. If you decide to plan a visit during a dance, understand that the Hopi do not share our Anglo clock fetish. Dances begin when they begin—no sooner, no later. They end when they are over. This can be one hour or six hours. Indians have a totally different concept of time. Bring patience, a chair, and a warm blanket or heavy jacket. Above all, *do not bring cameras.* Picture taking is not allowed during dances.

The Snake Dance. This dance is held in late August and currently is banned to anyone other than Hopi. It is, however, worth it to call the Hopi Reservation to check since rules may change. Tribal dances are pageants full of color and drama, and if you are fortunate enough to be invited, don't hesitate. Go! The snake dance is famous because for this ceremony men dance with live snakes in their mouths to invoke the gods' mercy to send rain for their crops.

WHERE TO GO

Walpi, First Mesa. All the ancient villages are off the main roads, situated high atop the mesas. In the past, a mountaintop location protected the village from intruders.

As you drive through the reservation on A–264, you'll see signs pointing to Polacca, an Indian village. At Polacca, you'll spot a gravel road that leads north to Walpi. (There are no names on the few streets leading to these ancient villages.) The narrow road climbs and makes several sharp turns. Although the pueblo buildings may appear to be closing in on you, don't worry. This road is fine for passenger car travel. Once on top of the mesa, park. Proceed immediately to the visitor center. You will be assigned to a guide. You'll see the ancient plaza, still used for ceremonials with its kiva (underground ceremonial chamber) near the center. While you may freely explore the plaza and old pueblo dwellings, the kiva is off-limits.

Walpi is an especially picturesque village that comes to life during important ceremonies. You will find that the Hopi who live here are extremely friendly, and you may be invited inside some homes to see handcrafted art items. If you are interested in native arts, by all means, accept the invitations.

Don't take Hopi hospitality for granted. Observe all the signs posted in the ancient villages that ask you not to take any photographs, make sketches, or make any sound recordings. *Remember:* When you are in Hopi (or any other reservation), you are a guest in another country.

When you leave First Mesa, continue west on A–264 and you'll see signs leading to Shipolovi (Shi-pah-lo-vee) and Shongopovi (Shun-gó-pa-ee), other well-known old villages on **Second Mesa**. You may either visit or see them from a distance. Continue toward

Oraibi. Soon you'll see the Hopi Cultural Center, a cluster of pseudo-pueblos, on your right. If you're hungry, thirsty, or tired of driving, this is a good place to stop. You'll find a restaurant, gift shop, small museum, and overnight accommodations here.

Oraibi, Third Mesa. From the cultural center, continue west on A–264 to Oraibi. You may want to take a quick trip to Old Oraibi. Like Walpi, this community hovers on a high, narrow, rocky ledge. The road to Old Oraibi heads off to your left (south) shortly after you pass Oraibi (sometimes called "New Oraibi"). Although parts of the settlement are in ruins, the village is very much a part of modern Hopi life. When you're finished visiting here, drive west on A–264 toward Hotevilla to see that village.

WHERE TO EAT AND STAY

The Hopi Cultural Center. On A–264, 5 miles west of the junction with A–87. The dining room is big and airy, and you'll be served by Hopi women in native dress. Order the Hopi specialties: Hopi stew made with chunks of lamb and anything made with blue corn, a special type of corn grown and used here. $-$$; (CC).

If you plan to spend the night, call ahead for reservations and be prepared to rough it some. You will not find the same quality of service and accommodations on the reservation as you'll find in the cities, but unless you are pulling a camper or driving an RV, this is your only choice for an overnight stay. $$; (CC). (520) 734-2401.

METEOR CRATER

Leaving Flagstaff, drive east on I-40 toward Winslow. Twenty miles before you reach Winslow, you'll see an exit for Meteor Crater. Head south on the well-marked, paved road to this fascinating natural site.

Meteor Crater was formed in 20,000 B.C. when a meteoric mass, traveling 33,000 miles per hour from interplanetary space, struck the earth. The impact, blasting nearly a half-billion tons of rock from the surface, destroyed all plant and animal life within 100 miles. In contemporary times this perfectly preserved, huge hole in the ground has tantalized scientists who use it as a living laboratory. Meteor Crater hit the news when the Apollo astronauts used it as a practice surface to train for their lunar walk. Discovered in 1871, the crater has impressive statistics. It measures 4,150 feet from rim to rim, is more than 3 miles in circumference, and is 470 feet deep. In addition to staring at the crater, you can visit the Museum of Astrogeology, the Astronaut Hall of Fame, and well-appointed gift and lapidary shops. Open daily. Call for extended summer hours. Fee. (520) 774-8350.

From Meteor Crater, continue to Winslow on I-40. The town is named for F. Edward Winslow, who was president of the St. Louis and San Francisco Railroad, and like its neighbor, Holbrook, is devoted to transportation. Situated 30 miles west of the Mogollon Rim, this community serves as a conduit for more remote and scenic areas of the state. Unless you need to stop here, continue east on I-40 for 33 miles to Holbrook.

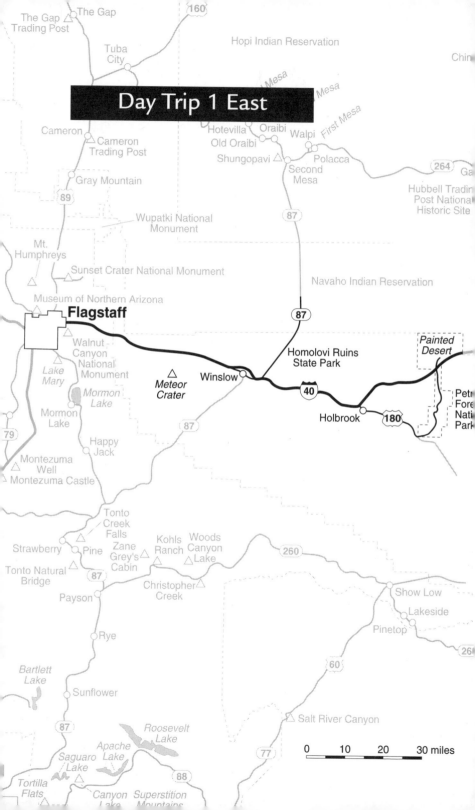

Known as "The Hub City," because of the transportation lines that intersect here, Holbrook also serves as the seat of Navajo County. It caters to tourists who are on their way to the Painted Desert and Petrified Forest National Park. It's a good place to stretch your legs, pick up a snack, or fill up the car with gas before going on.

HOMOLOVI RUINS

Homolovi Ruins State Park is located approximately 3 miles northeast of Winslow. Take I-40 to exit 257; then go 1.3 miles north on A-87. The park consists of over 300 archaeological sites, including four major fourteenth-century pueblos you can roam through. There is also a campground and several hiking trails that wind through the ruins. Open daily. Fee. (520) 289–4106.

PAINTED DESERT

From Holbrook continue on I-40 approximately 19 miles to exit 311. As you approach the parks, the Painted Desert is the area due north of the highway; the Petrified Forest National Park lies south of it. Although the parks are referred to as separate entities, in fact they are contiguous. The Painted Desert offers a superb backdrop for travelers who enjoy the desert at its most delicately pastel, but the Petrified Forest is the better attraction.

Try to time your arrival during the early morning or late afternoon hours. At sunup or just before sunset, the fallen logs in the Petrified Forest seem most lifelike and the colors of the Painted Desert appear most vibrant.

WHERE TO GO

Painted Desert Inn. One mile north of I-40 at the entrance to the park. This is your first stop. Inside you will learn how both the Painted Desert and the Petrified Forest were formed. Exhibits illustrate the evolution of the Painted Desert, and a short film describes how natural forces turn the forest to stone.

Wander around the displays and pick up information for a self-guided tour of both parks. Check for summer and winter hours. Fee. (520) 524–6228.

PETRIFIED FOREST NATIONAL PARK

The Petrified Forest National Park is the greatest and most colorful concentration of petrified wood ever discovered on earth. The park, which consists of 93,431 acres of brilliantly colored stone logs, preserves the glassy remains of an ancient coniferous forest. About 200 million years ago, the trees grew in the highlands to the west and southwest. The area of the present forest was swampland, and as streams carried the dead logs down to this flat, depressed area, they were buried in sediment rich with volcanic ash.

Over eons the chemical process worked its magic. The logs were slowly impregnated with silica until they turned to solid stone. Iron oxide and other minerals then stained the silica, producing the stone rainbows we see today. In the process, the logs became stony jewel boxes for quartz and other gemstones that developed in the wood during petrification.

Today each chip and rock is carefully protected. No one is allowed to pick up even the tiniest souvenir. But in ancient times, the people who lived here carved on the petrified wood, chiseled messages on the rocks, and fashioned tools and weapons from the rainbow forest.

You'll want to take a slow drive through the area. If you've stopped at the Painted Desert Visitor Center, you've picked up a pamphlet describing a self-guided drive. This brochure explains all the places you'll want to see. If you don't have a brochure, don't worry because you'll find, as you approach each site, a written description clearly posted. Be sure to stop and get out of your car to see these unusual rock formations. You should hike to **Agate Bridge** in the First Forest. Here a petrified tree fell across a canyon, forming a stony bridge for eternity. Plan to climb down the 120 steps to **Newspaper Rock**, a large boulder covered with ancient writing. No doubt this served as a kind of local bulletin board, announcing activities and goings-on to the Indians who lived in the area. If you follow all the side roads that are marked in this stony forest, you'll drive about 38 miles before you reach the south entrance, which is your exit point.

WHAT TO DO

Rainbow Forest Museum. Near the south entrance. This is your final stop before leaving the Petrified Forest. Inside you'll see geological exhibits. If you didn't stop at the north entrance, you can learn how the forests were formed here. Check for summer and winter hours. Fee. (520) 524-6228.

Return to Flagstaff by following US-180 northwest to Holbrook where you'll pick up I-40 west to Flagstaff.

Day Trip 1 Southeast

180

89

Gray Mountain

Wupatki Natio
Monumen

40 Seligman

Fairfield
Continental
Snow Bowl

Sunset Crater National Mon

Museum of Northern Arizona

Ash Fork   Williams

Keibab

Humphreys

Flagstaff

Bill Williams
Mountain

Lowell
Observatory

Pioneer
Historical
Museum

Walnut
Canyon
National
Monument

Meteor
Crater

89

White
Horse
Lake

Oak Creek
Canyon

Lake
Mary

Mormon
Lake

Mormon
Lake

87

Tuzigoot
National
Monument

Perkinsville   Sedona

Cottonwood

179

Happy
Jack

Jerome State
Historic Park

Clarkdale

Ace
Springs

Granite Basin

A89

Bridgesport

Jerome

279

Montezuma
Well

Montezuma Castle

Tonto
Creek
Falls

Prescott

Camp Verde

17

Skull Valley

Dewey

96

89

Humboldt

Groom Creek

Camp Verde
State Historical
Park

Strawberry   Pine

Zane
Grey's
Cabin

Kohls
Ranch

W
Ca
L

Wolf
Creek

Mayer

69

87

Christopher
Creek

Peeple's
Valley

Cordes Junction   Arcosanti

Tonto Natural
Bridge

Payson

Yarnell

Stanton

3   89

Octave

Sunset Point

Rye

Pioneer Arizona
Living Museum

Wickenburg

Lake
Pleasant

Carefree

Bartlett
Lake

Sunflower

74

Cave
Creek

87

Roosevelt
Lake

93

Fountain Hills

Apache
Lake

60

White Tank
Mountains

Surprise

Peoria

Saguaro
Lake

88

Youngtown

Litchfield
Park

Sun
City

Paradise
Valley

Tortilla
Flats

Canyon
Lake

Superstition
Mountains

10

Phoenix

Glendale

Scottsdale

Apache Junction

Miami

Tempe   Mesa

Guadaloupe

Superior   60

Chandler

0   10   20   30 miles

Gila River
Indian Crafts
Center and
Heritage Park

287

Sacaton

79

Boyce
Thompson
Arboretum

MORMON LAKE

Approximately 30 miles southeast of Flagstaff on Mormon Lake Road, Mormon Lake is an optimum destination for a quick, easy, scenic loop through some of Flagstaff's best outdoor country.

To get there from Flagstaff, follow I-17 south to the Lake Mary Road exit. Stay on Lake Mary Road until you reach the Mormon Lake area. As you drive, the road will wind through the Coconino National Forest and will take you near some great fishing lakes. Lake Mary is one of the favorites.

This area is long on scenery but short on facilities. Numerous campgrounds dot the countryside, but wise travelers will carry picnic hampers filled with lunch goodies. You won't find any fast food here, unless, of course, you are especially quick with hook and bait. What you will find, however, is serenity—ponderosa pines trimming lush meadows, backed up by a panorama of the San Francisco Peaks.

As you continue southeast, you'll see a dirt road off to your left (east), which leads to Ashurst Lake. Unless you have a four-wheel drive, avoid this. Dirt roads in this area can be hazardous to the health of your car. Unless you are driving a four-wheel-drive vehicle or a truck, it's advisable to stay on paved surfaces. During the rainy season you can get flooded out, and during the dry periods, these roads can be extremely rough.

Continuing on Lake Mary Road, you'll come to Mormon Lake Road, a dirt byway leading off to your right (west). Take this unpaved road, which will loop around Mormon Lake, the largest natural lake in Arizona. Cattle that roamed over the meadowland stamped down the earth, forming a natural dish that held the winter snowmelt. The Mormons, who remained in this vicinity for many years, ran a dairy and even built a cheese press here. It's not known why they left the area, but probably a drought forced them out.

Over the years the snowmelt continually refilled the depressed area and formed a large natural lake surrounded by open range where cattle graze. The lake is also a haven for ducks and duck hunters.

Adjacent to the water is the village of Mormon Lake, which consists of Montezuma and Mormon Lake lodges, a post office, a dance hall that seats 350 people, a steak house, and a general store. During big holiday weekends (including Fourth of July and Labor Day), the dance hall resounds with live entertainment.

WHAT TO DO

Cross-Country Skiing. During the winter you'll find some of the best cross-country skiing in the state. You can drive up and ski for the day or make overnight arrangements at either of two lodges in the area. (See Where to Stay.)

Bicycle Tours. Bicycle enthusiasts rave about touring the Mormon Lake area. Bring your own bicycle or arrange to join a group ride. If you go the entire distance, you'll ride 26 miles around the shoreline. To find out about bicycle tours offered in the Mormon Lake area, call the Arizona Bicycle Club in Phoenix, (602) 968-4997.

WHERE TO EAT

Mormon Lake Lodge. Mormon Lake. The menu features seven kinds of steak, all reasonably priced. During the summer, the lodge is open for breakfast, lunch, and dinner. In winter, only dinner is served during the week with all meals available on the weekends. $$-$$$; (CC). (520) 354-2227.

WHERE TO STAY

Montezuma Lodge. Mormon Lake. Follow the Mormon Lake dirt road 3 miles to the lodge. Guests can stay in twenty well-equipped kitchenette cabins nestled in the woods against the Mormon Mountains. This is a favorite "ride-in" stop for bicyclists who come, packs on their backs, to rest and then ride in the area. Closed in winter. Meals by prior arrangement only. $-$$; (CC). (520) 354-2220.

Mormon Lake Lodge. Mormon Lake. From Lake Mary Road turn right onto Mormon Lake Road and continue for 9 miles to the lodge. (You will pass Montezuma Lodge.) There are ten sleeping units—four motel rooms and six cabins (cooking facilities are in two of the cabins). $$$; (CC). (520) 354-2227.

HAPPY JACK

Another 12 miles southwest on Lake Mary Road is Happy Jack, a logging community. You'll see campgrounds and some private cabins tucked away on this not-so-beaten path. From Happy Jack you have a few options. You can continue to the junction with A-87 and follow A-87 northeast to Winslow. From Winslow, follow US-180 back to Flagstaff.

Or you may follow Lake Mary Road to the junction of A-87 and take A-87 to Strawberry and Pine, and then follow General Crook Highway west to Camp Verde. There you can pick up I-17 north and continue to Flagstaff. Along the way, you can stop at Montezuma Castle and Montezuma Well. (See Day Trip 2, North from Phoenix.)

WORTH MORE TIME: PAYSON

A third option is to follow Lake Mary Road south to A-87 and continue on A-87 to Payson. See Day Trip 2, Northeast from Phoenix for more details on what to see and do around this community.

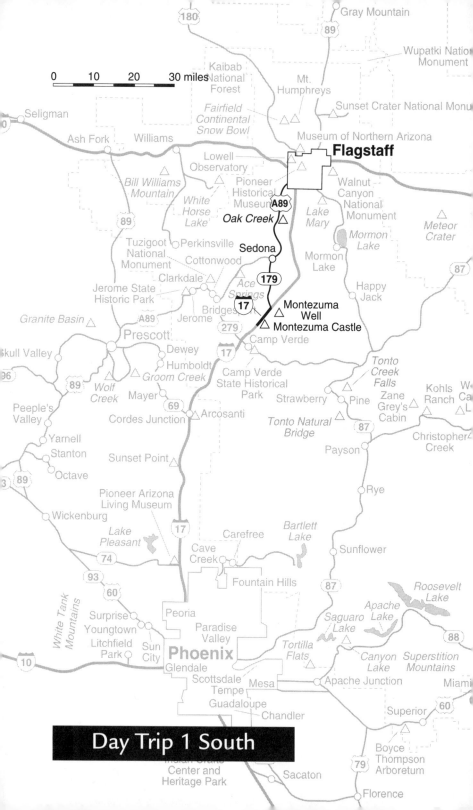

Day Trip 1 South

Oak Creek/Sedona
Worth More Time: : Montezuma Well
and Montezuma Castle

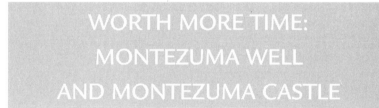

OAK CREEK/SEDONA

From Flagstaff, head due south on US-89A to A-179 to Oak Creek
and Sedona. (Refer to Day Trip 4, North from Phoenix for all there
is to do and see here.) From Flagstaff, the trip to Sedona takes less
than an hour.

WORTH MORE TIME:
MONTEZUMA WELL
AND MONTEZUMA CASTLE

From Sedona, stay on A-179 south to its junction with I-17. To visit
Montezuma Castle or Montezuma Well, drive south on I-17 to the
exits marked for each. (See Day Trip 2, North from Phoenix for additional information on these historic sites.) One fee covers both the
castle and the well. (520) 567-3322.

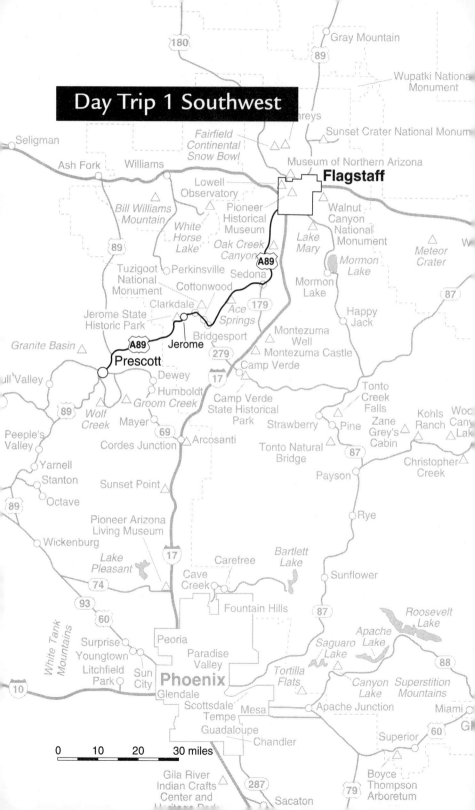

JEROME

Follow US–89A due south from Flagstaff. You'll drive about an hour to reach Jerome, a charming semi-ghost town. (Read about Jerome in Day Trip 2, North from Phoenix.)

PRESCOTT

From Jerome, continue 41 miles southwest on US–89A to Prescott, Arizona's picturesque community famous for its Victorian homes and historical significance. Here territorial Arizona springs to life. The first capital of the Arizona Territory, Prescott ultimately lost its bid to become the permanent state capital to Phoenix. Still, much Arizona history was made here and, fortunately for visitors, remains well preserved. For more information, see Day Trip 1, North from Phoenix.

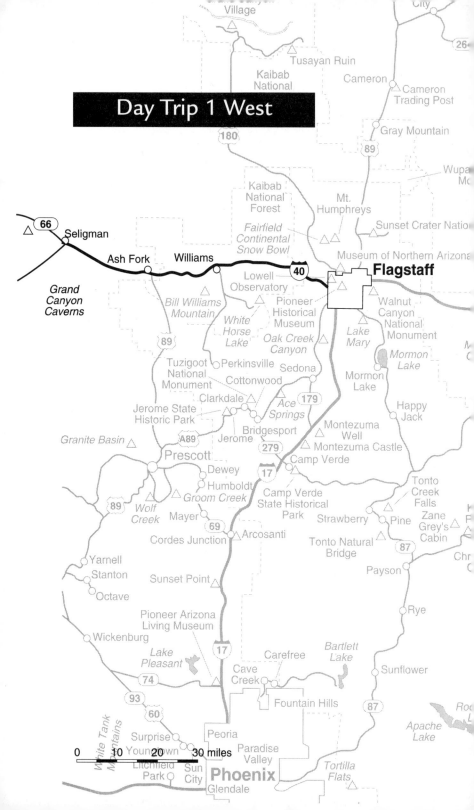

Day Trip 1 West

Grand Canyon Village

Tusayan Ruin

Kaibab National

180

26

City

Cameron

Cameron Trading Post

Gray Mountain

89

Wupatki Mo

66

Seligman

Ash Fork

Williams

40

Kaibab National Forest

Fairfield Continental Snow Bowl

Mt. Humphreys

Sunset Crater Natio

Museum of Northern Arizona

Flagstaff

Grand Canyon Caverns

Bill Williams Mountain

White Horse Lake

Lowell Observatory

Pioneer Historical Museum

Oak Creek Canyon

Lake Mary

Walnut Canyon National Monument

Mormon Lake

M

89

Tuzigoot National Monument

Perkinsville

Cottonwood

Clarkdale

Jerome State Historic Park

Sedona

Ace Springs

179

Mormon Lake

Happy Jack

Granite Basin

A89

Bridgesport

Jerome

279

Montezuma Well

Montezuma Castle

Camp Verde

Prescott

Dewey

Humboldt

Groom Creek

17

Camp Verde State Historical Park

Tonto Creek Falls

89

Wolf Creek

Mayer

69

Strawberry

Pine

Zane Grey's Cabin

F

Cordes Junction

Arcosanti

Tonto Natural Bridge

87

Chr

Yarnell

Stanton

Octave

Sunset Point

Payson

Rye

Pioneer Arizona Living Museum

Wickenburg

Lake Pleasant

17

Carefree

Bartlett Lake

Sunflower

74

Cave Creek

87

93

60

Fountain Hills

Apache Lake

Roc

F

Surprise

Youngtown

Peoria

Paradise Valley

Tortilla Flats

Litchfield Park

Sun City

Phoenix

Glendale

White Tank Mountains

0   10   20   30 miles

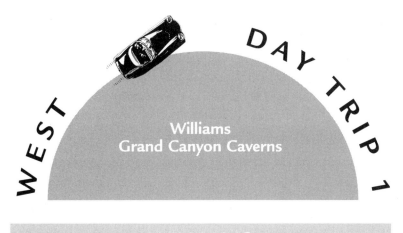
WILLIAMS

From Flagstaff, drive west 32 miles on I-40 across the golden meadowland known as Garland Prairie. During spring and summer, the meadow is a carpet of wildflowers. The fields shimmer with azure blues and dashing reds. As you continue toward Williams, you drive through the pine-scented, lush greenery of the **Kaibab National Forest.**

Called "The Gateway to the Grand Canyon," Williams is named for William S. (or Old Bill) Williams, a master trapper and Indian Scout who traveled on the Santa Fe Trail during the 1820s. A rugged six-foot-one-inch eccentric, he was known to drink and gamble excessively. Called the "lone wolf" of trappers, like many of the mountain men of his day, Old Bill spent most of his time working and sleeping in the wilderness. He only emerged from the mountains long enough to lose his money fast. Then he'd retreat to the wilds to trap and restock his supply of furs. Soon he'd reappear in town, get cash, and start the cycle again.

Although mountain men like Old Bill Williams are remembered primarily as trappers, they played a key role in Arizona history. True, they were an environmental disaster, wiping out the entire populations of grizzlies and beavers that once roamed through the forests and swam in the streams. But as explorers, mappers, and later guides for the military, these reclusive individuals provided invaluable services. Their knowledge of the wilderness made it possible to open the land for the settlers who followed.

Today the spirit of Old Bill Williams is kept alive through the Bill Williams Mountain Men, who have their headquarters in Williams. If you are in town during any of the town's celebrations (see Festivals section), you may have an opportunity to see them in full regalia, dressed in furs and leather. This group of Williams men meets regularly to celebrate the spirit of Old Bill and reenact the mountain men's unique period of frontier history. They ride in parades, take part in rodeos, and whoop it up in festivities in Williams and elsewhere throughout the state.

Like many northern Arizona communities, Williams is a sportsman's paradise. The town sits in the shadow of Bill Williams Mountain, a 9,286-foot-high peak just south of this small community. Good walking trails scale both sides of the mountain. Seven fishing lakes, many with cabins and boating facilities, surround the town. During the winter, there's a small (450-foot vertical drop) downhill ski run. In addition to skiing, **The Benham Snow Play Area,** just south of town on County Road 173, echoes with "snow tubers," kids and adults careening down snowy slopes in inner tubes. For complete information on camping, fishing, and hiking in the vicinity, visit or write the Williams Grand Canyon Chamber of Commerce, 820 West Bill Williams Avenue, Williams, 86046 or call (520) 625-4061.

WHERE TO GO

Grand Canyon Deer Farm. 6752 East Deer Farm Road. As you drive toward Williams from Flagstaff, you'll see this unusual petting zoo facing I-40 8 miles east of Williams, some 24 miles west of Flagstaff. This is a fun stop for families with children. Adults who enjoy observing eight varieties of these graceful animals will also like this farm. Some deer are common to Arizona and other areas of the U.S. but there are more unusual types such as Japanese Sika deer and a herd of Spotted Fallow, a type found in the Mediterranean. Phone for specific hours. Fee. (520) 635-2357 or (800) 926-DEER.

The Little Grand Canyon (also called Sycamore Point). Twelve miles south of White Horse Lake on Forest Service Road 110. This is a side trip for adventurous explorers. Locals call this "The Little Grand Canyon," and when you see it, you'll understand why. Follow the paved County Road 173, south of Williams (toward Perkinsville and Jerome) to the unpaved Forest Service Road 110, which leads to White Horse Lake. Drive 12 miles south on Forest Service Road 119, a rugged, bumpy road to Sycamore Point. When you arrive, feast your eyes on the steep limestone walls and pillars of sandstone that form this canyon.

Although Oak Creek Canyon offers a more dramatic vertical drop, and the Sedona area has more rocky sculptures, the Little Grand Canyon exudes a solitary beauty. With its rocky spires and stands of aspen, oak, and sycamore, it is largely undiscovered and appeals to those individuals who like the thrill of discovering a majestic, pristine jewel. Rugged adventurers can hike among the cliffs and rock formations. Since there are no established trails or facilities here, inexperienced hikers should not attempt to walk in this wilderness.

Planes of Fame. At Grand Canyon Valle Airport near the junction of A-64 and A-180. Aviation enthusiasts will find this museum to their liking. The original museum is in Claremont, California, and was founded in 1957 by Edward T. Maloney. The collection has grown remarkably since then. This branch of the California museum houses 30 aircraft, all of which are flyable. Among those on display is the aircraft that General Douglas MacArthur used as his personal transport plane. Called the "Bataan," it is a Lockeed Constellation, and tours of the plane are available for an additional charge. The entrance to the museum is through the airport's terminal at the Gift Shop. It is the only Gift Shop in northern Arizona specializing in aviation artifacts, gifts, books, etc. Open 9:00 A.M.–6:00 P.M. in summer, and 9:00 A.M.–5:00 P.M. in winter. Fee. (520) 635-1000.

Steam Train from Williams to the Grand Canyon. Grand Canyon Railway, 235 Grand Canyon Boulevard, Williams 86046-2704. Take I-40 to exit 163. Then follow Grand Canyon Boulevard, 1¹/₂ miles south to the depot. Steam engines opened the West, so what better way to see the territory than aboard one? The Grand Canyon Railway uses a 1923 Iron Horse to pull restored 1920s Harriman coach cars along original 1901 rails from April 1 through September 30, and a diesel engine October 1 through March 31. Passengers are delivered to the threshold of the Grand Canyon. The train travels at a top speed of thirty-five miles per hour, so the trip takes about 2¹/₂ hours. Entertainment and refreshments add to the fun, and complimentary soft drinks and snacks are provided. Box lunches may be purchased.

Spend around three hours at the Canyon and come back, or stay the night. Summertime is a popular time to ride the rails to the Grand Canyon, but winter snows bring a unique beauty to the Grand Canyon. Ride the new first-class glass-domed car which gives a 360-degree view of the ever-changing landscape of northern Arizona.

The Grand Canyon RR offers numerous value packages which combine the vintage train travel with a stay at the Fray Marcos and other hotels in both Williams and the Canyon. Round-trips operate daily year-round, leaving Williams at 9:30 A.M. $$; (CC). For information on fares, schedules, and special overnight packages at the Canyon, call (800) THE–TRAIN (800–843–8724).

WHERE TO STAY

The Fray Marcos Hotel. 235 North Grand Canyon Boulevard, Williams, 86046. From I–40 take Williams exit 163 to Grand Canyon Boulevard. Go ¹/₂ mile south to the Grand Canyon Rail Road Depot complex. This new hotel offers eighty-nine rooms all decorated in classic Southwest style. Spencer's Lounge features a beautifully carved wooden bar, which was bought in London and lovingly re-assembled in Williams. It was originally carved in England by George O. Spencer, a London cabinetmaker. As part of his agreement, he had the privilege of drinking free at the bar! He lived into his 70s and drank daily at Spencer's bar. $$. Reservations: (520) 635–4010.

GRAND CANYON CAVERNS

Continue west approximately 44 miles on I–40 through Ash Fork, which calls itself the flagstone capitol of the world, and go on to Seligman. Exit the interstate and pick up A–66, or "Old 66." Follow A–66 about 25 miles to the Grand Canyon Caverns.

Here is one of the world's largest completely dry cave systems. Meandering twenty-one stories beneath the earth, well-preserved Grand Canyon Caverns are known to be closely related geologically to the Grand Canyon. Yet because of the off-the-beaten path location, tourists often ignore them. Professional cave explorers are well acquainted with the caverns, and excavation goes on continually because experts are certain that more rocky rooms wait to be discovered.

You'll enter through a commercial center, which has a coffee shop, motel, gift shop, and airstrip for private planes. A forty-five-minute guided tour leads you through the expanse of vaulted rooms filled with colorful rock formations. You'll wander through mysterious passageways and hear an intriguing commentary about the history of the caves. But for all its wild beauty, this is a comfortable experience for explorers of all ages. The paths are paved and the formations well lit.

The caverns became general knowledge in 1927 when a heavy rain widened the natural funnel-shaped opening to the upper level. However, the Hualapai (Wal-pee) Indians, a tribe that lived here centuries ago, were familiar with that level of the caverns. Even today, elders caution young people that the original entrance is a sacred place and should be observed as such.

From fossils embedded in the redwall limestone, scientists have determined that many prehistoric sea and land dwellers once lived in these caves. Fossils of a giant ground sloth, estimated to have lived here over 20,000 years ago, were also discovered in the caverns. Call for hours. Fee. (520) 422-3223.

To return to Flagstaff, follow old A–66 east to Seligman. Pick up I–40 east through Williams to Flagstaff.

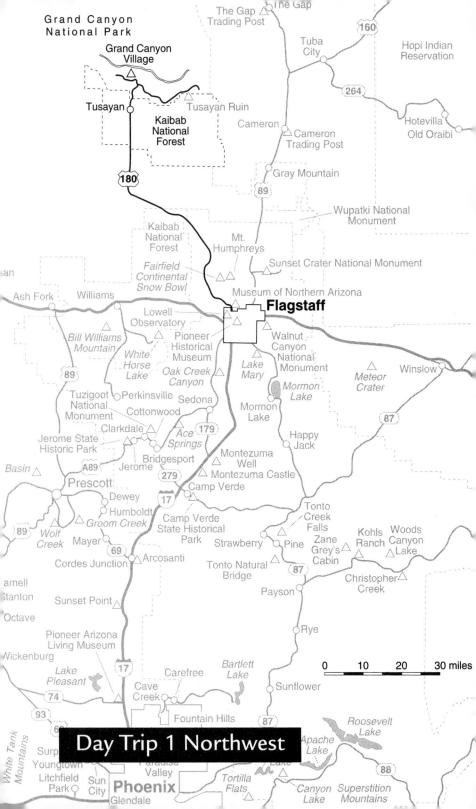

Grand Canyon
National Park

Grand Canyon
Village

Tusayan

Kaibab
National
Forest

Tusayan Ruin

The Gap
Trading Post

The Gap

160

Tuba
City

Hopi Indian
Reservation

264

Cameron

Cameron
Trading Post

Hotevilla
Old Oraibi

180

Kaibab
National
Forest

Fairfield
Continental
Snow Bowl

Mt.
Humphreys

Gray Mountain

89

Wupatki National
Monument

Sunset Crater National Monument

Museum of Northern Arizona

Ash Fork

Williams

Lowell
Observatory

Pioneer
Historical
Museum

Flagstaff

Walnut
Canyon
National
Monument

Winslow

Bill Williams
Mountain

89

White
Horse
Lake

Oak Creek
Canyon

Lake
Mary

Mormon
Lake

Meteor
Crater

87

Tuzigoot
National
Monument

Perkinsville

Cottonwood

Sedona

Mormon
Lake

Clarkdale

Ace
Springs

179

Happy
Jack

Jerome State
Historic Park

Jerome

Bridgesport

Basin

89

279

Montezuma
Well

Montezuma Castle

Tonto
Creek
Falls

Kohls
Ranch

Woods
Canyon
Lake

Prescott

Dewey

Humboldt

Groom Creek

17

Camp Verde

Camp Verde
State Historical
Park

Strawberry

Pine

Zane
Grey's
Cabin

89

Wolf
Creek

Mayer

69

Cordes Junction

Arcosanti

Tonto Natural
Bridge

87

Christopher
Creek

arnell

Stanton

Sunset Point

Payson

Octave

Pioneer Arizona
Living Museum

Rye

Wickenburg

17

Carefree

Bartlett
Lake

Lake
Pleasant

74

Cave
Creek

Sunflower

93

66

Fountain Hills

87

Roosevelt
Lake

White Tank
Mountains

Surp

Youngtown

Litchfield
Park

Sun
City

Phoenix

Glendale

Paradise
Valley

Tortilla
Flats

Apache
Lake

Canyon
Lake

Superstition
Mountains

88

0   10   20   30 miles

Day Trip 1 Northwest

THE SOUTH RIM OF THE GRAND CANYON

From Flagstaff, drive north on US–180 approximately 60 miles to Grand Canyon Village, headquarters for this most spectacular national park. All visitors to Arizona put the Grand Canyon at the top of their "must see" list, but few realize that the Grand Canyon is actually two parks: the North Rim and the South Rim. The South Rim is closer to Phoenix. It is located 223 miles north of that city, and is open to tourists all year. The more rugged and remote North Rim is a 230-mile drive from the southern park. Although it is possible to "do" the South Rim of the Grand Canyon in a long day's trip starting and ending in Phoenix, the experience is exhausting. It is far better to use Flagstaff as your headquarters if you plan to see the canyon in one day. Better yet, stay overnight in the Grand Canyon park area.

Should you decide to see both rims, you'll be in for two distinctly different experiences. The North Rim, more than 1,000 feet higher than the South Rim, is the more remote and rugged park. It is closed from late fall to mid-spring because the roads are snowed in from about late October to mid-May. Facilities at the North Rim exist on a smaller, more rustic scale. In contrast, although the facilities at the South Rim are superb, it's often crowded during the summer.

The fascination with the Grand Canyon spans every age, nationality, and experience. The view into the chasm appears pure illusion, for it seems that nothing can be that deep, that mysterious, that endless. While volumes have been written about its majesty, no words or pictures can contain the happy shock of coming upon it. One writer notes that people who stare across and into the magnificent abyss, no matter how many pictures they've seen of it, find themselves instinctively looking back to check that the earth they're standing on is solid.

Although you may suppose that it will be enough for you to just stand and gaze at this massive split in the heart of the earth, once you arrive you'll discover that you may want to participate more fully in the canyon experience. Then you must decide how to do it, for there are many ways to see the South Rim. You can travel on foot, on horseback, or cling to a mule. You can view the Grand Canyon from the top down: flying over it in a small plane or helicopter; or from the bottom up: riding the torrents of the Colorado River rapids. For more information on the South Rim, call the National Park Service (520) 638-7888. During the busy tourist season (spring, summer, and early fall), you'll need reservations for either camping or lodging facilities. You must also make prior arrangements if you plan to journey into the canyon for an overnight hike or pack trip, because overnight hikers and campers must have permits. As with all national parks, there is an entrance fee.

WHERE TO GO

Grand Canyon IMAX Theatre. Seven miles south of the South Rim on A-64/US-180 in Tusayan (Too-see-an). If you haven't experienced an IMAX film, you're in for a treat. An IMAX film puts you into the action. You sit surrounded by a six-track soundtrack, looking up at a 70-foot-high screen. Even if you've seen any of the other IMAX films (they cover many subjects, from time to outer space), see this one especially if this is your first trip to the Grand Canyon. The IMAX Theatre is a superb introduction to the history and geology of the Kaibab Plateau and the Grand Canyon and is a film that children and adults of all ages will greatly enjoy. "The Grand Canyon—The Hidden Secrets" is the most popular of IMAX productions shown in this country. In thirty-four minutes you get a crash course on the Grand Canyon and the Colorado River and their geography, geology, history, and anthropology.

Thanks to the wonders of photographic magic, you even experience a wild river ride down the rapids of the Colorado River. The film is shown daily. For schedule information, telephone or write to The Grand Canyon IMAX Theatre, P.O. Box 1397, Grand Canyon, AZ 86023-1397. Fee. (520) 638-2203.

Visitors Center. In the Grand Canyon National Park, 1 mile east of Grand Canyon Village on Village Loop Drive. This should be your first stop once you enter the park. No matter how you choose to experience the canyon, you'll get more out of it if you have an understanding of how grand it really is.

Spend some time studying the exhibits and dioramas describing the formation of the canyon and the flora and fauna in the area. You'll find brochures and information on several self-guided walking tours that traverse the rim. Here you can also pick up trail maps for hiking into the canyon and get information on driving tours along the East Rim and West Rim drives.

East Rim Drive. A paved road leads from the visitors center past the **Yavapai Museum,** a delightful and informative geological facility, to Mather, Yaki, and Grand View points. The road continues to Desert View, a spectacular lookout 25 miles east of Grand Canyon Village. Along the way, you may stop at any of the turnouts to experience the panorama of the Canyon. This is an especially impressive drive in the early morning hours or just before sunset when the colors of the canyon are their richest.

West Rim Drive. This takes you past Powell Memorial and Hopi, Mohave, and Pima points—equally outstanding places from which to observe the majesty of the canyon. This drive ends at Hermit's Rest. From April through September, the West Rim road is limited to tour buses to relieve traffic congestion and help preserve the ecological integrity of the canyon. For information about the bus tours, inquire at the visitors center.

Don't leave the visitors center without browsing through the selection of scientific and illustrated books for sale. The more you can learn about the canyon, the more you'll enjoy your visit. Even nonscientific types should know that this region encompasses five of the Northern Hemisphere's seven ecological zones, and that no other place in the world so clearly illustrates such a vast panorama of Time. Free. (520) 638-7888.

El Tovar Hotel. On Village Loop Drive, Fred Harvey, Inc., P.O. Box 699, Grand Canyon, AZ 86023. From the visitors center follow Village Loop Drive west about a half mile to the first right turn. This road takes you to the parking lot for El Tovar. Even if you do not intend to stay or eat at this hotel (see Where to Eat and Where to Stay sections), make it a point to visit this historic place. El Tovar is a rambling, wooden hotel that has long served as headquarters for activity at the South Rim. On any day, as you stand in the spacious, high-ceilinged lobby, you may hear a dozen different languages, see sunburned hikers who have just emerged from the canyon floor, listen to river rafters still riding high on their exhilaration, and see celebrities and dignitaries who have come to relax in the stately splendor afforded by this charming setting. (520) 638–2631.

Bright Angel Trail. As you leave El Tovar, turn left and follow the Rim Walk toward Bright Angel Lodge. There's a sign pointing to the Bright Angel Trail, a well-maintained hiking path that twists and turns 20.6 miles into the canyon floor.

For the first half mile, Bright Angel is gentle enough for even non-hikers to negotiate without any special equipment other than good walking shoes. However, as you peer down the trail from the Rim, you'll see a splash of deep green in the distance. The green glistens against the sun-bleached yellows, oranges, and peach tones of the Grand Canyon. This is **Indian Gardens,** a 4.4-mile hike from the top. The trek to Indian Gardens takes you through man-made tunnels and down a series of steep switchbacks. You can rest and picnic at this remarkable natural oasis, which is shaded by tall cottonwood trees. The hike to Indian Gardens is an excellent round-trip day experience that gives you a good workout and a sense of the serenity of the inner Canyon.

The less ambitious may prefer a fifteen-minute walk down Bright Angel Trail. Go at least as far as the first tunnel or hole-in-the-rock. Remember, it will take you twice as long, or a half hour, to walk back up. Even this short excursion will give you a feeling for the grandeur of the canyon, an understanding that you can never get from standing at the rim and looking down into it.

WHERE TO EAT

El Tovar. In the park on Village Loop Drive. Count on hearty breakfasts and superb views from the dining room window. Pancakes are light and fluffy, and the syrup hot. Lunches and dinners are more elegant. The food and the service rival those of any fine restaurant in the Phoenix or Tucson areas. During the spring, summer, and early fall, reservations are recommended for dinner. $$; (CC). (520) 638-2631.

WHERE TO STAY

El Tovar. In the park on Village Loop Drive, Fred Harvey, Inc., P.O. Box 699, Grand Canyon, 86023. Because this is an historic hotel, each room is different—some large and airy, others smaller—but the accommodations are uniformly charming. If you are looking for atmosphere and convenience, El Tovar is an outstanding choice. $$; (CC). (520) 638-2631.

Grand Canyon Squire Inn. One mile south of the entrance to Grand Canyon National Park and ¹/₂ mile north of Grand Canyon National Park Airport on US-180/A-64. The Grand Canyon Squire Inn is a newer resort and conference center with meeting rooms, continental cuisine, and tennis courts. For information, write to Grand Canyon Squire Inn, P.O. Box 130, Grand Canyon, 86023-0130. $$; (CC). (520) 638-2681.

For a complete listing of all motel accommodations and camping facilities available in the park, contact the Superintendent, Grand Canyon National Park, Grand Canyon, 86023, or call (520) 638-7888.

WHAT ELSE TO DO

Hiking and Backpacking. For information on hiking and trail services in the park, contact Grand Canyon Hiker Services or the National Park Service Concessionaire for hiking and backpacking. A network of trails of varying difficulty crisscrosses the canyon. Some lead to remote destinations; others are more accessible. Hikers of any skill and interest can have a rewarding experience. From April to November, inquire about hiking and backpacking by writing to Grand Canyon Hiker Services, P.O. Box 735, Grand Canyon, AZ 86023, or call (520) 638–2391. At any time during the year, you can write to Grand Canyon Hiker Services at P.O. Box 2997, East Flagstaff, AZ 86003, or call (520) 526–0924.

Muleback Trips. Mules descend the Bright Angel Trail at the South Rim on full-day, half-day, and overnight trips. This is a strenuous trip. Good physical condition is a must. Reservations are mandatory from May through October. Fee. For information about these excursions, contact Grand Canyon National Park Lodges, Reservations Department, P.O. Box 699, Grand Canyon, AZ 86023, or call (520) 638–2401.

Colorado River Trips. Motor-powered raft and rowing trips are regularly scheduled down the Colorado River during the summer months. Various kinds of boats and trips are geared to different types of travelers. You can choose anything from a rugged few weeks of boating and hiking to an exciting but still relaxing experience.

If you plan only one "outdoorsy" experience in your lifetime, this should be it. Nothing beats it. The Colorado River not only has the most rapids, but the most exciting rapids of any river, and there is only one Grand Canyon in the entire world to provide such a glorious backdrop for the thrills. If you're worried about roughing it, don't be. There are plenty of luxuries, including excellent food and even cakes baked fresh on the beach. For thrills in an incomparable setting, this trip cannot be equaled.

Would-be river rates (the local terminology for those who've run the river) should be in good physical condition. Each rafting company has its own list of requirements. Fee. for a complete listing of companies, write or telephone the National Park Service at the Grand Canyon. Addresss inquiries to the Superintendent, Grand Canyon National Park, Grand Canyon, AZ 86023, or call (520) 638–7888.

Directories

Festivals and Celebrations
National Parks
Indian Reservations
State Parks
Regional Information
Tourist Safety Tips

Festivals and Celebrations

JANUARY

Phoenix Area
Fiesta Bowl Day, Tempe. This is becoming one of the major college bowls in the country and each year attracts top university football talent. (602) 967-7891 or 350-0911.

Tucson Area
American Hot Rod Association's Winter Nationals, Tucson. The biggest national drag race goes on for four days at Tucson Dragway. (520) 791-4873.

FEBRUARY

Phoenix Area
Lost Dutchman Days, Apache Junction. The Lost Dutchman lives again each year during the three-day rodeo, parade, arts and craft exhibit, antique car show, and carnival. (602) 982-3141.

Parada del Sol, Scottsdale. Enjoy top professional rodeo, an elaborate horse-drawn parade, and wild west fun. Scottsdale celebrates the entire week as the town dresses, thinks, and acts western. (602) 945-8481.

Yuma Crossing Day, Yuma. This festival celebrates the "Crossing of the Fathers" when the Spanish crossed the Colorado River into Arizona to settle the territory. Dance performances and exhibits are held at cultural and historical facilities throughout the area. Horse-drawn wagons shuttle visitors to and from each facility. (520) 344-3800.

Quartzsite Annual Gem and Mineral Show, Quartzsite. Thousands of rockhounds flock each year to this tiny desert community to buy and sell at one of the world's largest gem and mineral shows. See demonstrations of rock tumbling and learn about the world of gems. (520) 927-6325.

Tucson Area

La Fiesta de Los Vaqueros, Tucson. This is Tucson's big rodeo. Usually held in February, it is kicked off by the longest nonmechanized parade in the world. (520) 792-1212.

Tubac Arts Festival, Tubac. A nine-day outdoor festival featuring international craftspeople. Demonstrations, exhibits, and food booths make this a perennial favorite. (520) 398-2704.

MARCH

Phoenix Area

Phoenix Rodeo of Rodeos, Phoenix. Professional cowboys converge on Phoenix to compete in a national indoor rodeo of top caliber. An impressive parade in downtown Phoenix highlights the week's festivities. (602) 254-5521.

Old Town Tempe Spring Festival of the Arts, Tempe. The center of Tempe becomes a shopper's paradise as artists and craftspeople from all over the country set up booths to show and sell their wares. You'll find everything from "junque" to true art—often at bargain prices. (602) 967-4877.

Tucson Area

Tombstone Territorial Days, Tombstone. This tiny town celebrates its beginnings with a carnival of fun. Shoot-outs, the Arizona Firehose Cart Championship, and a pet parade make this fun. (520) 457–2211.

APRIL

Phoenix Area

Arid Land Plant Show, Superior. Held at the Boyce Thompson Southwestern Arboretum, this show features a wide variety of drought-resistant trees, shrubs, cacti, and succulents from as far away as Australia and Africa. Gardeners find this a great place to look, browse, and buy. Learn how nature equips these beautiful, unusual plants to survive in water-short lands. (520) 689–2811.

Heard Museum Indian Fair, Phoenix. Stroll around the museum grounds and see dances, arts, crafts, and exhibits from many Arizona Indian tribes. Munch on delicious Navajo fry bread, made hot on the grounds, and other native delicacies. Bring the entire family for this popular, authentic Native American fair. (602) 252–8848.

Tucson Area

San Xavier (Ha-veer) Pageant and Fiesta, San Xavier Mission. This dramatic event is held the Friday after Easter and begins in late afternoon with over one hundred Indian dancers celebrating the history of the mission. As night falls, one hundred bonfires are lit and the coming of Father Garces, who built the present mission, and Father Kino, who opened the land for the Spanish, is commemorated through narration and drama. More than twenty costumed horsemen ride into the area lit by bonfires, and the evening ends with a spectacular procession of worshippers, the joyous pealing of bells, and fireworks. Throughout the weekend, the Tohono O'odham Indians host a food and crafts market. (520) 792–1212.

Fiesta de la Placita, Tucson. The Hispanic community of Tucson turns out for a bilingual, full-fledged Mexican fiesta full of slowly simmered Mexican food, piñata games, dancing, and music. Everyone, regardless of heritage, is invited to attend. (520) 792–1212.

Pioneer Days, Tucson. This two-day festival celebrates the history of Tucson during the nineteenth century and features dancing of all kinds—from Indian to barn dances. There are western food booths, mountain men, and brightly costumed camp ladies and military men. A spectacular Military Field Day includes reenactments of frontier battles. Be sure to sample the "Old West BBQ." Pioneer crafts are displayed and sold. (520) 792-1212.

La Vuelta de Bisbee, Bisbee. A three-day bicycle race attracts riders from all over the country who compete on the tortuously steep course through this mining town. (520) 432-5421.

MAY

Phoenix Area

George Phippen Memorial Invitational Western Art Show and Sale, Prescott. This show, held over Memorial Day weekend, attracts western artists from all over the country. Well-known names compete for medals, and unknowns have a chance to be discovered. There's an art auction and reception so that the public can meet the show's painters and sculptors. (520) 445-2000.

Flagstaff Area

Bill Williams Rendezvous Days, Williams. This festival is held on Memorial Day weekend. In addition to the in-town arts and crafts booths, cow-chip throwing contests, live music, and food booths, the Williams city park hosts an authentic Mountain Men Rendezvous. Here men and women from around the country camp (1840s style) in teepees and compete in authentic Mountain Man black powder events. The "Raw Egg Shoot" is a favorite. If a contestant misses the egg, he eats it. See Mountain Men compete in the "Seneca Run," which combines all wilderness skills into one marathon event. Men must shoot, throw a tomahawk, canoe, run, set a bear trap, and light a fire. (520) 635-4061.

JUNE

Phoenix Area

Old Time Country Music Festival, Payson. All kinds of bands, including bluegrass, country, and buck-dancing, compete in this nationally recognized music festival. (520) 474-4515.

Annual Chili Cookoff, Payson. If you think a chili cookoff is full of beans, think again. This is a world-class cooking event—complete with a parade. Sample all the chefs' best recipes. (520) 474-4515.

Annual Square Dance Festival, Prescott. Pick up some new twists and dips and watch teams from around the country compete in this most American dance experience. This is a fun festival for dancers and toe-tappers. (520) 445-2000.

International Innertube Race, Parker. Hundreds of people, dressed in outlandish costumes, converge on the Colorado River to compete in a 7-mile race. (520) 669-2174.

Tucson Area
Bisbee Renaissance Festival, Bisbee. A celebration of Bisbee's rebirth. Watch the jousting and enjoy the food, arts and crafts, and merrymaking. (520) 432-5421.

JULY

Phoenix Area
Prescott Frontier Days and Rodeo, Prescott. The town turns out for the Fourth of July weekend in flag-waving frontier style, with a glittering parade, rugged professional rodeo (the oldest rodeo in the country), dancing, and general wild fun. In Arizona, Prescott's Whiskey Row is the place to be this weekend. (520) 445-2000.

Championship Loggers/Sawdust Festival, Payson. This is one of the biggest sawdust festivals in the country where loggers come to show off their skills in competition. Among the events scheduled are rolling pin throws (a ladies' contest), crosscut sawing, precision cutting, and axe throwing. Loggers from all over the country converge here for this festival. (520) 474-4515.

AUGUST

Flagstaff Area
Arizona Cowpunchers' Reunion and Old Timers' Rodeo, Williams. If you want to see real, working cowboys, this is the place

to come. Only working cowboys are allowed to compete. All events involve skills cowboys use in their profession. Spectators can watch three-man teams compete in a wild-horse race where men must catch, saddle, and ride a wild horse across a finish line. Another favorite is the wild-cow milking contest where two-man teams rope and milk a cow, catching the milk in a Coke bottle. This is not as crazy as it sounds, because often a wild cow won't nurse her baby. Cowboys must catch and milk the cow, then put the milk into a Coke bottle so they can save the young calf. (520) 635-4061.

Phoenix Area
Payson Annual Continuous Rodeo, Payson. See the world's oldest continuously held professional rodeo. Watch cowboys from around the world ride bucking broncos and rope steers while they compete for big money. The rodeo weekend includes all kinds of western festivities. (520) 474-4515.

SEPTEMBER

Phoenix Area
Annual State Championship Old Time Fiddlers Contest, Payson. This is one of Payson's most famous festivals. You can hear fiddlers from all over the state compete with their fanciest fingerwork. This is a delightful art form for spectators as well as contestants. (520) 474-4515.

National Indian Day, Parker. This is celebrated in Manataba Park the last Friday of September and the following Saturday. The four tribes in the area, as well as others from throughout the Southwest, converge for traditional games, singing, dances, and other activities. Arts and crafts and traditional foods are sold. The celebration begins in midafternoon and picks up toward evening. (520) 669-2174.

Flagstaff Area
Annual Navajo Nation Fair, Window Rock. Window Rock is the headquarters for the Navajo Nation. Feast your eyes on fine Navajo arts and crafts and your tummies on hot Navajo fry bread dripping with honey. There's even a Navajo fry bread-making contest, as well as horse racing, rodeos, a parade, and an authentic Indian pow-wow.

Other events include a 10,000-meter run and traditional Navajo singing and dancing competition. (520) 871-4971.

OCTOBER

Phoenix Area
Arizona State Fair, Phoenix. Livestock shows, exhibits, big name entertainment, and a carnival are just part of the action when the annual State Fair comes to town. (602) 252-6771.

Tucson Area
Helldorado Days, Tombstone. This is the event that puts Tombstone on the map every year. If you ever wondered what the Old West was like, come to Helldorado Days and find out. Shoot-outs, a fast-draw contest, and a parade add to the general wild western craziness. (520) 457-2211.

NOVEMBER

Phoenix Area
Fountain Festival of the Arts, Fountain Hills. More than 200 artists, artisans, and craftspeople move into Fountain Hills for a three-day show and sale. The juried competition attracts some of the finest artists in the country. The pottery and sculpture are always outstanding. (602) 837--1654.
Annual Swiss Village Christmas Lighting, Payson. Set among Payson's pine forests, the Swiss village looks amazingly appropriate when dressed for Christmas. The celebration brings out the entire town. (520) 474-4515.

DECEMBER

Nearly every community has a Christmas tradition. Festivals abound. For a more complete listing, consult the Chamber of Commerce in each city. Below is a sampling of what happens during the holiday season.

Phoenix Area

Old Town Tempe Fall Festival of the Arts, Tempe. If you miss the Spring Festival, come to this one. Mill Avenue, the main street of town, becomes a bazaar of arts, crafts, and unusual collectibles as artists set up booths to show their wares. The art on display is often terrific and always interesting. (602) 967-7891.

Victorian Christmas at Heritage Square, Phoenix. Phoenix turns back the clock to the 1800s as Dickens comes to the desert. The dress at this celebration is heavy with velvet and lace. Christmas stories are read aloud, choirs sing, and the historical district glows with the spirit of Christmases past. (602) 262-5071.

Christmas Parade and Courthouse Lighting, Prescott. With its Victorian setting in place all year long, Christmas comes naturally to Prescott. The entire town turns out for the parade and comes to the square to see the courthouse blaze with colorful lights. (520) 445-2000.

Tucson Area

Luminaria Night, Tucson. The Tucson Botanical Garden is lit by hundreds of luminarias (lighted votive candles nestled in brown paper bags that are filled partway with sand). Mariachis, bands, Yaqui Indian dancers, and other musicians add to the festivities. (520) 624-1817.

Tumacacori Fiesta, Tumacacori. Folk dancing, music, food, and crafts from many of Santa Cruz County's cultural groups make this a special Southwestern holiday celebration. (520) 398-2341.

Christmas Boat Parade of Lights, Lake Havasu. Watch as gaily trimmed and lighted houseboats glide across Lake Havasu in an unusual salute to the season. (520) 855-2178.

Holiday boat parades also are held on Lake Powell, Lake Mead, and Lake Mohave. Check with the local Chambers of Commerce at Page, (520) 645-2741; Bullhead City, (520) 754-4121; and Parker, (520) 669-2174, for dates and times.

National Parks

Arizona is studded with a wonderland of national parks, monuments, and forests. Although the state is vast in its physical size, popular parks can fill up quickly. It's always wise to write or call ahead for information, instructions, camping permits, and other details when planning a visit to a national recreation site.

Grand Canyon National Park
Back Country Reservation Office
P.O. Box 129
Grand Canyon, AZ 86023
(520) 638-7888

Canyon de Chelly National Monument
Box 588
Chinle, AZ 86503
(520) 674-5500

Coconino National Forest
2323 East Greenlaw Lane
Flagstaff, AZ 86001
(520) 527-3600

Kaibab National Forest
Sixth Street
Williams, AZ 86046
(520) 635-2676

Apache-Sitgreaves National Forest
P.O. Box 649
Springerville, AZ 85938
(520) 333-4301

In addition to forests, monuments, and parks operated by the federal goverment, other public land in Arizona is under direction of the U.S. Bureau of Land Management (BLM). Information about hiking or camping on BLM lands is available from the following address:

Bureau of Land Management
Arizona State Office
Siete Square
3707 North Seventh Street
Phoenix, AZ 85014
(602) 417-9206

Indian Reservations

Arizona is home to twenty-one Indian tribes representing nearly 160,000 people. A total of twenty reservations cover more than nineteen million acres. As you read this list, you will see many hyphenated tribal names. Over the years, the U.S. government has combined tribes, giving them new homes together on a single reservation. Nevertheless, each has managed to retain its own distinct heritage.

Visitors who wish to travel on Indian reservations may do so without prior permission. If, however, you want to know where to go to buy arts or crafts or observe dances, celebrations, or rodeos, you should call ahead or write to the tribal office for dates, times, and locations. Following is a brief description and location of each tribe.

Ak-Chin Reservation, 56 miles south of Phoenix in Pinal County. This tribe is noted for basketry. Ak-Chin Indian Community, Route 2, Box 27, Maricopa, AZ 85239, (520) 568-2227.

Camp Verde Reservation, 94 miles north of Phoenix in Yavapai County. This reservation includes Montezuma Castle National Monument and Montezuma Well. Basketry is the major art form. Yavapai-Apache Indian Community, P.O. Box 1188, Camp Verde, AZ 86322, (520) 567-3649.

Cocopah East and West Reservation, 12 miles southwest of Yuma in Yuma County. This tribe is well known for its intricate beadwork. Cocopah Tribal Council, Bin "G," Somerton, AZ 85350, (520) 627-2102.

Colorado River Reservation, 189 miles west of Phoenix in Yuma County. Collectors may want to buy baskets, beadwork, and Indian motif wall clocks made by these tribes. Colorado River Indian Tribes, Route 1, Box 23-B, Parker, AZ 85344, (520) 669-9211.

Fort Apache Reservation, 194 miles northeast of Phoenix in Apache, Gila, and Navajo counties. The Apache Tribe owns and operates Apache Sunrise Resort, a ski lodge and resort facility. Skiing aside, the people create excellent beadwork and the highly prized "Burden Baskets," wonderfully woven baskets that are trimmed with leather thongs and silver metal "bells." White Mountain Apache Tribe, P.O. Box 700, Whiteriver, AZ 85941, (520) 338-4346.

Fort McDowell Reservation, 36 miles northeast of Phoenix in Maricopa County. The Fort McDowell Indians manufacture jojoba bean oil, which is a superb substitute for the environmentally scarce whale oil. Basketry is a specialty. Mohave-Apache Tribal Council, P.O. Box 17779, Fountain Hills, AZ 85268, (602) 837-5121.

Fort Mojave Reservation, 236 miles northwest of Phoenix in Mohave County. This reservation borders Arizona, Nevada, and California; tribal headquarters are located in California. The Fort Mojave Indians are noted for their beadwork. Fort Mojave Tribal Council, P.O. Box 888, 500 Merriman Avenue, Needles, CA 92363, (619) 326-4591.

Fort Yuma Reservation, 185 miles southwest of Phoenix in Yuma County. This reservation borders Arizona and California. Information may be obtained by writing to an Arizona address or by calling the tribal headquarters in California. Collectors may buy beadwork and other artifacts from this tribe. Quechan Tribal Council, P.O. Box 1352, Yuma, AZ 85364, (520) 572-0661.

Gila (Hee-la) River Reservation, 40 miles south of Phoenix in Maricopa and Pinal counties. Pima basketry and Maricopa pottery are prized native items produced by the Pimas and Maricopas. Gila River Indian Community, P.O. Box 97, Sacaton, AZ 85247, (602) 963-4323 or (602) 562-3311.

Havasupai (Have-a-sue-pie) Reservation, at the bottom of the Grand Canyon via an 8-mile trail from Hilltop to Supai. The people of the "Blue-Green Waters" are best known for their exquisite, remote reservation reachable only by mule or foot. The Havasupais produce basketry and beadwork. Havasupai Tribal Council, P.O. Box 1, Supai, AZ 86435, (520) 448-2961 or (520) 448-2731.

Hopi (Hoe-pee) Reservation, 323 miles northeast of Phoenix in Coconino and Navajo counties. The Hopi produce an assortment of art and collectibles. Basketry and plaques are exquisite, but Hopi are better known for hand-carved and painted kachina dolls, which are spirits of the gods worshipped by this tribe. The Hopi are also leaders in silver and gold jewelry, crafts, and pottery. Hopi Tribal Council, P.O. Box 123, Kyakotsmovi, AZ 86039, (520) 734-2445.

Hualapai (Wall-pie) Reservation, 252 miles northwest of Phoenix in Coconino, Yavapai, and Mohave counties. Dolls and basketry are the primary art forms of this tribe. Hualapai Tribal Council, P.O. Box 168, Peach Springs, AZ 86434, (520) 769-2216.

Kaibab-Paiute (Kigh-bab–Pie-ute) Reservation, 398 miles north of Phoenix in Mohave County. This tribe specializes in coiled shallow baskets known as "wedding baskets." Kaibab-Paiute Tribal Council, Tribal Affairs Building, Pipe Springs Route, Fredonia, AZ 86022, (520) 643-7245.

Navajo Reservation, 356 miles northeast of Phoenix in Apache, Coconino, and Navajo counties. Best known for their museum-quality, hand-woven rugs and blankets, the Navajo also create magnificent silver crafts and some basketry. Cultural Resources Department Visitor Services, P.O. Box 308, Window Rock, AZ 86515, (520) 871-4941.

Tohono O'odam Reservation, 136 miles south of Phoenix (adjacent to the city of Tucson). This reservation stretches across Maricopa, Pinal, and Pima counties. Best known for its distinctive and valuable basketry, the tribe also produces fine pottery. Tohono O'odam Tribal Council, P.O. Box 837, Sells, AZ 85634, (520) 383-2221.

Pascua-Yaqui Reservation, 135 miles southwest of Phoenix (adjacent to the city of Tucson) in Pima County. Collectors appreciate the "Deer Dance" statues and cultural paintings created by the children of the tribe. Pascua-Yaqui Tribal Council, 4821 West Calle Vicam, Tucson, AZ 85706, (520) 883-2838.

Salt River Pima-Maricopa Indian Community, 15 miles northeast of Phoenix adjacent to the city of Scottsdale. The Salt River Indians produce basketry and pottery. Salt River Pima-Maricopa Tribal Council, Route 1, Box 216, Scottsdale, AZ 85256, (602) 874-8350.

San Carlos Reservation, 115 miles northeast of Phoenix in Gila and Graham counties. Along with basketry and pottery, the San Carlos Apaches create unusual jewelry set with peridots, pale green semiprecious gemstones found in that area. San Carlos Apache Tribal Council, P.O. Box O, San Carlos, AZ 85550, (520) 475-2361.

Tonto-Apache Reservation, 94 miles northeast of Phoenix in Gila County. Native crafts of basketry and beadwork are emphasized. Tonto-Apache Tribal Council, P.O. Box 1440, Payson, AZ 85541, (520) 474-5000.

Yavapai-Prescott Reservation, 103 miles northwest of Phoenix in Yavapai County. Best bet for collecting native baskets. Yavapai-Prescott Tribal Council, P.O. Box 348, Prescott, AZ 86302, (520) 445-8790.

For more information about Arizona's Indian tribes contact:
Arizona Commission of Indian Affairs, 1645 West Jefferson, #127, Phoenix, AZ 85007, (602) 542-3123.

State Parks

Land of the great outdoors, Arizona has nineteen state parks with historical and recreational settings. Each offers strollers, hikers, boaters, backpackers, and climbers a variety of experiences. Twelve of the recreational parks have hiking trails, and six of those include equestrian trails. Campground facilities are available at eleven of the parks, and seven offer boating opportunities. There is a nominal per-vehicle fee charged at each park. For more information on any of the state parks, call or write to:

Arizona State Parks, 1688 West Adams Street, Phoenix, AZ 85007, (602) 542-4174.

For specific information on Arizona trails and hiking, write for information to: **Arizona State Parks, Trails Coordinator,** 1688 West Adams Street, Phoenix, AZ 85007, (602) 542-4174.

Regional Information

Arizona is divided into fifteen counties; and not all of them have recreation departments. For information concerning local trails and bike paths, contact the Board of Supervisors in the area that interests you. Following is a list of recreation departments for Arizona's three largest metropolitan areas:

Phoenix

Maricopa County Parks and Recreation Department, 4701 East Washington Street, Phoenix, AZ 85034, (602) 506-2930.

Phoenix Parks, Recreation, and Library Department, 125 East Washington Street, Phoenix, AZ 85004, (602) 262-6861.

Tucson

Pima County Parks and Recreation Department, 1204 West Silverlake Road, Tucson, AZ 85713, (520) 740-2690.

Tucson City Parks and Recreation Department, 900 South Randolph Way, Tucson, AZ 85716, (520) 791-4873.

Flagstaff
Coconino County Parks and Recreation Department, Coconino County Courthouse, Flagstaff, AZ 86001, (520) 774-3464.
Flagstaff Parks and Recreation Department, 211 West Aspen, Flagstaff, AZ 86001, (520) 779-7690.

Tourist Safety Tips

Flash Floods
When a violent thunderstorm breaks out over the mountains and deserts of the Southwest, runoff from the torrential rains cascades into the steep canyons in a matter of minutes. Walls of water, sometimes 10 to 30 feet high, swirl through the canyons and arroyos picking up mud, boulders, trees, and other debris. Plants, animals, and sometimes humans are caught and swept along, for a flash flood stops for nothing that is unlucky enough to be in its path.

Flash floods can result from thunderstorms miles away and can occur in Arizona at any time of the year. However, the predominant seasons are summer and early fall. Isolated thunderstorms are the main cause from late June through mid-September, while tropical storms or Pacific storms are the main culprit from August through October.

A thunderstorm cloud, called a cumulonimbus, is a large, towering formation that frequently spreads out at the top into the shape of an anvil. This cloud usually appears dark and threatening when viewed from below, but very bright and white when seen from the side at some distance.

The National Weather Service issues a Flash Flood Watch when such a flood is a possibility. A Flash Flood Warning is issued when flash flooding has been reported or radar indicates heavy rain in a flood-prone area.

What to Do
1. Stay tuned to a radio station that gives flood watch warnings.
2. Keep an eye on the sky and watch for thunderstorms.
3. Avoid deep canyons and dry washes during stormy or threatening weather.

4. Camp on high ground but not on top of exposed peaks or ridges.
5. Never cross a flooded dip in the roadway. The water may be deeper than you think or the roadway washed away.
6. If your vehicle is stuck in a low-lying area, abandon it and move to higher ground.
7. If local authorities want you to leave an area—leave. People die needlessly because they ignore warnings to seek safety.
8. Inform someone of your destination and when you expect to return. Police should be notified immediately if you do not return on time.

Desert Survival

Having great weather year-round means that Arizonans spend more time outdoors than most people in the country. With the elegant Sonoran desert surrounding us, it's no wonder that the urge is to get out and enjoy it. Unfortunately, too many people go out into the desert unprepared. Here are some important desert survival tips to remember.

Three Rules of Desert Survival

Never Alone
Tell Someone
Stay Put

If you do get lost, make a large X — at least 14 feet long — where you are. This can be made by dragging your foot, breaking off bush branches, or any other means at your disposal.

Start blowing a whistle at regular intervals using three short blasts. This is the international distress signal.

Light three fires in the shape of a triangle near where you are. This is a good signal both day and night.

Don't eat in the desert. Eating draws fluid out of your body and makes you dehydrate faster.

Keep a water jug with a straw in the car. Remember that children dehydrate quicker than adults.

Remember these three points about water in the desert: *TAKE IT, DRINK IT,* and *DON'T SAVE IT!*

Finally, always tell someone the make of your car, its color, where you are going, and when you'll be back. This will make it easier for searchers to find you.

The Climate of Arizona

Arizona is a land of dramatic contrasts, as varied in its climate as in its beauty. Temperatures and rainfall vary tremendously throughout the three main topographical areas within the state, for extremes in elevation are matched by extremes in temperatures. These three topographical areas can roughly be divided as follows: The high plateau—elevations average 5,000 to 7,000 feet. The desert mountains and valleys. The mountains—with peaks from 9,000 to 12,000 feet.

Temperatures can range as much as 60 degrees in a single day due to the dry air normally over the state, but generally average temperatures are governed by elevation. As a rule of thumb, figure on a 3¹/₂ degree F difference for every 1,000-foot change in altitude.

When it comes to extremes, there are usually worse days on record! The hottest daytime temperature ever recorded was 127 degrees F at Parker in 1905. The coldest day on record was minus 40 degrees F at Hawley Lake on January 7, 1971. Of course new records are always being set. Both July 14, 1982, with 113 degrees F recorded, and September 6, 1982, with 110 degrees F, set new high maximum temperatures for those dates. From the beginning to the end of October, the greatest temperature changes are recorded in Phoenix—greater changes than any seen during the year in central Arizona. By November, the mild winter season is established in the Salt River Valley.

Sunshine in Phoenix averages 86 percent of the possible amount, ranging from a minimum monthly average of about 77 percent in January and December to a maximum of about 94 percent in June.

Elevation and season also affect the amount of rain and snow that Arizona receives. These amounts vary dramatically. On the average, some desert areas have only 3 to 4 inches of rain a year, while certain mountain areas receive up to 30 inches. Pacific storms cause most of the rainfall from November through March with winter snowfall totals sometimes reaching 100 inches on the highest mountains. Summer rainfall begins in July and extends through mid-September when moisture-bearing winds from the southeast and south cause the Arizona monsoon. The thunderstorms that result can cause strong winds, blinding dust storms, and local heavy rainfall. Heavy thunderstorms can cause flash flooding, and while major flooding is rare, it can—and does—happen.

Dry spells can last for many months but count on April through June as the driest part of the year anywhere in the state. However, when thunderstorms occur, they can be wild. The damaging winds accompanying these storms are usually straight-line winds that can move in at speeds upward of 75 miles per hour.

Heat Wave Safety Rules

If you are not used to the extreme heat that can occur in the desert, it's easy to overdo it and even get sick. Below are some basic rules for living in—and even enjoying—Arizona's high temperature times.

1. **Slow Down.** Your body cannot keep up with extremely high temperatures, especially when the humidity rises.
2. **Dress for Summer.** Lightweight, light-colored clothing reflects the heat and sunlight and helps maintain normal body temperatures.
3. **Put Less Fuel in Your Inner Fires.** Foods like proteins that increase metabolic heat production also increase water loss.
4. **Don't Dry Out.** Hot weather can wring the water out of you before you know it's happened. The first sign of dehydration is being cross. Recognize this symptom and drink lots of water when the weather is hot.
5. **Don't Get Too Much Sun.** Sunburn makes the job of heat dissipation that much more difficult. Not only is sunburn uncomfortable, but too much sun invites skin cancer. Wear a good, protective sunscreen whenever you are in the sun.
6. **Take Care of the Children and Pets.** Never leave the kids or animals in the car on a hot day—not even for that quick trip into the store.
7. **Vary Your Thermal Environment.** Try to get out of the heat for at least a few hours each day.

About the Author

Pam Hait is a freelance writer and award-winning author of thirteen books. She is Southwest Editor of *Metropolitan Home,* has covered Arizona for *Sunset* and *Travel & Leisure,* and has written for many national publications. She is a longtime contributor to *Arizona Highways.* Pam and her partner own Strategies, a media relations and marketing firm focusing on tourism with special expertise in eco and heritage tourism.

A member of the American Society of Journalists and Authors, she is a graduate of Northwestern University Medill School of Journalism. Pam Hait served as Deputy Director of the Arizona Office of Tourism, where she created domestic and international marketing promotions for the state. She lives in Paradise Valley with her husband, Glen, a plastic surgeon.